The Metaphysics of Powers

Routledge Studies in Metaphysics

The Metaphysics of Powers

Their Grounding and their Manifestations

Edited by Anna Marmodoro

Routledge
Taylor & Francis Group

NEW YORK AND LONDON

First published 2010
by Routledge
711 Third Avenue, New York, NY 10017

Simultaneously published in the UK
by Routledge
2 Park Square, Milton Park, Abingdon, Oxon OX14 4RN

Routledge is an imprint of the Taylor & Francis Group, an informa business

First issued in paperback 2013

© 2010 Taylor & Francis

Typeset in Sabon by IBT Global.

Library of Congress Cataloging-in-Publication Data
   The metaphysics of powers : their grounding and their manifestations / edited by Anna Marmodoro.
      p. cm. — (Routledge studies in metaphysics ; 2)
   Includes bibliographical references (p.) and index.
   1. Power (Philosophy)   I. Marmodoro, Anna, 1975–
   BD438.M47 2010
   111—dc22
   2009047166

ISBN13: 978-0-415-87685-8 (hbk)
ISBN13: 978-0-415-83442-1 (pbk)
ISBN13: 978-0-203-85128-9 (ebk)

Contents

Figures

Introduction

Anna Marmodoro

The importance and centrality of powers in various domains of philosophical inquiry has been argued for by many.[1] Powers are properties like fragility and electric charge, whose possession *disposes* their bearer in a certain way. The instantiation of fragility in the glass disposes the glass to break if struck in the appropriate circumstances. The striking is the stimulus, and the breaking the manifestation of fragility.

Consider the electric charge of an electron. Is the electron's charge a property like its mass and its shape? Is it as primitive a property of the electron as they are? If not, is it reducible to such properties? Or is it grounded on such properties? Can we make sense of the notion of ungrounded powers? *Can there be a world of powers only?* This has become one of the driving questions in the investigation into the metaphysics of powers, and it is central to nearly all the volume's essays.

THE GROUNDING OF POWERS

The question of whether there can be a world of powers only divides metaphysicians into two camps, according to what kinds of properties they think are required at the fundamental level to provide an adequate account of the manifest world. On the one side there are those who hold *Property Dualism*: there are two irreducible kinds of properties, both fundamental: the so called categorical (or qualities) and the dispositional ones. On the other side there are those who hold *Property Monism*: there is only one fundamental kind of property.

But if there is only one kind of fundamental property, what is it?

Some hold that *only dispositional* properties are fundamental, while non-dispositional properties, if they exist, are higher order. This view is also known in the literature as Pandispositionalism. Strong Dispositional Essentialism for example is a view of this kind, and is held e.g. by Sidney Shoemaker and most notably in the current debate by Alexander Bird.

Others argue that there is only one kind of property at the fundamental level and such properties are *powerful qualities*; namely, all fundamental properties are *both categorical and dispositional*. This position was put forward by Charlie Martin and John Heil and has been labeled the Identity Theory of Properties.

A further monist position, Categoricalism, holds that fundamental properties are essentially non-dispositional and that dispositions are conferred to objects on the basis of contingent laws of nature. David Armstrong has argued for this position, which has already been discussed extensively in the literature.

Arguments in favor and against the view that all fundamental properties are dispositional are investigated in this volume, focusing on a series of *regresses* that critics of the all-powers view have put forward in the recent literature. Jonathan Lowe claims that the view that powers are ungrounded faces a 'No Identity Fixation' vicious regress; Stathis Psillos argues that the very notion of ungrounded powers is epistemologically and metaphysically incoherent, because ungrounded powers have a regressive nature; and Richard Swinburne charges the all-powers view with an epistemological regress.

The regresses are aimed at probing the all-powers view on the following issues: *Do powers need to be grounded in non-powers?* And what is the nature of the grounding-relation, if there is any? These questions have to be addressed both by those who hold that all fundamental properties are 'pure' powers (that is, powers with no grounding in categorical properties) and by those who hold that there are at least some pure powers.

The charge of incoherency is the first challenge to the all-powers view addressed in this volume. Anna Marmodoro, in her 'Do Powers Need Powers to Make Them Powerful? From Pandispositionalism to Aristotle', engages with one of the most recent arguments of this type, put forward by Stathis Psillos, who claims that pure powers have a regressive nature which makes them incoherent to us. Marmodoro shows that Psillos's regress is but an instance of the regress developed by Aristotle on the assumption that an entity is related to its essence. She compares Aristotle's, Bradley's, and Psillos' regresses, showing that Bradley's and Psillos's (different) conclusions from their regress arguments lead to impasses. She argues that, contrary to what Psillos concludes, pure powers *do not (regressively) need further powers* to make them powerful; rather, they do what they do because they *are* powers. This lifts the hindrance that Psillos had claimed to admitting pure powers into the ontology, if physics gave us reasons to posit them.

Other regress arguments against pure powers are discussed in this volume by Kristina Engelhard and Jennifer McKitrick, with different conclusions.

Engelhard in her 'Categories and the Ontology of Powers. A Vindication of the Identity Theory of Properties' is motivated by the idea that the difference between an object with a disposition and one just like it without that disposition is qualitative; so we should think of dispositions as making qualitative contributions to objects. Engelhard calls this the 'dualist intuition', which she sees as driving Lowe's and Swinburne's regress arguments against Pandispositionalism. She puts forward the position that all properties are powers *with an intrinsic 'dual structure'*, qualitative and dispositional.

But can we have epistemic access to powers if all properties are powers? McKitrick engages with this issue, raised most notably by Swinburne. In her 'Manifestations as Effects' she examines regresses recently advanced against pandispositionalism, with a view to the question of what the metaphysical status of a power's manifestation is. McKitrick shows the force of the Swinburne-style argument that, on the pandispositionalist view, all manifestations become unobservable. She concludes that non-powers must be posited.

The same conclusion, namely that there are two irreducible kinds of properties, is argued for in this volume also by Jonathan Lowe and Brian Ellis. Lowe in his 'On the Individuation of Powers' investigates the question of whether the pandispositionalist view provides adequate criteria of individuation for powers. His starting point is the widely held and plausible position that powers are individuated, at least partly, by their manifestations. But on a pandispositionalist view the manifestations of powers themselves always consist simply in the instantiation of further powers. Thus, Lowe argues that pandispositionalism is prey to a 'No Identity Fixation' vicious regress, or else to circularity in the individuation of powers. He engages with the most recent arguments that have been put forward to avert this kind of threat by a number of philosophers who appeal to structuralist considerations, but argues that their responses are inadequate and thus concludes that some properties must be non-powers.

Can causal powers even exist if ontology admitted no categorical properties? Ellis in his 'Causal powers and categorical properties' offers arguments for the *ontological dependence* of all causal powers on categorical properties. For, the instances of causal powers must all have contingent locations, i.e. spatiotemporal relations to other things. Powers must act from somewhere. But the instances of location do not have locations contingently; they *are* locations. Nor do the instances of location have any causal powers essentially. For, any such causal powers would have to be immovable. Furthermore, Ellis argues, causal powers must all have defining laws of action, specifying manifestation and circumstances, and such laws of action of all causal powers involve categorical properties essentially.

But if one holds, like McKitrick, Lowe, and Ellis in this volume, that both powers and non-powers are to be admitted in our ontology, the question arises of what the relation of powers to non-powers is.

A position which is discussed in this volume is that neither the categorical nor the dispositional are reducible; neither is higher order; rather, each property is both categorical and dispositional. *Are powers, then, metaphysically simple or do they have an internal structure?* Martin and (in this volume) Heil have put forward the Identity Theory of Properties. They hold that properties are metaphysically simple; Heil (2003) suggests as a model for his theory a Necker cube, that can be *seen now one way, now another.* The dispositional and the categorical are not different aspects of a property; rather, they are *different ways of considering the property.*

Heil addresses directly the question of whether powers have an internal structure in his contribution to this volume 'Qualities and Powers', by engaging critically with a position put forward by Peter Unger. Unger and Heil agree in holding that non-powers figure ineliminably in the individuation of powers. But Unger also posits a contingent relation of covariance between the categorical and the dispositional, for all properties—from which it follows that powers are internally structured. Heil offers reasons why contingency should be rejected and properties should be conceived as *powerful qualities.*

THE NATURE OF A POWER'S MANIFESTATION

What is the nature of a power's manifestation? This question is particularly central to Toby Handfield's and Jennifer McKitrick's essays. Handfield in his 'Dispositions, Manifestations, and Causal Structure' explores the idea that the manifestations of a disposition are causal processes that constitute a *natural kind.* In order to form a natural kind, such processes must have a common intrinsic structure. For causal processes, the relevant structure must be in some sense causal. Handfield examines various ways in which such an intrinsic causal structure might be represented, and considers whether or not it is plausible that such a structure exists in fundamental physical processes.

In her 'Manifestations as Effects' McKitrick discusses whether manifestations are events, or instantiations of properties, or both. On the pandispositionalist view she engages with, if manifestations are instantiation of properties, and all properties are powers, regresses follow (most importantly in her view the one concerning the non-observability of the manifestations of powers, as we have seen previously). On the other hand if manifestations are events, this is also problematic in cases where what actually occurs is not the kind of effect that the power is a power for, but rather a complex interaction of various powers. An alternative is to think of manifestations as *contributions* to effects rather than effects, as e.g. George Molnar has suggested. McKitrick examines and then argues against this proposal, and for the view that a single kind of power can have different kinds of effects, some of which involve the instantiation of non-dispositional properties.

Can powers have more than one manifestation-type? For example, are the cracking and the breaking of a glass both manifestations of the very same power, fragility? In his 'On the Individuation of Powers' Lowe challenges this view by posing a dilemma for those who suppose that a single power could have more than one manifestation-type.

An ice cube cools the lemonade, and the lemonade melts the ice cube. Cooling and melting are manifestations of two different but somehow interrelated powers. The slamming of the door for example bears no such relation to either the lemonade's cooling or the ice's melting. Manifestations such as the lemonade's cooling and the ice's melting are the *mutual products* of powers through interaction. But *what explains their coupling?* Williams in his 'Puzzling Powers: the Problem of Fit' raises this issue as a difficulty for those who hold there are irreducible causal powers (whether all properties are pure powers or only some). The difficulty is to explain how it is that powers are intrinsically powerful and yet *causally harmonious*— that is, mutually interrelated. Williams proposes as a way forward building an appropriate metaphysical framework in which powers can be accommodated: Power Holism (which bears analogies with semantic holism).

DISPOSITIONAL ANALYSES OF CAUSATION

Under the hammer's blow, the glass shatters. *Can causation be adequately explained by a dispositional theory of properties?*

Causes dispose towards their effects and often produce them. But a set of causes, even though they may succeed in producing an effect, cannot necessitate it since the effect could have been counteracted by some additional power. Stephen Mumford and Rani Anjum in their 'A Powerful Theory of Causation' argue for this view and note that powers compose additively and subtractively, as vectors do. They develop a model for representing *powers as constituent vectors* within an n-dimensional quality space, where composition of causes appears as vector addition. This model throws new light on causal modality and cases of prevention, causation by absence, and probabilistic causation.

Also exploring the prospects of a dispositional account of causation, Bird in his 'Causation and the Manifestation of Powers' suggests an account of causation that identifies it 'with activity of the underlying ontology'. On an all-powers view, one simple proposal for accounting for causation is that A causes B when A is the stimulus of some disposition and B is the corresponding manifestation. Bird examines some of the advantages and disadvantages of this simple dispositional analysis of causation. He argues that it avoids some of the counter intuitive consequences of the counterfactual approach to causation and offers a promising way of accounting for the distinction between cause and condition. Furthermore, the dispositional analysis offers insights into the modality of the relation between cause and effects (see the following section).

THE NECESSITY OF THE RELATION BETWEEN A POWER AND ITS MANIFESTATION(S)

Are powers and manifestations related by necessity? Ellis in his 'Causal Powers and Categorical Properties' argues for a full commitment to an anti-Humean position with respect to causation. His line of argument assumes that Hume's causal phenomenalism is the only plausible alternative to causal realism. But causal processes necessarily involve causally related states of affairs. What is the nature of this relationship? Hume's causal phenomenalism leaves this relationship unexplained. This is why, Ellis argues, causal realism is the better metaphysical option. If one is a causal realist, one must suppose that causal powers are dispositional, i.e. have identities that depend essentially on what they would dispose their bearers to do in the circumstances in which they would be effective.

But such a commitment is not without difficulties, some of which are raised in this volume by Marcus Schrenk in his 'Antidotes for Dispositional Essentialism'. Dispositional essentialism draws (part of) its anti-Humean strength from the idea of metaphysical necessity put forward by Kripke and Putnam. Kind Essentialism claims that tigers have certain features necessarily or else they would not be tigers; by analogy Dispositional Essentialism claims that dispositions have their manifestation-type M necessarily (in appropriate circumstances C, which include the stimulus) or else they would not be the dispositions they are. But, Schrenk notes, there are two major dissimilarities between Kind Essentialism *à la* Kripke and Putnam and Dispositional Essentialism: firstly, for the latter, the relata are not only individuals or kinds or properties but also include world state types and events; secondly the manifestation of powers unfolds in time; it is not expressed by a-temporal statements such as those about metaphysical necessity.

Handfield in his 'Dispositions, Manifestations, and Causal Structure', pursues what he calls a 'Humean Dispositionalism' program: he wants to retain the Humean principle of recombination: there are no necessary connections between distinct existences; which leads him to claiming that there are no necessary connections between a property and the causal powers it confers to the bearer. Rather than necessary connections, Handfield argues, a property and its process kind (manifestation kind) stand in virtue of their intrinsic natures in a relation such that they would not be the things they are if the relation did not hold. Handfield sees Humean Dispositionalism as an advancement on Dispositional Essentialism which says that natural properties are essentially such as to confer certain powers on their bearers without any further explanation (e.g. Bird and Ellis); and also as an advancement on the mere appeal to brute modal facts of some variety (e.g. Mumford).

Mumford and Anjum in their 'A Powerful Theory of Causation' argue that "dispositionality has an important, *real, and irreducible modal force of its own*". They hold that causes do not necessitate their effects; they produce them but in an irreducibly dispositional way, in a way that is less than necessary but more than purely contingent. And so does Bird in his 'Causation and the Manifestation of Powers'. He sees the relation between a disposition and its manifestation in response to stimulus as *ontologically basic and not reducible*. The sufficiency of the stimulus for the effect of a disposition is of a subjunctive kind, and so has modal force, but less than full metaphysical necessitation.

NOTE

1. The terms 'powers' and 'dispositions' are used interchangeably in what follows.

1   On the Individuation of Powers

E. J. Lowe

INTRODUCTION

It is often maintained—I think with considerable plausibility—that powers are individuated at least partly by their manifestations. But it is also sometimes held that the manifestations of powers themselves always consist simply in the acquisition of *further powers*. This seems to raise the threat of a vicious circularity (or else an infinite regress) in the individuation of powers, requiring us to acknowledge the existence of at least some power-manifestations—and hence some properties—that are *not* powers. Recently, a number of philosophers have appealed to structuralist considerations in order to avert this kind of threat, but in what follows I shall argue that such a strategy is doomed to failure. Some properties, I shall conclude, must indeed be non-powers.

IDENTITY AND INDIVIDUATION

Suppose we believe that *powers exist*, perhaps because we espouse Quine's criterion of ontological commitment—"To be is to be the value of a bound variable"—and are convinced that scientific theories that we believe to be true quantify over powers.[1] Perhaps we shall then also want to espouse Quine's other famous dictum—"No entity without identity"—and thus accept that we are obliged to offer a *criterion of identity* for powers, on the grounds that no clear sense can be made of certain entities being possible values of our variables of quantification if no principled account can be offered of the identity and distinctness conditions of such entities.[2] A criterion of identity for entities of a kind K is supposed to be a principle which specifies the identity (and thereby also the distinctness) conditions of Ks in an *informative or non-trivial* way—a principle that can be stated in the following form:

(CI) If x and y are entities of kind K, then $x = y$ iff x and y stand to one another in the relation R_K, where 'R_K' denotes some equivalence relation (other than identity itself) on entities of kind K.[3] It is often assumed that one condition on the adequacy of a criterion of identity is that such a principle should be *non-circular*, not just in the obvious way which is excluded by not allowing R_K to be the relation of *identity*, but also in any more roundabout way. However, this last assumption has been questioned in some quarters: and this is an issue to which I shall return later. It is also often assumed that talk about identity criteria is interchangeable with talk about *principles of individuation*—that an 'identity criterion' for *K*s *just is*, in other words, a 'principle of individuation' for *K*s. But this is an assumption that I myself certainly want to challenge.

Here is how I would distinguish between the two kinds of principle. Criteria of identity concern 'identity' conceived as a *relation*—the relation that logicians standardly represent by means of the *equality sign*, '='. Hence, it is such criteria that are required in order to put on a firm footing statements of *number* concerning entities of any kind. On the other hand, principles of individuation concern 'identity' understood in the sense of *individual essence*: what John Locke famously called 'the very being of any thing, whereby it is, what it is'.[4] Individuation, in the metaphysical (as opposed to the cognitive or epistemic) sense, is a *determination relation between entities*: the relation that obtains between entities x and y when x determines or 'fixes' (or at least *helps* to determine or 'fix') *which* entity of its kind y is.[5] When x stands in such a relation to y, x is the (or at least an) *individuator* of y. Entities that *have* individuators obviously warrant being called 'individuals'. We shouldn't automatically assume that *all* entities are individuals in this sense, however. Nor should we automatically assume that *only individuals* can be provided with criteria of identity. For instance, it is debatable whether sub-atomic particles—such as electrons—are individuals in our sense, even if they can be supplied with a satisfactory criterion of identity. For it seems that there may be circumstances in which it is a determinate fact that we have *two distinct electrons* (orbiting, say, a helium nucleus) and yet there is no determinate fact as to *which* electron each of these two electrons is.[6] Much more can and should be said about these general issues concerning identity and individuation, but now we need to turn more specifically to the topic of *powers*.

POWERS AND THEIR MANIFESTATIONS

What are powers supposed to *be*? Some will say that they are *properties* of a certain kind—properties, moreover, of *concrete objects*. Even if true, that is, however, not very informative. 'Property' is a very general term indeed. We want to know what is supposed to be distinctive about powers. As usual, the best place to start (though *only* to start) is our customary ways of talking about powers—the 'language of powers'. What, then, do we typically say about powers, quite generally? We always say, or at least imply, that a power is a power *to do something*. When an object possesses a power to do something, we say that its *doing* that thing is its 'manifesting' or 'exercising' that power. Sometimes, a power is a power *to acquire another power*, in which case an object manifests the first power when it acquires the second. In such a case, we may say that the former power is a 'higher-order' power. It might be thought that not *all* powers could be 'higher-order' powers in this sense, on pain of a vicious infinite regress. Some powers, it may be assumed, must be *first-order* powers, whose manifestations are *not* acquisitions of other powers. For example, it seems natural to say that *solubility* is a first-order power, which an object manifests by *dissolving*—where dissolving is conceived not to be the acquisition of another power, but rather something else. *What* else, though? Well, we intuitively take dissolving or dissolution to be a certain kind of physical *activity*. So, on this view of powers, the manifestation of a first-order power consists in some distinctive kind of activity on the part of the object possessing the power. Of course, it might be said that *acquiring a power* is just a kind of 'activity', so that we haven't yet ruled out the idea that all power-manifestations might be acquisitions of other powers. We can only rule this out if we can argue that some activities are 'pure' activities, which don't just consist in the acquiring of further powers. However, it does seem relatively clear, at least *prima facie*, that there are 'pure' activities in this sense. For instance, *rolling* seems to be one. When a ball rolls down an inclined plane, its rolling surely does not consist merely in its acquiring some power or powers which it formerly lacked. Rather, it consists in its undergoing a combination of rotational and translational motion: it at once turns on an axis through its centre and moves as a whole along a line down the plane. However, there is much more to be said about this issue, so I shall return to it later.

We have said that a power is always a power *to do something*. But an important question that we can raise in this connection is this. Is a power always a power only to do some *one* thing, or can there be powers that are powers to do a range of *different* things? Indeed, is it perhaps the case that *all* powers are powers to do a range of different things? This, it seems clear, is a question concerning the *individuation* of powers—assuming powers to *be* 'individuals' in our technical sense. For it seems correct to say that a power is at least partly individuated by *what it is a power to do*—in other words, by its type (or types, if there can be many) of manifestation.[7] It cannot be a merely *accidental* feature of a given power that it is a power to do such-and-such: rather, it must be a part of its *essence*. For example, we might venture to say, at least as a first approximation, that *magnetism* is the very power that it is at least partly in virtue of its being an object's power to *attract ferrous metals in its vicinity*. Of course, an object possessing the power of magnetism need not always be *manifesting* that power by attracting ferrous metals, not least because there may be no such metals in its vicinity. Furthermore, even if an object *is* manifesting its power of magnetism by attracting some ferrous metals in its vicinity, it needn't be the case that those ferrous metals are consequently *undergoing motion* towards the magnetic object: for it is always possible for the object's force of magnetic attraction to be counteracted by another force. However, what does *not* seem to make sense is the thought that an object might genuinely be *magnetic* and yet not in any circumstances be capable of attracting ferrous metals. It *must* be capable of doing this if it is to be magnetic, where the 'must' has the force of metaphysical necessity.

But what about the question of whether the same power may have more than one manifestation-type? For instance, could *magnetism*—that very power—be essentially not only a power to attract ferrous metals but also a power *to do something else*? I don't think so—not if we really are correct in characterizing it as being essentially a power *to attract ferrous metals*.[8] If we really can think of 'something else' that it is a power to do, such as to *induce an electrical current* in certain circumstances, then I suggest that this merely shows that we need to think more carefully about how we should describe the 'manifestation-type' of this power, in order to find a description which covers in a unified way *all* of the supposedly 'different' things that the power is a power to do. If we can't do that, then we should conclude that we are not really dealing with *just one power*. And I suspect that this might in fact be the correct conclusion to draw in the present case: that the phenomena of magnetism involve a number of different, albeit related, physical powers.

We can pose a dilemma for those who suppose that a single power could have more than one manifestation-type. Either those supposedly different types fall under a single unified description or they do not. If they do, then there is really only one manifestation-type. If they don't, then what reason is there to suppose that there is really just *one* power involved rather than two or more—one for each genuinely different manifestation-type? It might be replied that all powers must be 'grounded' in *non*-powers, such as 'structural' properties of the objects possessing the powers, and that powers with the same grounds are identical—but that this may be consistent with powers having multiple manifestation-types. However, first of all, it seems plausible that there may be 'pure' powers which are 'ungrounded' and, secondly, why should we suppose that powers with the same grounds must be identical? For instance, an object may have both a power to cast a rectangular shadow and a power to go through a round hole, with both of these powers being 'grounded' in the object's 'structural' property of having a cylindrical shape. But are they therefore the same power? It is not at all obvious that they are—and the reason for this, I suggest, is that the two manifestation-types in question are not only different but don't seem to fall under any single unified description. Once we allow that powers may genuinely have multiple manifestation-types which don't fall under any unified description, it becomes unclear why we should think that a single object may have many different powers rather than just *one*—a power to do all the things that it can do. And that would render the notion of power a rather feeble and trivial one.

Suppose I am right in contending that each power has just one fundamental manifestation-type which is essential to it, so that a power is at least partly individuated by its manifestation-type—that type being, thus, one of the power's 'individuators'. Then we can ask: what else, if anything, besides its manifestation-type, is needed to individuate a power? That depends on whether we are speaking of *types* of power or of 'tokens' of those types. A *type* of power is, I think, completely individuated by its manifestation-type—one implication of this being that the same type of power may in principle have different types of 'grounds'. But a *token* power is plausibly individuated by its manifestation-type only in conjunction with the power's *possessor* and *time of possession*. For instance, a particular grain of salt's *particular* or *token* power to dissolve in water is individuated by its manifestation-type—the activity of dissolving in water—together with that grain of salt and the time at which it possesses the power. The identity of that token power is entirely determined or 'fixed' by its being the power *to dissolve in water* that *that grain of salt* has at a certain time, t—where t may be either an instant of time or, more probably, a continuous period of time. If the same object has a power to dissolve in water at two successive times, between which it lacks any such power, then I think we should say that it has *two different token powers* at the successive times, not just one token power whose existence has been temporarily interrupted.

IMPREDICATIVE IDENTITY CRITERIA AND THE CIRCULARITY PROBLEM

Although I said earlier that we should not *confuse* identity criteria with principles of individuation, it is also clear that a principle of individuation for Ks can provide us with a criterion of identity for Ks, but not necessarily *vice versa*. Thus, suppose we are right to say that token powers are individuated by their manifestation-types, possessors, and times of possession. Then we may state the following as a criterion of identity for token powers:[9]

> (CIP) If P and Q are token powers, then $P = Q$ iff P and Q have the same manifestation-type, M, possessor, O, and time of possession, t.

Now, (CIP) *seems* to meet all the desiderata for an adequate criterion of identity. First, it is *non-trivial*. An important point in this connection is that a power, P, is never identical with its manifestation-type, M. This is obviously true of *token* powers, since types cannot be identical with tokens. But it is also true of power-*types*. Clearly, even though a power can be a power to acquire *another power*, a power cannot be a power to acquire *itself*: it cannot *be* its own manifestation-type. Secondly, (CIP) is *formally correct* inasmuch as it specifies the identity conditions of token powers in terms of *an equivalence relation* (distinct from identity itself) on powers, namely, the relation of having the same manifestation-type, possessor, and time of possession. However, there is a further issue that we need to consider here and that is whether (CIP) involves any kind of *circularity* that would serve to vitiate it as a criterion of identity. This is where we must return to the question of whether or not the manifestation-types of all powers are or involve the acquisition of other powers; for if they do, it may be worried that (CIP) is implicitly circular in a vicious way.

An obvious analogy here is with the well-known criterion of identity for token *events* once proposed (and later retracted) by Donald Davidson:[10]

> (CIE) If *e* and *f* are token events, then *e* = *f* iff *e* and *f* have the same causes and effects.

The first thing to observe about (CIE) is that it illustrates our earlier point that criteria of identity are not just the same as principles of individuation. It is not plausible to maintain that an event's causes and effects are *essential* features of it and thus qualify as its *individuators*, because it is very plausible to suppose that the same event *could have had* different causes and effects from those that it actually has. Another illustration of this point is provided by the 'Lockean' criterion of identity for *material objects*— 'Lockean' because Locke maintained that no two material objects of the same sort (for example, two *cats* or two *tables*) could exist in the same place at the same time:[11]

> (CIM) If *x* and *y* are material objects, then *x* = *y* iff *x* and *y* are objects of the same sort and have the same spacetime trajectory.

For, once again, it is not plausible to maintain that a material object's spacetime trajectory is an *essential* feature of it: any cat or table, for instance, *could have occupied* different spacetime locations from those that it actually occupies. More immediately important for present purposes, however, is the fact that (CIE) appears to be *viciously circular*, at least if one supposes that all causation is *event* causation, for this implies that all of an event's causes and effects are *themselves events* and so subject to (CIE). In short, (CIE) is an *impredicative* identity criterion, because the equivalence relation on events to which it appeals in order to specify the identity conditions of events itself involves *identity relations between events*.

Now, a number of philosophers, including myself, have observed that such impredicativity *as such* need not be fatal in a criterion of identity.[12] For instance, it is not a fatal objection to the status of the Axiom of Extensionality as a criterion of identity for sets that *sets themselves* may be members of sets. That criterion may be stated thus:

(CIS) If x and y are sets, then $x = y$ iff x and y have the same members.

For, at least in standard set theory, every set has in its transitive closure either certain *non*-sets or at least the (unique) empty set, with the consequence that, by repeated applications of (CIS), we can be guaranteed that that criterion will serve to identify or distinguish *any* two sets x and y, even if they contain other sets in their transitive closure. (CIS) itself, of course, establishes the uniqueness of the empty set, because sets with *no* members trivially have *the same* members. And it might be thought that similar considerations can save (CIE) from vicious circularity. Thus, it may be pointed out that the causal structure of events in a given world could be such that, *as a matter of fact*, each event's place in that structure is uniquely specifiable in causal terms, in a way that makes (CIE) applicable to those events.[13] In a very simple case, for example, such a structure might contain just three events, e, f, and g, such that e has no causes and has f as its only immediate effect, while g has only f as its immediate cause and has no effects. See figure 1.1 at the bottom of the page.

In this structure, there is *just one* event with no causes and exactly two effects (event e), *just one* event with exactly one cause and exactly one effect (event f), and *just one* event with exactly two causes and no effects (event g). (Here we are assuming, of course, that causation is transitive, but it would make no material difference for present purposes if it were not.) Thus, each event is uniquely specified by its place in the causal structure, in a way that makes (CIE) applicable to those events: for, given the above causal facts about the structure, it follows that each member of the pairs $\{e, f\}$, $\{f, g\}$ and $\{e, g\}$ differs from the other member in respect of at least some of its causes or effects. And who is to say that the *actual* world is not a world whose causal structure similarly provides a unique specification for every event in it, in a way that makes (CIE) applicable? In which case, would not (CIE) be vindicated?

No, it would not. What philosophers who take this line of thought forget is that a criterion of identity for entities of a kind K is supposed to be a *metaphysical* principle, telling us what the identity and distinctness of Ks *consists in*, to use Locke's well-known phrase.[14] As such, it is a principle that should hold for Ks in *any* possible world in which they exist. (CIE) does not meet this desideratum, because there are evidently worlds in which there are events but in which, owing to a *symmetry* in the causal structure of the world in question, (CIE) *fails to determine*, with respect to every pair of events in that world,

Figure 1.1   A causal structure in which (CIE) is applicable.

whether or not they are identical.[15] See Figure 1.2 at the bottom of the page, in which events *g* and *h* are distinct but (CIE) is incapable of distinguishing them, because they both have the same causes (*e* and *f*) and effects (none).

The mere fact that, in a certain world—perhaps even the actual world—a certain principle happens to reflect the fact that a unique place within a certain structure is occupied by *every entity* of a kind *K* in that world does not mean that that principle qualifies as a *criterion of identity* for *K*s in that world. We should not be misled in this regard by the set-theoretical example discussed earlier: for, of course, given the correctness of standard set theory, (CIS) serves to determine, with respect to every pair of sets *in any world whatever*, whether or not they are identical. (CIE) only does the same for events in *some* worlds—and that is not good enough for it to qualify as a genuine criterion of identity for events. For it doesn't serve to tell us what the identity and distinctness of events, considered purely as such, *consists in*. This cannot be supposed to depend on contingent features of just some worlds in which events exist, since it is a fact about the very nature of events.

POWER-STRUCTURES AND THE INDIVIDUATION OF POWERS

Perhaps it will be guessed, now, in what direction we are being taken with regard to the question of the identity and individuation of powers. Suppose it is maintained, contrary to what I myself proposed earlier, that the manifestation-types of all powers either are or involve the acquisition of other powers. It might still be thought that this fact would not necessarily vitiate a criterion of identity for powers framed in terms of their manifestation-types, such as (CIP). For it might be supposed, analogously with the case of (CIE), that the *power-structure* of a world could be such that every power in it occupies a unique structural position with respect to all other powers in that world.[16] There might be a kind of circularity involved, in that the identity or distinctness of every pair of powers in that world turns on the identity or distinctness of *other* pairs of powers in that world—but not, it may be urged, a *vicious* one. (It is important to note that it is not at all crucial whether or not I am right in supposing that a single power has only *one*

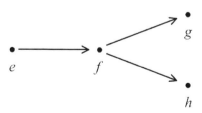

Figure 1.2   A causal structure in which (CIE) is not applicable.

manifestation-type, so we can set aside that issue with regard to the matter now in hand.) So, the thought might be that, whatever might be the case in *some* possible worlds, at least in the *actual* world (CIP) might turn out to be an adequate criterion of identity for powers, even though the equivalence relation on powers to which (CIP) appeals itself involves *identity relations between powers*, rendering (CIP) *impredicative* like (CIS) and (CIE). Of course, my objection to this suggestion is, as with the case of (CIE), that an adequate criterion of identity for entities of any kind K must be applicable to Ks in *any* world in which Ks exist. And while (CIS) passes this test, (CIP) does not if the supposition now at issue is true, any more than (CIE) does— this supposition being, recall, that the manifestation-types of all powers either are or involve the acquisition of other powers.

At this point, it is worth returning to another important matter discussed earlier: the difference between *criteria of identity* and *principles of individuation*. I remarked that a criterion of identity may be derived from a principle of individuation, but not necessarily *vice versa*. A significant difference between (CIP) and (CIS), on the one hand, and (CIE) on the other is that the former derive from principles of individuation but the latter does not. One way to think of the difference is as follows: (CIP) and (CIS) both have the status of putative *transworld* identity criteria, but (CIE) has only the status of a putative *intraworld* identity criterion. In advancing (CIE), Davidson had no intention of implying that any event must have the same causes and effects in every possible world in which it exists—just that any two events in a possible world that have the same causes and effects *in that world* are for that reason identical events, that is, that no two distinct events can be such that there is some possible world in which they have the same causes and effects.[17] By contrast, because (CIS) derives from the principle of individuation of sets—which is that they are individuated by *their members*—it *does* serve as a transworld identity criterion for sets: any set must indeed have the same members in every possible world in which it exists, for *which* set it is is entirely determined by which things are its members. Likewise, then, because (CIP) derives from the putative principle of individuation of powers, it should serve as a putative transworld criterion of identity for powers: if (CIP) is correct, any token power must have the same manifestation-type, possessor, and time of possession *in every possible world in which it exists*. In this connection, it is important not to confuse the point that some criteria of identity, such as (CIS), are *transworld* criteria of identity with the point that any adequate criterion of identity must be *applicable in every possible world*. The latter point applies equally both to criteria like (CIS), which are transworld criteria, and to criteria like (CIE), which purports only to be an intraworld criterion. The mere fact that (CIE) purports only to be an intraworld criterion does not exempt it from the requirement of being applicable in every possible world—a requirement which, as we have seen, it fails to satisfy.

Now, if a criterion of identity qualifies as a transworld criterion, because it derives from a principle of individuation, then we know that it must be applicable in *every* possible world if it is applicable in *any*. A criterion of identity, C, cannot be applicable *across* certain possible worlds unless it is also applicable *within* all of those worlds. To deny this commits one to the absurdity of having to allow that there might be two entities, x and y, both of which exist in each of two worlds, w and v, such that, according to C, x in w is identical with y in v and yet C *does not determine* whether or not x in v is identical with y in v. If C determines that x in w is identical with y in v, then *a fortiori* it determines that x in v is identical with y in v. For if C applies across w and v, then it must, obviously, determine that x in v is identical with x in w—whence, by the transitivity of identity, it determines that x in v is identical with y in v. See Figure 1.3 at the bottom of the page.

Thus, for example, Davidson's putative criterion of identity for events, (CIE), could only turn out to be applicable in some possible worlds but not in others because it is supposed to qualify only as an intraworld criterion.

The foregoing fact gives us an additional reason for contending that (CIP) is inadequate as a criterion of identity for token powers if it fails to be applicable even in just *one* possible world. For (CIP), like (CIS), is derived from a principle of individuation and so should be applicable in every possible world if it is applicable in any. Adherents of (CIP) cannot therefore allow that there should be *any* possible world in which it would not be applicable (even setting aside my own contention that all adequate criteria of identity should, in any case, be applicable in every possible world in which entities of the kinds that they concern exist). But it appears that this is what they *must* allow, if they think that the manifestation-types of powers always are or involve the acquisition of *other powers*. For then it seems that they must allow that there are worlds containing powers in which the power-structure is such that (CIP) does *not* serve to identify a unique position in that structure for every power, on account of some kind of symmetry in the structure. If powers really are *individuals*, there cannot be a

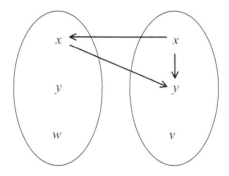

Figure 1.3   Transworld applicability entails intraworld applicability.

world in which there are *unindividuated* powers. But if powers are always individuated at least in part by *other powers*, there can be no guarantee that all of the powers in a possible world are fully individuated, because 'two' powers may stand in the same power-structure relations to all 'other' powers, such that nothing in that structure determines *which* power either of these powers is. It surely will not do to proclaim as an *a priori* truth that the power-structure of any possible world *must* exhibit asymmetries which permit the assignment of each power in that world to a unique position in the structure. (Essentially the same objection may be raised against any philosopher who, unlike Davidson himself, maintains that (CIE) qualifies as a transworld criterion of identity: it simply isn't credible to suppose that causal structures like that of Figure 1.2 are *metaphysically impossible*— and yet this is what must be maintained by any philosopher who holds that (CIE) derives from the *principle of individuation* of events.)

I conclude that those philosophers who think that only a benign circularity need be involved in the claim that all powers are at least in part individuated by other powers are deceiving themselves. First, they are failing to distinguish properly between criteria of identity and principles of individuation. Second, they are failing to recognize that even those criteria of identity, such as (CIE) and (CIM), which purport only to function as *intraworld* criteria, still need to be *applicable* in every possible world in which entities of the kinds that they concern exist—which is why (CIE) itself turns out to be inadequate.

IS THERE A PROBLEM ABOUT NON-POWER PROPERTIES?

But why should any philosopher even be tempted to suppose that the manifestation-type of any power always is or involves the acquisition of other powers? This is worth asking because, of course, it is only this supposition that has raised a dispute about the adequacy of (CIP) as a criterion of identity for powers. If it turns out that there must be a *hierarchy* of power-types of descending orders, such that for every power-type of order n there is a sequence of $(n-1)$ successively lower-order power-types, with each power-type in the sequence having as its manifestation-type the *next* lower power-type in the sequence and terminating in a first-order power-type whose manifestation-type is a *non*-power, then (CIP) is guaranteed to be free of vicious circularity, for the same sort of reason that (CIS) is according to standard set theory. Why should any philosopher doubt that this must be the case? Well, they might think that the very notion of a '*non-power* property' of a concrete object makes no sense because, they suppose, such a property would be causally *perfectly inert*. For this sort of reason, some philosophers contend that there are really no purely 'categorical' or 'qualitative' properties—*only* power properties, even if some of them may also be in some way 'qualitative' or have a 'qualitative aspect'.[18] For instance, they urge that even a *shape* property, such as sphericity, cannot be coherently thought of as being a pure non-power, because that would imply that sphericity made no difference whatever to a spherical object's causal behaviour—in which case we couldn't even *tell* whether or not an object was spherical, because perception of an object's properties requires some sort of causal interaction between the perceiver and the object. Such philosophers typically urge that part of what it is *to be* a spherical object— part of the *essence* of sphericity—consists in the powers that an object has in virtue of its sphericity, such as the power to roll down an inclined plane or to cast a circular shadow when it is illuminated from a suitable angle or, indeed, to *look* spherical to a normally sighted person.

However, this suggestion, it seems to me, rests upon a confusion. *Of course* we should acknowledge that a spherical object's sphericity is at least partly responsible for some of its powers, including some of its causal powers. It is partly because a spherical object is *spherical* that it has a power to roll down an inclined plane—only partly, because it doesn't have such a power unless it is also heavy and rigid, unlike a spherical soap bubble. But that is no reason to think that *what it is*, at least in part, for an object to be spherical is for it to have such a power when it also has such other properties.[19] We know perfectly well precisely *what it is* for an object to be spherical and it has nothing whatever to do with such powers: rather, what it is for an object to be spherical is simply for the object to have as its boundary a surface all the points of which are equidistant from a given point. Sphericity as such is a *purely geometrical property*, fully definable in the way just stated.[20] It is easy to understand, given some basic laws of mechanics, *why* an object possessing this property along with rigidity and weight has a power to roll down an inclined plane, whereas a cube-shaped object does not. But the power in question is *quite distinct* from the property of sphericity as such. At most, sphericity is part of the *ground* of that power in such an object. Other geometrical properties, such as cylindricality, can be part of the ground of the same power (that is to say, of the same power-*type*) in other objects. An object's sphericity *by itself* apparently confers no specific causal power upon it, but it can certainly *contribute* to the grounds of an object's causal powers and in that way 'make a difference to the object's causal behaviour'. Sphericity doesn't *itself* have to be some sort of power in order to do this. Thus, there is no good argument in the making here for the conclusion that there are no purely non-power properties of concrete objects. Indeed, there are many other plausible examples of such properties (in a broad sense of 'property'), such as the very activity of *rolling* that takes place when an object possessing the power to roll down an inclined plane manifests that power. Rolling has a purely geometrical-cum-kinematic definition and is not *itself* a power to do anything, even if it is, no doubt, *part of the ground* of various powers.

These observations also help to undermine another line of argument that is sometimes used against the idea of there being non-power properties, namely, that unless a property is a power with one or more manifestation-types which link it *necessarily* with other properties, there is nothing to ground the identity of the *very same* property existing in other possible worlds, so that transworld identity for non-power properties would have to be primitive and hence mysterious. Two possible worlds could thus be indistinguishable in respect of their natural laws, it is suggested, apart from the fact that wherever in one of those worlds the non-power property *P* is exemplified, in the other the numerically distinct non-power property *Q* is exemplified, and *vice versa*. And this, it is said, makes no sense for any natural property. For instance, it makes no sense to suppose that there is another possible world whose natural laws are indistinguishable from those of the actual world apart from the fact that the properties of negative and positive unit charge are 'swapped' for each other. Commitment to the possibility of 'primitive' transworld identity for certain properties is sometimes called 'quidditism' and is often rejected for the same sort of reason that 'haecceitism' is frequently rejected where the transworld identity of *objects* is concerned—this latter being understood as the doctrine that two possible worlds can differ *merely* with respect to the numerical identity of one or more objects existing in those worlds.[21]

This line of argument is mistaken, I think. As we have seen, there is every reason to suppose that *sphericity* is a purely geometrical property and as such a pure non-power property. It is also clear that sphericity is numerically distinct from various other such properties, such as *cylindricality* and *cubicness*. Each of these properties has a distinct purely geometrical 'real' definition which expresses its essence and therefore serves as a ground of its transworld identity—without any implication that the latter is 'primitive' and 'mysterious'.[22] At the same time, it is clear that two possible worlds *couldn't* be indistinguishable in respect of their natural laws apart from the fact, say, that sphericity and cubicness were 'swapped' for each other. For some of those laws will be mechanical laws governing the dynamic and kinematic behaviour of objects possessing various shapes—and such laws are obviously not indifferent to the geometrical properties of objects. There could not be a world with laws exactly like those of this world except that all of the laws that actually apply to spherical objects applied instead to cubical ones and *vice versa*. One such law in the actual world is that a heavy, rigid, spherical object will, if unobstructed, roll down an inclined plane. But there is *no* possible world in which a heavy, rigid, *cubical* object rolls down an inclined plane. A cubical object simply cannot *roll*, while remaining cubical. It can at best *tumble*. We don't have to build into the very *definition* of sphericity the principle that a spherical object, when it is also rigid and heavy, has a power to roll down an inclined plane, in order to rule out the possibility of 'swapping' sphericity for cubicness in the fanciful manner just envisaged. That is, we don't have to say that the reason why such a 'swap' makes no sense is that it is part of the *essence* of sphericity that an object possessing it, along with rigidity and weight, has a power to roll down an inclined plane, with the consequence that a spherical object couldn't behave just like a cubical one does. We can perfectly well understand, on the basis of the purely geometrical definition of sphericity, why such a 'swap' is impossible.

FURTHER CONSIDERATIONS

My conclusion so far is, thus, that (CIP) is a perfectly adequate criterion of identity for powers and is not threatened by vicious circularity because *not* all powers have as their manifestation-types the acquisition of other powers. There are and must be first-order powers whose manifestation-types are *non*-power properties. If this were not so, then (CIP) would indeed be inadequate because viciously circular. However, there are some further considerations that we need to address before we can take this conclusion to be quite secure.

Suppose a philosopher were to agree that powers (that is, power-*types*) are individuated by their manifestation-types, maintain that the manifestation-type of any power always is or involves the acquisition of other powers, but simply *accept*, as a consequence, that it must also be maintained, in order to secure the applicability of (CIP), that the power-structure of *every possible world* containing powers exhibits no relevant symmetry analogous to that illustrated (in the case of events) by Figure 1.2. Such a philosopher might contend, perhaps, that although this latter thesis may not have much immediate intuitive plausibility, commitment to it is not too high a price to pay for an otherwise attractive view of powers.[23] Is there anything more that we can say to shake the confidence of such a philosopher? I think that there certainly is. For it simply doesn't seem intelligible to suppose that different entities of the same kind can be *each other's sole individuators*. Imagine, for instance, that someone were to try to counter my earlier suggestion that the two electrons orbiting a helium nucleus are not 'individuals' (in my sense) by contending that *each* of them is in fact *the other's* individuator: the obvious and correct reply would be that this suggestion is futile, because viciously circular. Two different entities of the same kind cannot both individuate *each other* any more than—to use the memorable analogy exploited by Russell[24]—two people can make a living by taking in each other's washing. Nor indeed, more generally, can *any* plurality of entities of the same kind all be individuated solely by other members of the same plurality. Consider first the two-entity case. Two distinct Ks cannot *each* determine *which* K the other one is, because unless it is *already* determined which K one of them is, this K cannot fix the identity of the other. And the two-entity case surely generalizes.

Note that the point at issue here exclusively concerns *principles of individuation* as such, not *criteria of identity*. It may well be argued that (CIP)—which is itself only a criterion of identity, albeit one that is *derived* from a principle of individuation—will be applicable in every possible world containing powers, even if all powers have other powers as their manifestation-types, provided that every such world has a suitably asymmetric power-structure. But that doesn't entail that in any such world all of the powers will be properly *individuated*—only that, for every pair of powers in such a world, (CIP) will determine *whether or not the members of that pair are identical*. And this is not at all the same as saying that the *identity* of every power in such a world will be fixed. Once again, we always must distinguish clearly between 'identity' understood as a *relation* and 'identity' in the sense of *individual essence*—and it is the latter notion that is now in play.

It is instructive to consider, here, the case of the *natural numbers*: 0, 1, 2, 3, . . . It seems entirely reasonable to say that each number in the series *except the first* is individuated *by its predecessor* and hence solely by another number in the series. The first number, 0, is not individuated in this way, however. In fact, 0 seems to be *self*-individuating, in virtue of its *essentially* being the sole natural number with *no* predecessor. Exactly the same may be said of the empty set: it too is self-individuating, in virtue of its essentially being the sole set with no members. But it is only *because* there is one number in the natural number series that is *not* individuated solely by other numbers in the series that *other* numbers in the series can be individuated by their predecessors and thus solely by other numbers in the series. So, even if there are no relevant symmetries in the power-structure of a world, I still contend that it cannot be the case that every power in that world is individuated *solely by other powers in that world*. Either some power would have to be somehow self-individuating, by analogy with 0 or the empty set, or else some powers would have to be individuated by *non*-powers. However, a moment's reflection reveals that no power *could* be self-individuating, given that all powers must have manifestation-types and that every power is individuated by its manifestation-type. For, as was pointed out earlier, no power can be *its own* manifestation-type and hence every power's individuator must be an entity that is distinct from itself. The conclusion must therefore be that some powers must have *non*-powers as their manifestation-types.

Suppose now, however, that a philosopher who holds that all powers have other powers as their manifestation-types were also to hold not merely that the power-structure of any possible world containing powers is suitably asymmetric, so as to make (CIP) applicable in every such world, but additionally that any power *belongs to the same power-structure* in every possible world in which it exists. Wouldn't that imply that any power is in fact *individuated* by its position in the power-structure to which it belongs, rather than by its manifestation-type(s)—in which case, it would seem that our preceding objections are ineffectual against such a philosopher? No, it wouldn't, as we shall now see. First, we have to ask what is meant by 'the same power-structure' in this context. By this one could either mean 'the *same* set of powers structured in the same way', or else one could mean '*a* set of powers structured in the same way'. If the *former* is meant, however, then the assertion that any power belongs to the same power-structure in every possible world in which it exists already *presupposes* a transworld criterion of identity for powers and hence a principle of individuation for them (since the same *set* of powers exists in two or more worlds only if the same *powers* do). And nothing that has so far been assumed implies that the principle of individuation in question must be the one that is now under consideration. On the other hand, if the *latter* is meant, then the assertion in question seems to allow that the same power could have different powers as its manifestation-type(s) in different possible worlds. If a power merely needs to stand in the same power-structure *relations* to other powers co-existing with it in any possible world, then it seems that nothing prevents it from standing in those same relations to different sets of powers in different possible worlds, provided only that those sets have the same cardinality. But that means, of course, that powers cannot be *individuated* by their positions in the power-structure to which they belong, since different powers can occupy those positions in different possible worlds.

Very well: but suppose, nonetheless, that a philosopher were to propose that this *is* in fact how powers are individuated—by their positions in the power-structure to which they belong. What would follow? Well, clearly, if all powers are individuated in this fashion, then sets of powers with the same power-structure relations must in fact be *identical*, not merely of the same cardinality. Now, however, we seem to have lost all grip on the notion of *power* itself. What entitles the envisaged philosopher to call a certain structure a *power*-structure? Bear in mind that this philosopher has now abandoned the view that a power is individuated by its *manifestation-type(s)*, since he holds instead that it is individuated solely by its position in a certain structure. (This raises the further question of whether such a 'position' in a structure is to be considered an *entity* in its own right, as it would need to be to qualify as an *individuator* of anything: I shall return to this question shortly.) He calls this kind of structure a *power*-structure, but in fact he seems to be able to tell us no more about *what a power is* beyond saying that it is something that is individuated by its position in such a structure—and that is clearly vacuous, because circular. Even if this charge can somehow be deflected or rebutted, however, the envisaged philosopher is still committed to a remarkably implausible metaphysical thesis, namely, that no two possible worlds can contain different powers but exactly the same power-structure relations. If that is so, then it appears that we cannot really know *which* powers the actual world contains without knowing the power-structure relations of the actual world—and this is something that we almost certainly do not and probably never will know. So, one heavy price of the present proposal is that it seems to generate a radical *power-scepticism*. Even if, as I rather doubt, it can avoid the charge that it leaves us in the dark as to *what* powers are, it almost certainly commits us to ignorance regarding *which* powers there are. And it is hard to see how such a position is any better, epistemically speaking, than *quidditism* is.

There is now a little unfinished business to deal with, adverted to a moment ago. If a power is supposed to be *individuated* by its position in a power-structure, then we need to ask whether such 'positions' and 'structures' are themselves genuine *entities* of any kind. What seems clear is that if they are, then they can only be *abstract* entities of some kind. However, powers themselves—and certainly *token* powers—are surely *concrete* entities, existing in space and time: for they are properties of concrete objects.[25] And how plausible, or even intelligible, is it to suppose that concrete entities of any kind are individuated by abstract ones? The reverse of this is unproblematic. Sets are abstract entities, but can be individuated by concrete ones: they are so whenever they have concrete entities as their members. I suggest, however, that only *abstract* entities can be individuated by other abstract entities—in which case, the proposal now under scrutiny seems to be committed to regarding powers as mere *abstracta*, with nothing *more* to their nature than their positions in certain structures.[26] But in that case, powers are not just *individuated* by those positions: they *are* those positions. And that seems manifestly absurd.

ACKNOWLEDGMENTS

I am very grateful for comments received when previous papers on some of the topics of this paper were presented to audiences at the Universities of Durham and Geneva, and when an earlier version of the present essay was delivered at the conference on 'Powers: Their Grounding and Their Realization' held at Oxford in July 2008.

NOTES

1. See Quine (1969a).
2. See Quine (1969b).
3. See Lowe (1989a).
4. See Locke (1975), III, III, 15.
5. See further Lowe (2003). I say more about individuation in this sense as well as in the *cognitive* sense—the sense in which individuation is the singling out of an entity in thought—in Lowe (2007).
6. See Lowe (1998: 62–3), and Lowe (2005). See also French and Krause (2006).
7. This is George Molnar's view in Molnar (2003), where he says that "each power gets its identity from its manifestation . . . [and] each power has one manifestation" (195). For the view that a single power may have many different manifestations, see Heil (2003: 83).
8. It is said that pigeons, unlike humans, are able to sense the earth's magnetic field and use that ability in navigation—which might lead one to suppose that one of the manifestation-types of magnetism is a certain kind of sensation

in pigeons (so that magnetism would be, for pigeons, a 'secondary' quality, as Locke understands this notion). However, what presumably happens is that the earth's magnetic field has an attractive effect on certain ferrous materials in pigeons' brains, which subsequently gives rise to the sensations in question—in which case we do not have here an example of magnetism manifesting itself *other than* by attracting ferrous metals. (The broader lesson might be that there is something problematic about Locke's notion of a secondary quality as a power to produce sensations of a certain kind, and indeed about his distinction between secondary and 'tertiary' qualities, these last understood as powers to produce effects in other material things.)

9. David Robb has put it to me that two different token powers, possessed by the same object at the same time, might have the *same* manifestation-type: for example, a round ball of soft clay can be pushed through a round hole, both because the clay has the same shape as the hole and because the clay is soft (so that it would squish through the hole regardless of its shape). But it seems to me that we are really dealing with two different manifestation-types here, each corresponding to a different token power: *sliding* (without deformation) through a role hole and *squishing* through a round hole (though it is also clearly true that these are both *ways of passing through a hole*). Only the first of these token powers seems to be manifested when the round ball is pushed through the hole. However, the example does usefully serve to reinforce the point that we need to think carefully about how exactly we should describe a power's manifestation-type.

10. See Davidson (1980a). He retracts it in his reply to Quine in LePore and McLaughlin (eds) (1985). Note that Davidson himself does not distinguish, as I think we should, between criteria of identity and principles of individuation.

11. See Locke (1975), II, XXVII, 1.

12. See Lowe (1989b).

13. I discuss this point in Lowe (2002: 226–8). See also Leon Horsten (forthcoming) and Ladyman (2007).

14. See Locke (1975), II, XXVII, 9.

15. Perhaps we are entitled to assume that there is no possible world in which there are events that are *causally isolated* from one another. But if there are such worlds, then (CIE) clearly fails in, for example, a world in which there are *six* events, each belonging to just one of two three-event structures of the form depicted in Figure 1.1.

16. See Bird (2007a).

17. Some philosophers do, however, appear to believe that any event has its causes and effects essentially, because they hold that causal necessity is nothing other than metaphysical necessity: see, for example, Shoemaker (1998). But it is evident that this view is not compatible with an endorsement of (CIE), given the metaphysical possibility of causal structures like that illustrated in Figure 1.2.

18. Compare Heil (2003: 76–8 and 111–13), although he emphatically eschews all talk of 'aspects' in this connection. Molnar, on the other hand, does countenance the existence of some non-power properties—but very few, and he doesn't include properties of shape: see Molnar (2003: 160). For further discussion of Molnar's theory, see Lowe (2006a: 136–40). For further discussion of Heil's theory, see Lowe (2006b).

19. Note that we attribute sphericity not only to material objects but also to such items as *cavities* and *regions of empty space*: but it doesn't really make sense to say of items like the latter that, for example, they would roll down an inclined plane *if they were heavy and rigid*—for it is *metaphysically*

impossible for such items to be heavy and rigid, or indeed to roll, so that counterfactuals like this one come at as being, at best, merely vacuously true. Hence, I don't concede, in reply to David Robb (personal communication), that 'if a spherical object has other properties (is solid, etc.), then it must roll'. A spherical cavity (for example, in a block of marble) cannot be solid and cannot roll, but is a spherical 'object' nonetheless: and sphericity in such an object is surely not a different property from sphericity in a material object.

20. Louis de Rosset has put it to me that the sphericity of a concrete object *does* involve powers, because its having a *boundary* does—this being defined in terms of *space-occupancy* and the latter involving powers, such as resistance to penetration. However, I don't see how (as de Rosset's contention would apparently require) the sphericity of a concrete object and that of a region of space—which apparently has *no* powers—can be regarded as being *different* properties. Space-occupancy does indeed plausibly involve powers, but a concrete object's boundary—and hence its shape—is surely just that of the (largest) region of space that it fully occupies, where this boundary and shape themselves have purely geometrical definitions involving no powers. To this it may perhaps be replied that some theories of space(time) imply that it does in fact possess powers. However, in the first place, whether such theories are true remains an open question—and one which is not to be settled by current considerations—and, secondly, it is in any case still clear that regions of space, even if they do have powers, cannot have powers at all like those of material objects, such as a power to roll down an inclined plane (see the preceding footnote).

21. See Black (2000). For further discussion, see Hawthorne (2001) and Schaffer (2004).

22. It may be objected that properties like sphericity and cylindricality, precisely because they are *definable*, are not 'basic' properties, in the way that the 'fundamental' properties of physics might be taken to be. However, this controversially assumes that, where natural properties are concerned, there is indeed a 'fundamental level'. For doubts about that, see Schaffer (2003). In any case, for present purposes it is enough to show that there *are* non-power properties, whether or not they are in some sense 'basic'.

23. I am grateful to Alexander Bird for pressing this line of thought with me.

24. See Russell (1927: 325).

25. David Robb asks me (personal communication) whether this means that I take token powers to be *tropes*. I answer that I have no objection to saying this, at least for the purposes of this paper.

26. For insightful discussion of closely related issues concerning the individuation of abstract objects in mathematical structures, see Linnebo (2008).

2 Do Powers Need Powers to Make Them Powerful?

From Pandispositionalism to Aristotle

Anna Marmodoro

THE PROBLEM OF PURE POWERS

The nature of powers is vigorously debated in the literature between, broadly, the dispositionalist camp and the categoricalist camp.[1] The main difference that divides the two camps is whether there are powers that do not depend ontologically on categorical properties—*pure* powers;[2] a secondary issue is whether, if there are pure powers in the world, there need to be categorical properties at all in the ontology.

There is general agreement among philosophers that the case for pure powers ultimately rests with physics. Stathis Psillos summarizes the reasoning behind it:

> "The fundamental properties (the properties of the fundamental particles) are powers. This argument is empirical. Physics . . . posits irreducible powers: mass, charge, and spin. . . . The fundamental properties are ungrounded ('bare') powers. And the argument for this conclusion is that the fundamental particles are simple: they have no internal structure. Hence, they have no parts (components) which can be deemed the bearers of further properties (be they powers or non-powers), which in turn, ground the properties of the particles" (2006: 151).

But Psillos skeptically withholds judgment on the conclusiveness physics has reached on the nature of the properties of the ultimate particles—it is still too early for a settled opinion on this issue (2006: 137; 154). For, granted that the fundamental particles are simple, what identifies and individuates the fundamental properties of the fundamental particles is still an open question.

For Psillos, that the evidence from current physics for the existence of pure powers is inconclusive is good news. The reason is, he argues, is that thinking of properties as pure powers leads to a *regress*, such that the ascription of pure powers to things is incoherent. It follows that physics will face a predicament if its best explanation is that the fundamental properties of particles are pure powers.

All, for Psillos, turns on the question: Do powers need powers to do what powers do? Psillos states they do, since

> "to say that, for instance, fragility is directed to its manifestations even when it is *not* manifested is to say that fragility (F) has the power to manifest itself even when it is not manifested. . . . It seems then that there is an answer to the . . . question [what do powers do when they are not manifested?]: when unmanifested, F has the *power* Q to manifest itself; that's what it does!" (2006: 139).

But this claim commits the dispositionalists to a fatal flaw, Psillos argues

> "I offer a *conceptual* argument against the view that all properties are pure powers. I claim that thinking of all properties as pure powers leads to a regress. . . . If successful, my argument undermines the view of properties as pure powers (*aka* pandispositionalism)" (2006: 137).

This description does not clarify whether Psillos's critique is epistemological or metaphysical. In fact, it turns out to be a combination of the two: it is an argument about the *conceivability* of pure powers, based on a *metaphysical* regress of pure powers that, as we shall see, is *independent* of the pandispositionalist commitment (although Psillos assumes he needs pandispositionalist principles to derive it).

Psillos concludes that the regress can be avoided if powers have categorical properties, not further powers, to help them do what they do. Yet this, he explains, is to take back to the drawing board the question of the ontological difference between powers and non-powers, if powers need *non*-powers to enable them to do what powers do when unmanifested.

I will argue that powers do not need powers to enable them to do what they do when unmanifested, and that no regress is undermining the nature of pure powers.

My strategy will be to begin by tracing Psillos's pure powers regress back to a regress of essences Aristotle developed in his metaphysics. I compare Aristotle's, F.H. Bradley's, and Psillos's regresses, showing that Bradley's and Psillos's (different) conclusions from the regress arguments lead to impasses. I then build on Aristotle's directive against regressive natures, arguing, with him, that an entity is not other than its nature (being divided from it by a relation between them); rather, an entity is an instantiated nature itself. The Aristotelian position I put forward explains how the *oneness* of the entity is achieved by its being an instance of that type. In conclusion, the nature of pure powers would pose no problems of an ontological or epistemological kind if physics gave us reasons to posit pure powers.

My aim is not to argue *for* pure powers but to remove an obstacle for the possibility of an ontology of pure powers. Yet the removal of this obstacle is of more general interest, as it invokes principles of wider metaphysical application.

THE ESSENCE OF A PURE POWER

Powers are entities that are in a state of "readiness for action." When given appropriate circumstances they interact with their environment. There are two aspects of this metaphor that are especially puzzling in the case of pure powers. The first is that "readiness for action" is *all* that pure powers are. The second is that this is a feature normally associated with the mental, not the physical.[3]

There is a history to the mentality aspect of the metaphor. C.B. Martin and K. Pfeifer put forward the idea that the (then) available characterizations of intentionality failed to distinguish "intentional mental states from non-intentional dispositional states" or powers (1986: 531). U.T. Place proposed in response that we think of intentionality as the mark, not of the mental, but of the dispositional (1996: 92).[4] At the present time, his influence is widening in the circle of power-ontologists who define a power in terms of its directionality toward its manifestation. George Molnar for example writes, "having a direction to a particular manifestation is constitutive of the power property" (2003: 60). In the case of pure powers, in John Heil's words, "*all there is* to [such] a property is its contribution to the dispositionalities of its possessors" (2003: 97).

Directedness captures the point of the comparison between intentionality and powers. Just as an intentional state is directed toward something beyond itself, so a power is directed toward its manifestation. Just as in the case of an intentional state, what it points to need not exist; similarly in the case of a power, what it points to need not come about, since a power may never be manifested (e.g. Molnar 2003: 62–3). A vase has the power of fragility that is directed toward breaking even when the vase never breaks, or an electric charge has the power to attract or repel even if no charged particle ever comes close enough to be attracted or repelled.[5] On the hypothesis that powers are pure, there is nothing more to fragility than the vase's disposition to breaking under certain circumstances, and nothing more to charge than the particle's disposition to attract or repel.

Molnar's thinking about powers along the model of intentionality directs the development of Psillos's argument, who describes powers as follows:

> "Physical powers . . . are intentional properties: they are *directed* towards their (possibly non-existent) manifestation. Accordingly, the distinctive feature of powers (as opposed to non-powers) is that they possess (or display) physical intentionality: they are *directed* towards their manifestations. . . . Molnar's appeal to physical intentionality

(directedness) can be seen as an answer to the . . . question [What do powers do when they are not manifested?]: when a power is not manifested, it is *directed* to its manifestation. Being directed to its manifestation is a property of a power" (2006: 139).

This is the core conception in Psillos's understanding of the nature of a power that plants the seed that will bloom into a regress. Based on this he will argue for the rejection of pure powers from ontology. Let us turn to the regress.

THE POWER REGRESS

The regress with which Psillos charges the nature of pure powers is based on the assumption we encountered in the last quotation, that physical-directedness toward a manifestation of φ-ing is a *property* of power F. In fact it is a necessary property of it.[6] The regress follows.

Let F be the power of an object to φ. That is, power F is directed toward its manifestation, the object's φ-ing. Let F's directedness toward its manifestation be called "Q". By Psillos's assumption, Q is a necessary property of F. Since Q is a property of F, it follows that F and Q are different entities.[7] Let us call this the non-identity premise. Thus, given power F, there is a further entity Q, and F has Q as a necessary property.

Here Psillos introduces the pandispositionalist assumption that all properties are powers. Q is a property of F, and as such, a power of F—F's power to manifest itself. As a power, Q is itself directed toward its own manifestation. By assumption, Q's directedness toward its manifestation is a necessary property of Q, call it "R". Since R is a property of Q, it follows that Q and R are different entities. From the pandispositionalist assumption, property R is a power of Q. As such it has the power S to manifest itself, where, S is different from R. And so on . . . Thus the regress takes off (Psillos, 2006: 139).

The pivotal point on which the regress turns is not the pandispositionalist assumption, but rather Psillos's assumption that the directedness of a power is a *property* of it and as such *different* from it. Thus, given a power, there is a second entity, its directedness-property. Pandispositionalism is then used by Psillos to replicate the phenomenon, but as we shall see it is not needed. So it is the non-identity premise in the previous derivation that generates the regress, and this premise is the metaphysical focus of the present investigation.[8]

There are two aspects to the regress: the assumption of the ontological *division* and the assumption of the *iteration* of the division within a pure power. I shall examine each of the two assumptions that lead to the regress.

THE POWER OF A POWER?

The ontological division between a pure power F and its "directedness towards a manifestation of φ-ing" is not justified by Psillos but assumed. For a start, the claim that directedness toward φ-ing is a *property* of a *pure* power F invites the question what is pure power F over and above the directedness toward φ-ing. It is presumably something that has this directedness, but what? What Psillos tells us is that:

"F is the power to φ" (2006: 139).

This is what F *is*. But then Psillos continues:

"Suppose we grant that when unmanifested, power F has the power Q to manifest itself, that is to φ" (2006: 139).

So, here F *has* the power to φ. How can this be? How can F *be* the power to φ, and also *have* the power to φ? Furthermore, if F and Q are two totally coincident powers that have the same definition (each being a power to φ), how can they be different? What sets them apart?

Psillos addresses this issue by stating:

"The intuitive idea here is that whereas fragility is the power of an object to break, Q is the power *of fragility* to manifest itself" (2006: 140).

This seems to offer us a different definition for Q than for fragility F; furthermore each of these two powers belongs to a different subject. Fragility is the power of an object to break, and Q is the power of fragility to manifest itself. The second definition is, at best, contracted. What does it mean that fragility manifests *itself*? It is not that the power of fragility comes to be, for the power of fragility has been present, actual, in the fragile object all along. Nor does fragility manifest itself in the sense of becoming apparent; only the breaking of the object becomes apparent. Rather, to see what it is that is manifested we need to look at what fragility is.

Fragility is a power of an object to break. That is, fragility is directed toward the breaking of the object. Hence, becoming manifested, for fragility, is reaching the target at which it is directed. But the target is the breaking of the object. Therefore, fragility's manifestation is the occurrence of the breaking of the object. Now Q was defined as "the power *of fragility* to manifest itself"; so, since fragility's manifestation is the occurrence of the breaking of the object, Q is the power of fragility to bring about the breaking of the object. But this is what fragility is, "the power of an object to break". So it is far from clear that a distinction has been made between Q and F, even after pursuing the "intuitive idea" of their difference. Is positing

Q as a distinct power from F ill-conceived? If so, the ontological division within a pure power is unjustified and the regress does not get started.

It seems prima facie that there is no need for Q; in fact, there is not even the possibility that Q be. A power does not seem to need a further power to take it from the unmanifested to the manifested state, since the power itself can take the object from potential φ-ing to actual φ-ing. So when Psillos says that "the intuitive idea here is that whereas fragility is the power *of an object* to break, Q is the power *of fragility* to manifest itself" (2006: 140), there does not seem to be an intuition to explore. Can we make sense, intuitively, of the object breaking and, over and above this, of fragility additionally manifesting itself at the same time with the breaking? What more does fragility do, beyond facilitating the breaking of the object, by manifesting itself? How can the breaking of the object not be the manifestation of fragility? Or are we supposed to understand here that the breaking is triggered by fragility manifesting itself? Is Q what drives the object's fragility? But then it would follow that fragility is powerless and that Q does all the work for it. Yet since Q is itself a power, it too would be powerless and R would do all the work for it; and so on. What appears to be the case then about this intuitive division between F and Q is that if Q's job is to *empower* fragility to become manifested, F and all other powers are powerless.

IS Q TO F AS GENUS IS TO SPECIES?

Psillos offers a metaphysical argument against the identity of F and Q, that is, fragility and its power to manifest itself:

> "Grant that the directedness of fragility is a *power* Q. If Q is a power, it is directed to its own manifestation. When is Q manifested? Exactly when fragility is manifested. But of course, this does not imply that Q and F (fragility) are one and the same property. To use a parallel (but not identical) case, the property of being red and the property of having colour are co-instantiated by a red rose but they are not the same property. Or the property of being trilateral and the property of being triangular are co-instantiated by triangles but they are not the same property"(2006: 140).

The argument for the difference between F and Q consists in the introduction of two parallel cases. The claim is that the relation between fragility and the power to manifest itself is analogous to the relation between being red and having color or the relation of being triangular and being trilateral.

Psillos's examples of having a color and being red and of being trilateral and being triangular are examples of the relation of a genus to its species (where being trilateral can include figures with curved sides). Whether a genus (for example, having color) is a distinct property over and above the species property (for example being red) is an ontological problem of its own that could hardly illuminate the present situation. But what is much clearer is that such examples do not provide a parallel to the present case. Q is the ability to be manifested. But the ability to be manifested is *not* a genus of species of powers such as fragility, magnetism, softness, and so on; it is a meta-description of powers, such as that of being a property is for properties or that of being a thing (or substance) is for things (or substances). Being a power is *not* a *generic type* of species of powers any more than being a substance is a genus of feline and canine. 'Being capable of being manifested' is a gloss on what we mean by the term power and provides a meta-description of items in a classificatory system. It is no more a property of powers than being a power is a property of powers or being a property is a property of properties. These terms or descriptions are formal characterizations of things in respect to how they are classified in the ontology, rather than in respect to their constitutive nature. Understanding the division in question thus leads to the following: the ability to be manifested is *not* a *constitutive power* of a power, but rather a classificatory description of the ontology.

Nevertheless, we should not (yet) give up on Psillos's division. We should explore a different direction the argument could have taken, in view of the way Q was initially introduced as a property that secures "a necessary connection between the power and its manifestation" (2006: 139). Maybe the division Psillos is after is between an entity and its *essence*, rather than what seemed to be between an entity and its classificatory qualification. In that case, herein would be the division between a power and its directionality. This way of conceiving of the division avoids the meta-description objection to it. Let us investigate this conception.

THE ESSENCE REGRESS

The division between an entity and its essence has already been explored in an ancestor of Psillos's regress, which makes a stronger and more universal case for the regress than we have so far encountered in his defense of it. The ancestor of Psillos regress was developed by Aristotle in his *Metaphysics*. We shall first see how it makes a stronger case for Psillos's regress, and then examine what it reveals about the nature of powers.

Saying that an entity F 'is a power to φ' expresses the nature of that entity. It is the answer to the question: 'What is F?' Psillos says that "the distinctive feature of powers . . . is that . . . they are directed towards their manifestations" (2006: 139), which, in light of Heil's clarification about pure powers (2003: 97) quoted earlier, leads to the conception that all there is to a pure power is directedness toward the manifestation of φ-ing. This is what an unmanifested power is: merely an instance of physical intentionality.

The Aristotelian regress that is the predecessor of Psillos's regress is built as follows. Consider the essence E of F: directedness toward the manifestation of φ-ing. E, being an entity of a certain kind, will itself have an essence, call it E_1: what it is to be directedness toward the manifestation of φ-ing. The essence of E_1 will be E_2: what it is to be what it is to be directedness toward the manifestation of φ-ing. E_2 will have an essence, E_3, . . . and so on to infinity. Aristotle writes,

> "The absurdity of the separation [between an entity and its essence] would appear also if one were to assign a name to each of the essences; for there would be another essence besides the original one, e.g. to the essence of horse there will belong a second essence . . . If they [say, the number one and its essence] were different, the process would go on to infinity; for we should have the essence of one, and the one, so that in their case also the same infinite regress would be found" (*Metaphysics* 1031b28–1032a4).

The generative principle at work is that every entity that makes a claim to *inherent oneness* is essentially a *type* of entity.[9] The main assumption for the regress is that the essential type is a *property* of the entity and so, different from the entity itself.[10]

Let us compare this regress to Psillos's regress. On the present reading of his argument, Psillos generates the division for the property regress by assuming the distinctness of a property from a further, necessary property it possesses, for example between fragility and its directedness toward breaking. The assumption that the directedness of fragility is an arithmetically different property from fragility itself gives the Aristotelian division between essence and entity. Psillos iterates the division using a different generative principle than Aristotle's, based on the pandispositionalist assumption—that all properties are powers, and so since a power has the necessary property of directionality, the property is a power, which is itself directed . . . and so on. The generative principle Aristotle uses for iterating the division between an entity and its essence, namely, that an essence has an essence, is independent of pandispositionalism, so it iterates the same division as Psillos's, but with a generality that takes this division beyond the domain of powers to all entities. Let us then use their common division between an entity and its essence, plus Aristotle's generative principle of the essence of an essence to reconstruct Psillos's property regress, but this time without the pandispositionalist assumption.

Let F be a property such as fragility. Psillos states that "F has the power Q to . . . φ", where Q is a property of F, namely F's directedness toward the manifestation of breaking (2006: 139). Fragility's directedness toward breaking, Q, is the essence of the property of fragility. Psillos's tacit assumption for his regress, which is explicitly Aristotle's assumption too for his own regress, is that the essential nature of an entity is a *property* of it. We now have a common division and a common principle of iteration: Q is the essence of property F and is arithmetically different from F; being itself a property, Q will have an essential nature of its own, different from itself, say property R; similarly R will have its own essence, . . . and so on to infinity. So Psillos's regress survives the abandonment of the pandispositionalist assumption, and is regenerated from his division as a regress of essential properties rather than of necessary powers.

ESSENCE AS SUBJECT—ESSENCE AS PROPERTY

We have seen from the previous analysis that it is Psillos's division that gives rise to his regress, not the pandispositionalist assumption. He defined F as "the power to φ" and then divided F from its essence Q: the power to manifest φ-ing (2006: 139). Let us consider the division between an entity and its essence.

Faced with the regress, Psillos concluded aporetically that perhaps the regress can be blocked if the essence of a power is not a further power but a non-power. This retains and firms up the initial division between a power and its essence but rejects pandispositionalism. As Psillos recognizes, this way of blocking the regress condemns powers to impotence since a non-power is called upon to empower a power to be directed to its manifestation. By contrast, Aristotle raised the same regress problem but reached just the opposite conclusion from Psillos, by giving up the division: *an entity is one with its instantiated essence.*

Aristotle, as we saw, makes the initial assumption that an entity has its essence as a property and from this division he derives a regress of essences. To block the regress, he concludes that an entity is its essence; namely, an entity does *not* have the *instantiation* of its essential type as a property, but rather is identical to the instantiation of its essential type:

> "Each . . . self-subsistent thing is one and the same as its essence" (*Metaphysics* 1032a2–4).

All that Socrates is is this instantiation of 'human being'. This still allows one to abstract from Socrates the general type 'human being', that is to abstract from *this* instantiation of 'human being' its general type, which Socrates shares with Xanthippe and Phaedo. But the conclusion Aristotle derived from this regress is that, whereas Socrates is not identical to this instantiation of wisdom or this instantiation of two-footedness, etc., he is identical to this instantiation of 'human being'. The instantiation of wisdom is a characteristic of a human being, but the instantiation of 'human being' is not a characteristic of a human being: it *is* the human being.

The argument for the oneness of a substance and its essence is developed by Aristotle in two steps. I will here only sketch it in the broadest terms to indicate its far-reaching significance. In *Metaphysics* VII.6, Aristotle undertakes to "inquire whether each thing and its essence are the same or different" (1031a15–6) and proceeds to argue, through the regress we examined before, for the oneness of an entity and its essence. The examples he uses in *Metaphysics* VII.6 are of immaterial, abstract entities. The reason for this is that material entities face the additional challenge to their oneness with their essence that they are constituted of material components. In consequence, Aristotle needs to investigate whether his hylomorphic account of material entities as composites of matter and form undermines their oneness with their essences. If a material entity is composed of matter and form, is the composite of the *two* different from the instantiation of the essential type of that entity or the same?[11] Aristotle addresses this in *Metaphysics* VII.17.

Aristotle's begins his second step in the investigation of the oneness of a thing with its instantiated essence with the Syllable regress in *Metaphysics* VII.17.[12] The Syllable regress is a metaphysical milestone that anticipates Bradley's regress by two millennia. Aristotle asks the following question: Suppose two letters, f and a, make up a syllable fa; what unites two separate letters into one syllable? If it is a further element in the syllable that unites the two letters into a syllable, Aristotle continues, then the syllable is composed of three elements—the two letters and their unifier; what is it then that unites these three elements into one syllable? If further unifiers relate the three elements to one another uniting them into a syllable, the argument applies again, questioning what unifies old and new elements into one syllable . . . and so on to infinity.

Importantly, Aristotle's conclusion from the regress is not that there are no unifiers or relations, which Bradley (1893) concluded. Realizing that unifiers are needed to explain how the many are one, he concludes that *there are* indeed unifiers, but they *cannot be further elements in the ontology*.[13] Rather, unifiers are *ways of unifying* the elements. According to Aristotle, a unifier of elements is *a principle of operation on the elements* that are unified. Unifying elements which are arithmetically and even qualitatively diverse into one entity is achieved by the elements changing or even transforming. A minimal change is such as when the boundaries of the elements are altered in one way or another, as in the case of a dollop of honey becoming one with the rest of the honey in a jar.[14] A maximal change is when the nature of the elements is changed in order to produce a unity, as in the case of the ingredients that go into making a loaf of bread. The result of the unification is a single entity that is individuated as an instantiation of the essential type; here it is the syllable fa.

I understand Aristotle's hylomorphism as a doctrine of *instantiation by change*: the material elements facilitate the instantiation of the essential type by being transformed in accordance with the essential type's organizational principle. When the essence is instantiated, the physical components are all unified into a single thing that is structured and qualified according to the principle the essence stands for—for example, fluids come to be an embryo or a plant, or food comes to be flesh. The transformation is full in the sense that everything about the component comes to conform fully to the organizational and qualitative principle the essence stands for. As a result, for example, the instantiated essence 'human being' differs from that essence in abstraction in that, when the abstract form 'human being' is instantiated, its instantiation is fully determined in quantity, quality, state, etc.; the instantiated 'human being' is not merely long, but so long, and weighs so much, etc. Furthermore, its instantiation involves the determination of every aspect of that form, not just of some modal aspects of it.[15] The instantiation of the essential form 'human being' is a human being.

The step of the determination from the level of the abstract essence 'human being' to the level of the individual human being has two aspects to it. First, it is a difference of a determination level. Second, it results in the maximal determination, namely in the level of the *determinate* rather than of a further determinable. The level of full determination is the level at which matter is involved. It should not be thought that matter enters the scene as a primitive particular; it only marks the level of the determinate instantiation of the essence without explaining it. For Aristotle, matter is indeterminate and has no number—particularity—associated with it. So it does not explain the determinateness of the essence but only flags the level of determinateness without accounting for it. The determinateness of the essence at the lowest level of determination, like the particularity of the instance, is a primitive, not explicable within the theory or for that matter, within any other metaphysical theory.

What Aristotle recognizes in the determinateness of essential forms is that at a certain level of determination, *recurrence stops*. This is just what 'being determinate' is for such forms.[16] What is significant for our purposes here is not to expound on Aristotle's account of the particularity of a thing,[17] but to explain that the introduction of matter marks the level of full determination of the essence primitively, without giving matter the role of a resident particular in the constitution of the thing. The individual human being differs from the abstract essential form "human being" by a level of determination, which is also the lowest level of determination. It does not differ in plurality: the individual human being is not two conjoined items, matter plus the instantiated essential form; rather, it is the essential form instantiated, that is, enmattered, namely, fully determinate.

But then, Aristotle's (assumed for the regress) and Psillos's ontological division between an entity and its inherent instantiated essence vanishes.[18] We cannot take even the first step in the regresses of essences in Aristotle's or Psillos's arguments. The instantiated essence of an entity is one and the same as the entity; the almond tree in the field is the instantiated essential type 'almond tree'.

Concluding the regress argument, Aristotle, but not Psillos, gives up the assumed premise that the instantiated essential type of a thing is a component-property in the thing; arithmetically different from the thing. The position reached by Aristotle in his Syllable regress argument is that the oneness of the thing is achieved by the essential form acting as a unifying principle on the material constituents, which results in their embodying (instantiating) the essential form. Psillos on the other hand endorses the distinctness of a power from its essence, for example of fragility from directedness to breaking, and so the regress commences. But what we now realize is that a pure power *does not* have directionality as a property; a pure power is this or that instance of directionality toward φ-ing. That is what a pure power does when unmanifested; it is an instance of readiness for action, of pure directedness toward φ-ing, and only that. No division, no regress. Anything that possesses such a power F, possesses directedness toward φ-ing, and so is disposed to φ.

CONCLUSION

Do powers need powers to do what powers do? If an entity needs another entity like it to make it what it is, it enters a quest for the untenable, since the second entity will be as deficient as the first: for example if a power needs another power to empower it, to make it manifestable. If on the other hand an entity needs another entity that is *unlike* it to make it what it is, then it wears the paradox on its sleeve: for example a power is made powerful by a non-power. Either way, the division between an entity and what the entity is is fatal.

I conclude, with Aristotle, that we should abandon the ontological division between an entity and its essence: "Each thing then and its essence are one and the same in no merely accidental way" (*Metaphysics*, 1031b19–20). A pure power has no property of directionality: a pure power *is* directionality towards the manifestation of φ-ing. If physics concludes that there are pure powers, philosophy would welcome them.

ACKNOWLEDGMENTS

Thanks are owed to the Editor of the *History of Philosophy Quarterly* for granting permission to reprint this paper, first published there in Vol. 26, No. 4, 2009, pp. 337–52.

NOTES

1. The latter camp includes advocates of a variety of ontological combinations of powers and non-powers.
2. Some philosophers in the dispositionalist camp allow that some properties are pure powers; whereas others, referred to as pandispositionalists, hold

that all properties are pure powers. Among the former are, e.g. Ellis (2001), Molnar (2003); among the latter, e.g. Bird (2007b), Holton (1999), Shoemaker (1984), Mellor (1974).

3. I will not examine here one further important issue relating to the first aspect, namely, whether there can be properties that exist as *pure potentialities* before they are manifested (even if their nature is not regressive), being ungrounded on categorical properties. This has been seen as being acutely problematic regarding pure powers in the literature; it therefore deserves its own separate treatment.

4. Mumford found shortcomings in Place's proposal and suggested that a better theory would be an understanding of a functional essence of dispositions (1999: 222). Place defended his position against the criticism and played down the difference between the intentional and the functional account of dispositions (1999).

5. I will not distinguish for the purposes of this discussion between sparse and abundant pure powers.

6. He follows Molnar who "takes it that there is a necessary connection between the power and its manifestation: 'A physical power is essentially an *executable* property' (2003, 63)," (2006: 139).

7. The non-identity premise is not explicitly stated by Psillos, but it is assumed in the derivation. I have supplied as the most plausible reason for it the subject-property distinctness.

8. Psillos believes that he can hold on to the division between a pure power and its directionality but still block the resulting regress–at a price. We are shown that he derives the regress by treating the directionality of a power as a necessary property of it, which, with the pandispositionalist assumption, delivers the regress. So Psillos assumes that the regress would be prevented if, abandoning pandispositionalism, we took the property of directionality to be a categorical property of the power rather than a power. He states that

   "Thinking of all properties as pure powers [that is, being pandispositionalist] leads to regress. The regress, I argue, can be blocked only if non-powers are admitted" (2006: 138). "What if one were to argue that Q is *not* a power. The regress would then stop by admitting non-powers . . . if Q (the directedness of F) is a categorical property of F" (2006: 141). "We need to view properties as being more-than-powers [i.e. powers and non-powers]" (2006:154).

   What Psillos is proposing here is not just that powers involve non-powers in some way (e.g. to provide a categorical grounding). What he is proposing is something much more radical: powers derive their powerfulness from non-powers. Directionality toward its manifestation to φ is what makes a power manifestable. It is this that gives the power the dynamic developmental character peculiar to a power, this that enables a power to point toward something other, something realizable, making the power powerful. But if directionality toward its manifestation is a categorical property of a power, namely a non-power, how can the power derive its powerfulness from it? Psillos is pessimistic about this way out (2006: 141).

9. Inherent oneness is what I take the central idea of *self-subsistence* as in *Metaphysics*, 1032a2–4 (quoted in the following section) to be for Aristotle's and for our purposes.

10. The difference between this regress and the property-of-a-property regress is that the essence of an entity is not a meta-description or a formal property of the entity; hence the regress of essential types is generated within the ontology, not about the ontology. It is a regress of essences, not of meta-descriptions of being an essence.

11. Scaltsas (1994: 128 ff.) is right to point us to the argument in *Metaphysics* VII.6 for the oneness of a thing with his essence, but as I argued before this is only the first step in showing the oneness of a concrete substance with its instantiated essence.

12. "What is compounded out of something so that the whole is one—not like a heap, however, but like a syllable—the syllable is not its elements, *ba* is not the same as *b* and *a*, nor is flesh fire and earth; for when they are dissolved the wholes, i.e. the flesh and the syllable, no longer exist, but the elements of the syllable exist, and so do fire and earth. The syllable, then, is something—not only its elements (the vowel and the consonant) but also something else; and the flesh is not only fire and earth or the hot and the cold, but also something else. Since then that something must be either an element or composed of elements, if it is an element the same argument will again apply; for flesh will consist of this and fire and earth and something still further, so that the process will go on to infinity" (*Metaphysics* 1041b11–22).

13. "But it would seem that this [i.e. the unifier of the elements in a syllable or in flesh] is something, and not an element, and that it is the cause which makes *this* thing flesh and *that* a syllable. And this is the substance [i.e. essence] of each thing; for this is the primary cause of its being; . . . which is not an element but a principle" (*Metaphysics* 1041b25–31).

14. Or as in the case of the letters 'f' and 'a' that lose their individuality—distinctness—in the syllable or a word.

15. A longer version of the account of the instantiation of an essence offered here would touch on the following further points: to each individual e.g. human being there corresponds a range of possible determinations of the abstract essence 'human being'; various combinations of possible determinations in the range are the same human being; this involves explaining the role of historical properties in the instantiation of an essence. But this project will not be carried out here.

16. It is captured as early as in Aristotle's *Categories* 1b3–7 in the concept of the *atomon* (indivisible). The indivisibility is within the categorical scheme, contrasted to recurrence and hence, not incompatible with the subsequent Aristotelian account of the compositeness of things out of matter and form.

17. I will not discuss here, either, how the previous account accords with the notion of physical continuity in the generation of things, which is significant for Aristotle's explanation of why transformations are not *ex nihilo* creations.

18. This is what Aristotle means when he says that a thing is said to be its essence in virtue of itself:

> "Necessarily, then, the good and essence of good are one, and so are fair and essence of fair, and so with all things that are not said in respect of another, but in respect of themselves" (*Metaphysics* 1031b11–3).

Once we understand the implications of e.g. a subject's being a human being in virtue of that subject itself, the vicious nature of Psillos's and Aristotle's regresses shows its face. How can we separate the instantiation of 'human being' from being a human being? Being a human being is all it is.

3 Categories and the Ontology of Powers
A Vindication of the Identity Theory of Properties

Kristina Engelhard

INTRODUCTION

Dispositional properties and powers have been a nuisance for analytic philosophy since its early days. According to strict criteria of empirical evidence, they have been rated unobservable and hence of dubitable ontological status, contrary to their manifestations that are reckoned to be observable and hence respectable citizens in our ontology. Yet, powers or forces figure as inevitable terms in laws of nature. Hence, they had to be taken seriously. Dispositional properties have become, and not only in very recent times, a central topic of debate among metaphysicians, some of whom hold that dispositions as such are real existing properties. According to these dispositionalists, the reason for analytic philosophy's uneasiness concerning dispositions is its basic ontological paradigm, that they call Humeanism. Hence, the dispositionalists' target is to replace Humeanism with a dispositional paradigm. A basic problem for dispositionalism is in finding a persuasive account of the basic ontological structure of dispositional properties.

The aim of this chapter is to show that an identity theory of dispositional properties, that claims that the dispositional and the qualitative are two features of one and the same property, is a desirable candidate for dispositionalism, because it avoids serious objections against pandispositionalism and because it is intuitively more plausible. In the first section of the chapter I give an introductory overview of different accounts of dispositionalism and their problems. A much discussed view is pandispositionalism, the view that all properties are dispositional. I want to show that there is a persuasive argument in favor of pandispositionalism, and yet there are very good reasons to reject this view, mainly regress arguments. These regress arguments are persuasive because of what I call "the dualist intuition", which says that there is some ontological duality between powers and their manifestations. In the second section of the chapter I outline what I mean by dualist intuition. In the third section I delineate the predominant models of dispositionalism in more detail. I try to show how plausible it is that these theories as they stand do not satisfy the dualist intuition. I also deal with the identity theory because it seems to be the best candidate to answer dualist worries, and yet it is at least able to hold that all properties are powers. Nevertheless, I will show that the identity theory, as outlined by Heil and Martin, falls victim of serious objections. In the last section of the chapter I investigate whether the identity theory enriched by a category system might solve these problems. In order for this to be achieved, a plausible case must be made that a category system can provide metaphysical dualism of powers and manifestations within pandispositionalism.

METAPHYSICAL PROBLEMS OF A REALIST ACCOUNT OF POWERS

Those who defend realism about powers are involved in a two-sided conflict. On the one hand they face external arguments against a realist assumption concerning dispositional properties or powers. There are objections of a broadly anti-metaphysical provenance doubting or rejecting the possibility of metaphysics in general. But there are also arguments from metaphysicians, like David Armstrong, who don't believe in dispositional properties, and hence don't believe in fundamental irreducible powers. But power realists are also engaged in a wide discussion concerning the question of what kinds of properties there are, and which theory of powers to adopt. One of the central issues here is whether one should embrace a theory of properties with a dual or with a monistic architecture.

Powers are understood as causally efficacious properties. Their identity conditions involve their typical or specific manifestations. Hence powers like dispositions sustain conditionals consisting of their manifestations; an ascription of a power to some object additionally includes the typical manifestation conditions. The paradigmatic example of a power is 'being charged' or 'having mass' as properties of elementary particles or objects in physics. Paradigmatic examples of non-dispositional properties are shape properties like 'triangularity',[1] spacetime relations, and structure-properties (Molnar 2003; Ellis 2001).[2]

The distinction between dualism and monism concerning properties is effective on at least two levels, the ontological, and the epistemic or linguistic level respectively. There are basically four options among dispositionalist theories.

(I) *Ontological Dualism* argues that there are two inherently different kinds of properties: dispositional, and non-dispositional, spelled out as categorical or occurrent properties or qualities.

(II) *Neutral Monism* holds that there is ontologically only one kind of properties that are as such neither dispositional nor categorical, whereas there are two ways of referring to these properties: they can either be seen as dispositional or as qualitative or 'occurrent'. According to the *dual aspect account* the distinction between the dispositional and the categorical is merely linguistic. The dispositional and the categorical are two aspects of the same property (Mumford 1998: 190 ff.). A different account, that combines an ontological property monism with a dualism concerning predicates, grounds that dualism in terms of basic ontological categories: the dispositional and the occurrent are two kinds of interpretation of predicates *via* basic ontological categories (Lowe 2006a: 124).

(III) *Identity Theory*: according to the Identity Theory the dispositional and the qualitative are two modes of one and the same property (Heil 2003: 119); or "different ways of being of the same unitary property such that they may be necessarily or contingently covariant" (Martin 2008: 63). The claim of identity theory is that properties are dispositional as well as qualitative (Martin 2008: 64). According to Martin the two ways properties are, are "approachable as limits" in abstraction.

Ontological dualism is unattractive for dispositionalists, because it is in danger of collapsing into categoricalism, the view that all properties are categorical non-dispositional properties (Mumford 1998: 112–6), because both properties involve different concepts of causation. So, either we also have to accept two kinds of causation, which seems unpersuasive, or—if we only accept one concept of causation—one kind of property is absolutely inert and hence a candidate for reductive accounts (cf. Prior, Pargetter and Jackson 1982). Even if neutral monism and the identity theory are ontologically monistic, both of them still keep a dualistic architecture on the epistemic or at least the linguistic level; the identity theory claims that there is some kind of ontological dualism, despite the basic monism. The reasons for these dualistic remainders in neutral monism are arguments against the forth option:

(IV) *Pandispositionalism, or dispositional monism*: this theory holds that at least all sparse fundamental properties are inherently dispositional or that they are all nothing but powers.[3] Only a few dispositionalists hold the view of pandispositionalism (Mellor 2000, Bird 2007b, Mumford 2004) even though the other options face constructive difficulties too and pandispositionalism seems to be the clear-cut choice for dispositional realists.

In the first place, why should we accept powers as real properties? There is a basic metaphysical intuition that motivates dispositionalism: there is something flawed in the view that properties are passive. Descartes held the par excellence paradigm of passivism: objects in themselves are passive—that is their essential nature is inertia and all action is extrinsically transferred from one object to the other. This view seems implausible for several reasons. It engenders paradoxes regarding the origin of motion and change, and it leads to a theory of extrinsic causation that has many undesirable consequences, such as problems with cases of causation by absence. Intuitively more persuasive is the paradigm of activism or dynamism or, as Rom Harré calls it, "Van Helmont's Paradigm" (Harré 1970: 82), according to which objects are intrinsically active or have intrinsic powers. Hence, action is brought about by an object's intrinsically efficacious powerful properties.

There are basically four kinds of arguments in favor of dispositionalism: (i) linguistic, (ii) epistemic (iii) naturalistic and (iv) metaphysical arguments.[4] Out of these arguments I pick out the epistemic argument, because it is perhaps the strongest support for dispositionalism, since it is direct and supposed to show immediately that all properties are dispositional, hence that pandispositionalism is true. In addition it is the target of very challenging counterarguments against pandispositionalism. It runs as follows: no property can be experienced unless it bestows powers to the object that has it. For, if observation presupposes a causal relation between observer and observed, in that the object causes the observer to observe the object having this or that property, then epistemic access to objects presupposes properties that are causally efficacious that is, powerful properties. Furthermore, if we can only experience properties according to their effects or distinguish between different properties by their different effects on things, properties must be causally efficacious—that is, they must be powers (Shoemaker 1980a). Note first that there are two things in play within this argument: first, the causal impact of a property on an observer as necessary for experience; and second, the causal roles that a property has in relation to other properties in general. Note also that conversely this argument implies that we only have epistemic access to the manifestation or the manifesting of powers, because they are the effects of powers. But we do not have epistemic access to unmanifested powers as such.

So, why don't all metaphysicians embrace pandispositionalism? There are basically two kinds of arguments against it. Arguments of the first kind concede that it is a consistent view, but argue that it is contrary to contingent facts, because as a matter of fact at least in our world there are non-dispositional properties (these are 'contrary to fact arguments'). Molnar claims that there are basic symmetries in physics that cannot be conceived of as dispositions or powers (Molnar 2003: 163); Ellis (this volume) thinks that spatiotemporal relations and structures cannot be spelled out as powers. Since these properties are indeed instantiated in the actual world, pandispositionalism does not hold in the actual world.

Arguments of the second kind try to show that pandispositionalism has fatal consequences (these are 'fatal consequence arguments'). Some of them are vicious regress of circularity or objections. They can be grouped together in two variants of objections. One variant aims at modality; e.g. Armstrong's "always packing never traveling" argument.[5] The second variant aims at the identity conditions of powers. These objections are directed dispositionalism in general. But they are particularly destructive for pandispositionalism. For, while dualistic accounts (ontological as well as descriptive dualisms) are able to readjust their metaphysics of powers in light of these objections, pandispositionalism has to reject them.

I will now take a look at two of these arguments that seem to be the biggest threats for pandispositionalism: Swinburne's regress argument and Lowe's "No identity fixation" argument.

Swinburne's regress argument: Manifestations of powers are changes of the properties or relations of objects.[6] If all properties were powers, these changes would be changes of an object's powers. Since we can only know of powers through their manifestations, these changes of powers would have to get manifested to be known. But if such manifestations in turn were just changes of powers these changes could not be known, if they were not manifested, and so on to infinity.[7] As I understand it, this objection is not only directed against the causal relation between observer and observed with respect to the causal power of the observed manifesting in the observer in order to cause a mental state.[8] It is also based upon the premise that we do not have epistemic access to powers as such, but only indirectly through their effects on things, which are changes that are observable—like mass being observable only through its effects on objects in making them accelerate in a certain way, which is a change between the object's having a certain speed to the object's having some other speed. If it is granted that powers are not observable as such, but only under the condition that they cause their specific manifestation, then the manifestation of a power has to be something different in character from the corresponding power, if our epistemic access to powers is to be explained. We infer from the acceleration of an object that there is an acting force. But the acceleration itself cannot be a power; it bestows power to the object traveling at a certain speed. If it is taken as granted that we do not have epistemic access to properties as such but only to their causal effects, the effects of powers must be different in kind from the causing powers. As it stands Swinburne's regress argument clearly accepts the premise that powers are not observable as such.[9]

Lowe's "No identity fixation" argument: If the identity of a power is fixed by its manifestation, then if this manifestation in turn were a power, its manifestation would be necessary to fix its identity. But again, if this power's manifestation were in turn a power, its identity would have to be fixed by its manifestation, and so forth (Lowe 2006a: 138). According to Lowe this leads to a vicious infinite regress or circularity. I agree with Bird that this argument needs some clarification in order to be a serious obstacle for pandispositionalism (Bird 2007b). As Bird shows, the objection cannot prove the inconsistency of pandispositionalism; rather, it shows that pandispositionalism entails an irresolvable problem for defining determinate identity conditions for powers. This is undesirable anyway, and may be reckoned a serious problem for pandispositionalism. Along these lines, the argument says that properties must be determinate, in the sense that there must be satisfiable identity criteria for a property for it to count as a real property. The identity of powers is determined by their manifestations. Now, if manifestations were themselves powers, their identity would have to be fixed by yet other manifestations. Hence, if a power is to be determined, then within the chain of manifestations there must be some manifestation that is not itself a power.

Bird grants this argument as it stands, but rejects a tacit premise, in pointing out that the identity of powers does not have to be determined by its intrinsic features, as the argument must presuppose to be effective against pandispositionalism (Bird 2007b). Rather the determination of powers can be purely relational, which is to say that the identity of a power is fixed by its relations to other properties. The "No identity fixation" argument works only if the identity of properties necessarily depends on explicating the intrinsic determinations of the property, that is: determinations that a property has irrespective of what else is the case. However, if, as Bird tries to show, a purely relational determination of properties is possible, the regress would not be vicious, since it would be possible to identify a certain power if the relation the power is connected to is instantiated.

If one accepts the regress arguments what follows from it? Must every power manifestation be a non-power property, or is it sufficient for the power's observability and identity to be fixed if somewhere in the chain of power properties there is a non-power property that is epistemically accessible, and that guarantees for the identity condition to be fulfilled? To stop the regress it suffices to take the weaker stance that somewhere in the chain of power manifestations there must be a non-power property. The arguments that both Swinburne and Lowe present may be driven by what I call the 'dualist intuition'.

THE DUALIST INTUITION

One reason why the question about dualism and monism is still controversial is that another issue is not yet settled. What is the ontological structure of powers itself? It is a semantic fact that powers are individuated through their manifestations; e.g. the meaning of the word 'fragility' is that it is the disposition to break. There is also reason to think that we have a different epistemic access to powers than their manifestations. We have direct epistemic access to phenomena like the breaking of a vase, but only indirect epistemic access to a property like fragility. Hence, there is a strong inclination to think that this reflects some kind of basic dualism in the ontological structure of properties. It leads us to think that there must be some ontological difference between power and manifestation, which is more than their numerical difference or different identity conditions; there must be some ontological difference in character, that is a difference in kind or type. I will call this 'the dualist intuition'. Of course, the dual semantic structure of powers does not immediately lead to ontological dualism, or descriptive dualisms of neutral monism. But dualist theories of powers have an easier tool kit at their disposal to provide semantic dualism with a metaphysical basis; they can say that two kinds of properties are the truth-makers of claims concerning the semantic difference between dispositional and categorical predicates or predicates of occurrent properties. In contrast to this, pandispositionalism has to account for the thesis that there is no intrinsic feature of properties that characterizes a manifestation as distinct in character from a power.

There are several aspects concerning the relation between a power and its manifestation to be considered. (a) There is a causal relation between a power and its manifestation, if the corresponding stimulus conditions are met. For, if something is a power, it is at least causally relevant to bringing about the manifestation in certain processes or events. We say that if the appropriate stimulus conditions are met the power (at least partially) causes the manifestation. (b) Since the identity of a power is defined *via* its manifestation, some kind of relation between the power and its manifestation holds even if the power is not manifesting and even if it never manifests. This relation can be taken neutrally as the directedness of powers towards their manifestations. It is an issue of debate whether this feature should be conceived of as a relation and whether there is such a relation.[10] Of course, directedness cannot be a real relation because the second *relatum*, the manifestation, is not actual.[11] If directedness is a relation, it is asymmetrical, because if the identity of the manifestation would in turn be defined through the power, there would immediately be a vicious regress. (c) We can also speak of a manifestation-relation, which is the feature of the actualization of the non-actual manifestation, if the appropriate stimulus conditions are met; so the power causes the transition from its non-actual manifestation it is directed towards to its actual manifestation. Hence, there are at least three distinctions that have to be taken into account with respect to powers: the distinction between cause and effect, between the possible and the actual manifestation, as well as between the first and second *relatum* in an asymmetrical relation, that we could take as 'directedness'. These distinctions correspond to three relations: the causal relation, an actualization relation, and the directedness relation.

To give an example: the power of being inflammable, instantiated by a match, stands in certain relations to its manifestation, which is 'burning'. If the stimulus conditions are not met, the match's dispositional property of flammability is nevertheless directed toward burning; it is "ready to go".[12] If the stimulus conditions are met, there is a causal relation between the match's properties that altogether constitute its power to burn and its actual burning. There is an actualization relation between the probable manifestation of flammability and the match's actual burning if the stimulus conditions are met. We can take the burning of the match as the process of its inflammation and its burning; but we can also take the burning of the match as a property of the match that it instantiates at a given time and place.

Now the question is whether there is a metaphysical basis for these distinctions, meaning that some entity is intrinsically a power and some entity is intrinsically a manifestation of a certain power. Or does the obtaining of the relation between two entities decree the character of the *relata* as being a power and as being the manifestation of this particular power? The latter might be called a relational account of property character, whereas the former is an intrinsic account. Is burning intrinsically the manifestation of the power of flammability? Or is burning a manifestation of flammability only because a certain relation between the two properties obtains? The relational account holds that the identity criteria for a power are purely relational in the sense that the power, as well as the manifestation, is identified *via* the relation between the two. The non-relational account holds that there are identity criteria for the manifestation of the power independent of the power, but there are no independent identity criteria for the power.

The 'dualist intuition' says that there is a metaphysical basis for the semantic distinction between a power and its manifestation; that there is something about things in the world that makes them either a manifestation or a power; that there is something about an entity that makes it a manifestation rather than a power.[13] I call the dualist claim an 'intuition' because, although there might not be a waterproof argument from which the necessity of an ontological distinction between a power and its manifestation might be inferred, there are nevertheless good reasons to hold the view that there is an ontological difference between powers and their manifestations, leaving indeterminate exactly which kind of ontological difference.[14] There is sometimes good reason to take an intuition as such seriously, even if we do not have a watertight argument for its truth.[15] Nevertheless, my claim is not that in this case the intuition is true, but that it is a phenomenon that asks for an adequate interpretation. The intuition is vague in suggesting only that there is an ontological difference between a power and its manifestation that is not merely numerical difference; it says nothing about what kind of difference is involved. Hence it is left open to metaphysical analysis to determine the ontological difference between powers and their manifestation.

Now, given that we should take the dualist intuition seriously, the question arises: Is pandispositionalism able to integrate an ontologically dual structure of power and manifestation of some kind, even if all properties are powers?

DISPOSITIONALIST MODELS

Pandispositionalists seem to be aware of the problem of the dualist intuition. Their solution is to model the dual structure of powers in an all-powers view within a combinatorial model of powers. Pandispositionalists take Sidney Shoemaker's "cluster-theory" as their fundamental model. According to this theory the manifestation of a power is brought about by the interaction of several powers, with the manifestation itself being a power, but a different power (Shoemaker 1980b). To give an example: if fragility as (a passive) power of a glass has been manifested in its being broken, each fragment of the glass has the power to cut or scratch. In this respect pandispositionalism seems committed to reject the dualist intuition.

1. Pandispositionalism: Relationalism and the Cluster Theory

Pandispositionalism is the view that:

(PD) All sparse fundamental properties are intrinsically powerful, i.e. they are powers.[16]

To be 'intrinsically powerful' means that the property, or the object that has it, is causally efficacious not in virtue of some extrinsic law of nature or regularity, but just in virtue of itself or solely in virtue of the property or the object's having the property.[17] Since pandispositionalism does not have to claim that abundant properties like 'grey or weighing twenty pounds' are also powers, it does not have to claim that all properties are powers. Also the identity theory may be seen as a pandispositionalism, since it takes all properties to be powers.

Relationalism: According to Alexander Bird's pandispositionalism (Bird 2007a) the determination of powers can be purely relational which is to say that the identity of a power is fixed by its relations to other properties. By the model of graph-theory Bird tries to show that purely relational determinations of entities as *relata* of relations are possible. In this case the identity and distinctness of the elements of the structure supervene on the instantiations of relations that constitute the element's identity. From this he infers that it is possible to fix the identity of powers *via* their pattern of manifestations and stimuli even if manifestations are powers as well. The distinction between a power and its manifestation according to this relational account of property character is determined *via* the asymmetry of the manifestation-relation. Hence, all properties can be powers, and only its position in this asymmetrical relation makes a power the manifestation of some other power. The ontological difference between a power and its manifestation is merely a difference in relational dependencies.

This theory falls prey of a criticism raised by Barker (2009b). The objection is tantamount to saying that a theory of properties fixing property identity by relational constitution ends up in a dilemma. The argument picks out the identity fixing manifestation relation that constitutes the property character of a property. If on the one hand this relation itself is non-relationally determined it has to be a quiddity, i.e. it has identity across possible worlds independent of its causal or nomological roles. And since this relation is constitutive of the properties themselves, this quiddity is no ontological free lunch. It trickles down, because it grounds the character of the properties involved. Hence there are non-relational properties. If on the other hand the manifestation relation is also relationally determined, then there cannot be any identity fixing by the manifestation relation. According to Barker the graph theory is no solution to this problem either, because it offers too little structure to reconstruct the character of the manifestation relation (Barker 2009a).[18] One needs to know first what the manifestation of a power is in order to be able to understand the relation and the property character it is supposed to bestow to its relata.

What are the pandispositionalist's options to deal with the problems of integrating the dual structure of powers adequately?

The Cluster Theory: The predominant way of spelling out pandispositionalism is the so called cluster theory, which is as such independent of pandispositionalism. Within the cluster-theory, introduced by Sidney Shoemaker, and advanced by George Molnar and Stephen Mumford, the concept of a cluster serves two purposes (among others): (i) it is part of the analysis of properties fixing their identity, and (ii) it is supposed to explain the process of manifestation in particulars in causal terms.

(i) According to the cluster theory a property is a cluster of different powers. The identity of a property is fixed by its constituting powers, meaning: the property's identity is fixed by its causal roles in relation to other properties (Mumford 2004: 171). But because of the identity-fixing function of the manifestation for a single power, each single power within the cluster of powers fixing the cluster's identity can have only one typical manifestation; and conversely each power manifestation is linked with only one power (Molnar 2003: 195). Since powers only manifest themselves as clusters of powers, Molnar speaks of the contribution of a single power to a manifestation of a power cluster. To say that a power makes a 'contribution' is to say that a single power is part of the complete cause making a difference to the effect. A single power must always make the same contribution in whatever power cluster it is involved, if it is to count as one determinate power—which is necessary in order to fix the identity of a power.

(ii) The process of manifestation in causal terms goes as follows. The actual events in the world—that is, the causally being brought about of something by something else—turns out to be the result of the interaction of several co-instantiating powers, bringing about another power cluster or a property. One power cluster is the cause of another power cluster that is its effect. A single power-token is only part of this instantiated cluster that might be called a 'symphony of powers', since the different powers run together in a unified effect. The effect itself is a combination of the manifestations of the elementary powers of the causing power-cluster. Molnar's example is two horses dragging a ship through a canal, each walking on one shore of the river. The manifestation of one horse's power would be the ship's movement in the direction of the horse's pull towards one shore of the canal. But this manifestation does not occur because the two powers work together in a cluster. Hence the effect of the two powers is a straight movement along the canal. The manifestations of each power nevertheless contribute to the effect (Molnar 2003: 195).

Thus, if there is a sharp distinction between manifestations and effects, since manifestations in almost all cases are only part of the effect, as Molnar stresses, then there must also be a distinction between the causation relation and the manifestation relation and the power's directedness. So if the pandispositionalist wants to pay justice to the dualist intuition concerning the distinction between powers and their manifestations, she cannot make use only of the distinction between cause and effect; for this cuts the beast at a different joint, namely that of instantiated powers on the level of property-tokens as elements of events. By contrast, the distinction between powers and their manifestations cuts at the level of powers as types and elements of power-cluster-types. On this level there is the directedness-relation that fixes the identity of a power between the power and its typical manifestation, and the instantiation relation of a power being manifested in a power-trope (that is, part of a property instance).

The cluster theory needs a conceptual framework apart from the physical vocabulary of causation to model the dual structure of powers, for it cannot explain the asymmetrical manifestation relation. It can only take it to be a fundamental fact. But since this relation does a lot of explicatory work, we need to know more about it. What is missing is an ontology that allows for differentiating between these distinct aspects or relata and their relations without introducing different kinds of properties or different entities on the same ontological level. If there were an ontological difference between powers and manifestations without there being two different kinds of properties, then we would need something which allows for determining an ontological difference without different kinds of entities. The so called identity theory, such as held by Charlie Martin and John Heil, promises to fulfill this requirement.

2. The Identity Theory

According to the identity theory every property unifies two features, a dispositional feature, responsible for its modal characteristics, and a qualitative feature, responsible for its identity. But these two features are not second order properties of properties, like in neutral monism. Rather, identity theories have to make sure that the dispositional and the qualitative are strictly identical. Martin calls this the "surprising identity".[19] Therefore Martin and Heil would reject the description given in the first sentence of this paragraph, because in their eyes the expression 'two features' undermines the strict identity claim. Now, in either version these accounts fall victim of counter arguments that aim at showing their inability to specify the two features as distinct and yet identical, which leads to a dilemma. Either both features are determined as ontologically distinct features, then the identity theory collapses to the two-aspect account of neutral monism, where the dispositional and the categorical are two separate second order properties, leaving the first order property neutral on this distinction, or they are not determined as distinct, and then the identity theory is inconsistent or unintelligible, because it declares that there are two sides and at the same time that there aren't.[20] Concerning the first horn of the dilemma Barker (2009b) shows that the model used by Heil for explaining how this identity should be understood, the Necker cube (Martin's example is the duck-rabbit figure (2008: 68)), does not suffice to show what kind of identity is a work, because there actually are different aspects that explain why these figures satisfy different descriptions. Concerning the second horn, it is obvious that one cannot motivate why the property should be a disposition as well as a quality, if one refuses to give a description of functions on the basis of which the property should be conceived of as having these features.

If we could specify the features of a property ontologically, one feature as being dispositional and some other feature of the very same property as being qualitative, and if we could show that there is an ontological fundament to the identity of the property uniting both features, then we could undermine this dilemma. Of course this will only show that there is a version of the identity theory that does not fall prey of the inconsistencies of the identity theories so far, not that it is true in the actual world. A category-system might be a good candidate to serve this purpose. In an ontological sense categories specify ways things are. Properties make things be in a specific way. One property can make things be in different ways, without there being different properties.

IDENTITY THEORY AND CATEGORY-ONTOLOGY

Another option for modeling the dual architecture of powers is to give it an interpretation in terms of ontological categories. According to E. J. Lowe the difference between the dispositional and the occurrent, which is Lowe's version of the categorical, is not ontological, but only names different types of predication that he defines by his four-category-ontology (Lowe 2006a: 126). Unlike Lowe, I think that the category system solves the problems left open by Martin and Heil of giving an ontological fundament to the two features one and the same property exhibits. Thereby we can deal with the objections against the identity theory by addressing the problem that Martin's and Heil's versions of the identity theory had no means to solve, namely in which respect some property is dispositional and in which respect the very same property is qualitative—leading to the dilemma spelled out previously. To advance this idea it is helpful to see how Lowe interprets the duality of dispositions and occurrent properties. One version of Lowe's four-category-ontology is this (Lowe 2006a: 126):

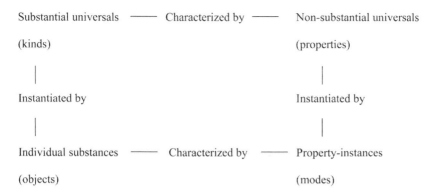

The occurrent interpretation of a predicate consists in attributing a property instance or trope to an object with respect to being a mode of the corresponding universal. '*a* is occurrently *F*' means '*a* possesses a mode of *F*-ness'. Whereas the dispositional interpretation of a predicate consists in attributing a property-universal to an object's substantial kind K. '*a* is dispositionally *F*' means '*a* instantiates *K* which possesses *F*-ness'. This theory enables framing the distinction of a power and its manifestation as follows. A certain property-type instantiated in a particular object characterizing this object irrespective of its possible kind is described as being an occurrent property, that is a property that a particular object has, like this particular match's burning. Whereas a power is a universal characterizing substantial kinds that can be instantiated by certain objects, like 'being inflammable'. The manifestation of a power may hence be seen as instantiation of a universal *qua* being the property characterizing a kind and hence being describable in terms of an occurrent attribution.[21]

How can this structure be implemented in pandisposionalism? What is particularly interesting for the line I want to pursue is that the difference between a power and its manifestation comes out as a difference in categories and their interrelations.[22] If we can make serious ontological sense out of categories as ways of being, rather than merely highest determinable predicates demarcating different entities, and different roles entities play, and if we accept a basic ontology of facts or states of affairs, then the following move, similar to Lowe's, can be made. To avoid problems, I dispense with kinds, but assume the three remaining categories: particulars, universals, and tropes.[23] Then we can say that properties have two ontologically valid aspects. Insofar as a property is the universal *in rebus* in abstraction from the fact or state of affairs it is part of, it stands in nomic relations to different properties that demarcate its manifestation and hence exhibits the manifestation relation of it as a power. We consider an entity's dispositionality if we consider the property of that particular in abstraction from the fact or state of affairs which it is part of. Focusing on the property we can detect the nomic relations that the property involves that are the expression of its modal character; this displays the property as a power. This is independent of what one thinks laws of nature are or what they do. Insofar as a property has a certain intrinsic nature it is a quality, meaning it is a mode of being of a particular.

The identity of a power is fixed by the way it makes things be, that is by being causally relevant something's qualitativity. We consider the property's qualitativity insofar as we do not abstract from the fact or state of affairs that it qualifies but take it as part of the fact in question involving one and the same property. As trope the property makes a particular being this or that way; by the same time the property fixes the nomic relations of the particular. Also we can perfectly well say that a power causes the instantiation of a numerically different property, namely that which it qua universal is directed to certain other properties are co-instantiated. I call this account semi-dualist pandispositionalism.

This account avoids the collapse of Bird's relationalism or graph theoretical account to haecceitism, as objected by Barker (2009b), since the nomic features of the property are intrinsic to them. It does not entail that the dispositional feature of a property is abstract, whereas its occurrent feature is concrete. The modal feature of the property, which is at work within the complex state of affairs, is merely extrapolated by abstraction. Now, we can take the directedness relation as connecting two inherently characterized relata: a property is the power P to F (in the sense of 'P is directed to F-ing') in virtue of its modal character that is extrapolated by abstraction from its instantiation, if it stands in a nomic relation to a numerically different property F which is characterized by qualitative features such that if appropriate powers are co-instantiated then F instantiates.

To give an example: we can determine the power of 'being negatively charged' as follows: the identity of 'negatively charged' is fixed by the qualitative aspect of a property, that is the way the property makes an object be; the instance of the property in a particular qualifies this particular as f, i.e. being an electron. It is a specific quality of this particular. We consider the qualitativity of 'being negatively charged' if we consider it as that which makes this particular be this way. The qualitative feature fixes the identity of the property. The qualitative feature of a property is considered in an instantiated property, as part of a state of affairs or of a fact. We consider the very same property as a power if we abstract from its making this particular being that way, but consider the nomic relations it makes a particular be involved with. We can say that we consider the property's power feature if we consider it as a universal. Being negatively charged is a power to repel or attract particulars with particular qualities. To spell out metaphysics by categories is a task of larger scope than can be done here.

NOTES

1. These examples are all controversial. There is a still ongoing debate whether geometrical shapes can be interpreted as dispositional too: Mellor (1982);

Prior (1985: 59–62); cf. Mumford (1998: 67–73); Mellor (2000); Bird (2009).

2. Some further clarification of terminology seems appropriate. Many metaphysicians take powers more or less simply as a kind of dispositional property (Molnar 2003; Ellis 2001: 124), whereas others think that there is a more fundamental difference between powers on the one hand, and dispositions and properties on the other.

3. I reserve the name 'pandispositionalism' for this thesis; identity-theorists too subscribe to the thesis that all properties are powers, but they also state that the very same properties are categorical too and deny that they are powers and only powers.

4. (i) According to the linguistic argument dispositions are not reducible to conditionals but only promote conditionals. The second premise says that all property terms or predicates at least support subjunctive conditionals. To take one of the most controversial examples 'triangular': if '*a* is triangular' is true it is also true that 'if *a*'s corners were counted correctly the result would be three'. Hence it is at least possible to analyse all predicates in terms of conditionals and accordingly give a dispositional account of all properties (cf. Mellor 2000). (iii) On the condition of a reductive or eliminativist naturalism one could launch an argument saying that the basic properties of physics, understood as fundamental building blocks of all physical reality, as a matter of empirical fact are dispositional in nature and hence that all properties supervening on these properties have dispositional bases. There is a discussion between philosophers of science about whether certain basic elements of contemporary physics allow for a dispositionalist reading, for instance symmetry groups (Psillos 2006) or the Principle of Least Action (Katzav 2004). (iv) Some arguments in favor of dispositionalism are metaphysical and aim at the merits of the theory as a whole in the overall cost-benefit-analysis in contrast to Humeanism. There are two strategies: one is indirect and says that there is no argument strong enough to force dispositionalism to accept any kind of ontological dualism. The other aims at dispositionalism's overall merits, like parsimony and explicative force.

5. The argument says: if all properties were powers and hence also the manifestations of powers were powers, this would amount to a mere shifting around of potencies. Nothing happen, since there would be no transition from potency to act (Armstrong 1997: 80). Armstrong clearly makes several presuppositions in this argument. One of them is that the distinction between power and manifestation is modal, in the sense that powers are mere potencies and their manifestations are actualizations of categorical properties according to laws of nature.

6. Swinburne (1980). Of course there are also powers that do not change something, but sustain a certain state that would change if the power wouldn't be there, like a magnet's power manifesting in a note's being fixed on the refrigerator-door. I think most of these cases come out as involving change anyway (at least counterfactually), because when entering into a system they must make a difference to it if they are causally relevant.

7. Swinburne's argument is originally tailored to refute Shoemaker's argument in Shoemaker (1980b).

8. This is Bird's reading of this objection (Bird 2007b). In this sense Swinburne's regress seems less destructive for pandispositionalism, since the pandispositionalist can claim that one of the traditional examples for dispositional properties are mental properties. So if a disposition causes a mental state which involves a mental property, then this could be seen as evidence that we have epistemic access to powers as such. If my reading of

the regress reducible to this, then we would have to deal with the issue was whether the identity of powers eventually is relative to human minds.

9. Of course this assumption could be tackled by the claim that it is possible to have immediate epistemic access to powers. But this move seems unpersuasive. If we take electric charge as a power property then it is natural to think that we know that something is electrically charged through the effects it has on things, such as attracting complementary charged objects or causing an electric shock. An object's power that does not act at all may be actual but it is not observable.

10. It might turn out to be a matter of importance whether 'directedness' is taken either as a property, or a genuine two-place relation or the power as such. Psillos (2006) has pointed out that there is a regress in the identification of powers if pandispositionalism is presupposed and directedness is taken to be a property of powers, since directedness would have to be a power too. There are difficult problems around this feature if pandispositionalism is presupposed. See also Marmodoro in this volume.

11. This has lead George Molnar to think that there is some structure equivalence with intentionality, insofar as the intended object of an intention does not have to exist for the intentional state to be real (Molnar 2003: 61ff.).

12. This is Martin's metaphor, hence he calls this feature "readiness" (2008: 2). He denies that it is a relation for the reason that the manifestations must not be actual in order for this feature to obtain.

13. The dualist intuition drives many seemingly inconsistent characterizations of the difference between powers and manifestations: first Martin calls the "having of a disposition" and the "displaying or manifestation of the disposition" "two very different things" but then he conceives of them as a conceptual distinction (2008: 48). On the bottom of this lies an identity theory he calls the "Limit View", that takes the dispositional and the qualitative as two different modes of consideration of one and the same property (2008: 63–9).

14. The "dualist intuition" does not necessarily imply ontological dualism. Categorical monism is also driven by the dualist intuition. "Intuition" should here be understood as rational intuition loosely in the sense used in contemporary epistemology as non-inferential state of belief. It is not necessarily a belief that everyone shares or that is necessarily true. I do not use the dualist intuition as evidence; I take it as an indication.

15. Cf. Cameron (2008).

16. A similar formulation of this thesis can be found in Bird (2007b: 45). It is certainly not the only possible version of pandispositionalism. It can also take a non-reductive and much stronger stance, claiming that all properties have dispositional essences.

17. What role the laws of nature play, if this view is accepted, is still a matter of dispute.

18. Furthermore, if relationalism of powers necessarily implies semantic holism, then out of structural similarity with semantic holism relationalism of powers faces objections like Fodor's argument against Davidson's holism about meaning. It says that semantic holism makes meaning hopelessly vague, since it is not possible to fully (or even roughly) specify the "network" of beliefs that a particular term is placed into (or is constituted by). Analogously it might be objected that relationalism makes identity of powers vague. (I owe this thought to Terry Godlove).

19. He tries to elucidate the relation between the dispositionality and the qualitativity of a property like this: "What is exhibited in the qualitative informs and determines what is the for-ness of the dispositional, and the for-ness of the dispositional informs and determines what is exhibited in the qualitative."

(Martin 2008: 65). But there is no description what the qualitative in a property is as apart from the dispositional; rather again and again Martin insists that both are strictly identical.

20. This is shown in detail in Barker (2009b).

21. "[O]n this view, individual objects possess their various natural 'powers' in virtue of belonging to substantial kinds which are subject to appropriate laws—these laws consisting in the possession by such kinds of certain properties (in the sense of universals), or in the standing of kinds in certain relations to one another." (Lowe 2006: 127). There are a number of problems connected with this account. But I do not think that my suggestion is affected, since it is sufficiently different from Lowe's.

22. Nothing depends on a universal system of categories here. What is needed is just, that there are ontological dependencies between the categories involved.—Note that the following problems do not affect Lowe's metaphysics, since he doesn't hold dispositionalism.

23. Of course it seems as a chimera to accept for both universals and tropes, since realism concerning universals does not seem to leave room for tropes. For the moment I take tropes only as the property insofar as it is particular in relation to the particular object that has it. Nothing depends on whether tropes that are instances of a universal are just similar or identical. Whether a category-ontology necessarily needs to hold that universals exist is a separate question. For a nominalist dispositionalism cf. Whittle (2009).

4 Powerful Qualities

John Heil

"The possibility of action . . . is the criterion of existence, and the test of substantiality" (Santayana 1930: 107).

My aim in what follows is less to advance a synoptic account of powers, than to call attention to aspects of powers that we turn of the century philosophers seem constitutionally incapable of appreciating. I read off with a consideration of problems with which any account of powers must wrestle. My thought is that a grasp of what drives these problems will make certain conceptions of powers more attractive than others.[1]

In working up to what I believe is a promising view of powers—or dispositionalities, or propensities, I employ the terms interchangeably—I will use Peter Unger's recent discussion of powers as a stalking horse (Unger 2006). My sense is that, although Unger is on the right track, he succumbs eventually to kinds of error that continue to plague contemporary discussions of powers.

SCIENTIPHICALISM

Unger's primary target is something he calls 'scientiphicalism'. Scientiphicalism is less a clearly articulated thesis than a *Weltanschauung*, a collection of implicit doctrines that inform the way we think about the world and our place in it. Central to scientiphicalism is the idea that the physical realm is bereft of qualities. The concern of science is to give an accounting of objects' capacities for interaction. Qualities play no role in this accounting. To the extent that our experiences are imbued with qualitative character, they stand 'outside'—at the limits of—the physical.

Electrons have a definite mass and charge. We characterize these (as John Foster puts it) 'topic neutrally' by spelling out their contributions to the capacities of electrons to act and be acted upon. When we reflect on electrons' intrinsic nature, it seems obvious that once we have set out their propensities to do this or that in concert with other elementary things, we have said all there is to say about them. So it is with the other particles, the forces, and the fields. We are left with a picture of the physical world as a colorless domain in which objects acting in ways that reflect their propensities combine to form more complex objects the nature of which is determined wholly by propensities of their constituents. The picture leaves no room for Technicolor boomings and buzzings. To the extent that we tolerate qualities in our thinking about the world, they appear to be, at best, epiphenomenal add-ons, byproducts of complex physical processes. To imagine that qualities themselves could affect or be affected by physical goings-on is to make a mistake of a fundamental sort, the mistake of imputing efficacy to the inherently inefficacious.[2]

All this is reminiscent of a conception of the world you find in Galileo. There are the primary qualities—mass, size, shape, a capacity for motion— and the secondary qualities—colors, sounds, tastes, odors. Science is concerned only with objects' primary qualities. It is these that determine how objects behave or would behave. The rest, the secondary qualities, are mental ephemera falling outside the purview of science, hence outside any respectable ontology of the physical world.

A conception of this kind dramatically bifurcates the mental and the physical. This bifurcation is codified in Descartes's characterization of the physical world as extended and unthinking, and minds as thinking and unextended. It is reflected today in the widespread presumption that mental and physical properties differ fundamentally.

I need not remind you of the many philosophical difficulties that attend this kind of division of reality. Attempts to surmount these difficulties so as to produce a unified picture of mind and world have, for the most part, embraced reductive strategies. Physicalists hope to reduce the mental to the physical. Idealists take the opposite tack, constructing the physical from the mental. The most prominent recent twist, 'nonreductive physicalism', endeavors to find a middle ground by conceiving of the mental as wholly dependent on and determined by, but nevertheless distinct from, the physical. The most compelling reason for embracing nonreductive physicalism is negative: the alternatives look much worse.

I might mention two philosophers who seem not to fit the scientiphicalist mold: Spinoza and Davidson.[3] Both embrace a thorough-going monism that turns mental–physical dualities into creatures of reason. This is not idealism, but neither is it physicalism, reductive or otherwise. There is no interesting sense in which the physical is privileged. How could it be, if the mental–physical distinction amounts to a distinction in mode of conception, not a distinction in reality?

I mention Spinoza and Davidson in order to set them to one side. The focus here will be on scientiphicalism, a conception of reality that accepts a sharp distinction between powers and qualities, the physical and the mental. Scientiphicalism excludes the mental, or whatever portions of the mental resist reduction, from the physical domain. Features of the world as we experience it that fail to turn up in our best physical theories are relegated to the mind. The task of making sense of mental phenomena is left to philosophers, who appear to have nothing better to do. If mental phenomena make no physical difference, they are excluded from the purview of serious science. Hence a conception of physical reality empty of qualities. There are the objects—the particles, the fields, space–time—and propensities of these to affect and be affected by one another in various ways. Qualities are, at best, mental projections, mental ephemera that, so far as the physical realm is concerned, we could do without.[4]

IDEALISM AND THE MYSTERY OF THE PHYSICAL

Unger argues that scientiphicalism, in removing qualities from the physical world, renders the physical world 'humanly unintelligible'. His argument (which I shall discuss in more detail subsequently) belongs to a family of arguments traceable at least to Berkeley. Berkeley argues that the elimination of qualities from the physical realm leads directly to idealism. He asks us to consider what follows from the supposition that qualities, or the secondary qualities, are exclusively mental. When we attempt to conceive of a material body, we inevitably conceive of it as having various qualities: it has a color, it makes a sound, it feels warm. Subtract these, and you are left with an empty conception.

> "Those who assert that figure, motion, and the rest of the primary or original qualities do exist without the mind, in unthinking substances, do at the same time acknowledge that colors, sounds, heat, cold, and such like secondary qualities, do not, which they tell us are sensations existing in the mind alone, that depend on and are occasioned by the different size, texture, and motion of the minute particles of matter. This they take for an undoubted truth, which they can demonstrate beyond all exception. If it is certain that those original qualities are inseparably united with the other sensible qualities, and not, even in thought, capable of being abstracted from them, it plainly follows that they exist only in the mind. But I desire any one to reflect and try, whether he can by any abstraction of thought conceive the extension and motion of a body, without all other sensible qualities. For my own part, I see evidently that it is not in my power to frame an idea of a body extended and moved, but I must withal give it some color or other sensible quality which is acknowledged to exist only in the mind. In short, extension, figure, and motion, abstracted from all other qualities, are inconceivable" (1710: § 10).

Berkeley's aim is to parlay the apparent inseparability of primary and secondary qualities into a defense of idealism. This theme is echoed by John Foster (1982) who argues that (as Unger might put it) scientiphicalist attempts to specify the intrinsic nature of material bodies yield at best 'topic neutral specifications', specifications that could be satisfied by immaterial states of affairs. We depict material bodies as spatially located, for instance, and extended three dimensionally. Space is presumed to be material because it serves as a medium for material bodies; bodies are taken to be material because they occupy regions of space. But

> "the two specifications cancel out, leaving us with a combined specification which is . . . topic neutral—a specification which characterizes matter-in-physical-space as a 3-dimensionally extended substance (of whatever intrinsic nature) in a 3-dimensionally extended medium (of whatever intrinsic nature)" (1982: 57).

When we turn to science for help in ascertaining the intrinsic qualitative nature of occupants of the physical realm we find little help.

> "Scientific analysis uncovers spatiotemporal arrangement and nomological organization, but does not reveal the intrinsic nature of the fundamental space-occupying substance or substances which are thus arranged and organized. It specifies the intrinsic nature of those substances only opaquely, in terms of their causal powers and sensitivities—the powers and sensitivities which, in the framework of natural law, their intrinsic properties sustain" (1982: 65).

The intrinsic qualitative nature of matter is, Foster holds, 'inscrutable'. Mental qualities, which constitute the intrinsic nature of states of mind are, in contrast, immediately evident. In so far as we think of powers as being grounded in the intrinsic natures of objects, we are left with an empty, purely formal conception of physical—that is, non-mental—reality: Unger's 'Mystery of the Physical'.

POWERS WITHOUT QUALITIES

Berkeley and Foster, along with various philosophers unsympathetic to idealism, object to attempts to detach powers from qualities on the grounds that descriptions of a world wholly in terms of powers manifested by objects populating the world, omit the intrinsic qualitative nature of the bearers of powers.[5] As Foster puts it, scientific descriptions are topic neutral, leaving the intrinsic character of the physical 'inscrutable'. The idea is that there is no reason to suppose that occupants of the 'physical role' are non-mental. If you couple this with the thought that the only intrinsic qualitative natures we have any conception of are those we encounter in conscious experience, you are on your way to the thesis that objects lacking mental qualities are flatly inconceivable.

One kind of scientiphicalist response to this line of reasoning begins by conceding its premises. We have no conception of what an intrinsic physical quality could be. Perhaps this poses no threat to scientiphicalist project, however. Perhaps it is of the nature of physical objects to have no intrinsic qualities. A physical object is constituted by powers to affect and be affected by other physical objects. In telling us about objects' powers, science is telling us all there is to know about the objects. As Foster puts it, on such a conception 'each particle is, in itself, no more than a mobile cluster of causal powers, there being no "substantial" space-occupant which possesses the powers and on whose categorical nature the powers are grounded.'[6]

Something like this seems to have been what Priestley, for instance, had in mind in defending the thesis that the physical realm is made up of

> "certain *centres of attractions and repulsions*, extending indefinitely in all directions, the whole effect of them to be upon each other; . . . a compage of these centres, placed within the sphere of each other's attraction, will constitute a body that we term *compact*" (1777: 239).[7]

Following Berkeley, Foster contends that such a conception of the physical world is incoherent.

> "The main problem is that if all the fundamental particles are construed in this way, there seem to be no physical items in terms of whose behavior the content of the powers could be specified, and consequently, it seems that, in the last analysis, there is nothing which the powers are powers to do" (1982: 68).

The difficulty, he thinks, manifests itself in a regress. Pretend the fundamental physical things are Newtonian atoms regarded as bundles of powers, 'mobile spheres of impenetrability'.

> "The problem arises when we ask: 'To what is a sphere of impenetrability impenetrable?' The answer is 'To other atoms, i.e. to other spheres of impenetrability.' But this means that the specification of the content of the atom-constituting power is viciously regressive: each atom is a sphere of impenetrability to any other sphere of impenetrability to any other sphere of impenetrability . . . and so on ad infinitum. From which it follows that the notion of such a power is incoherent, since there is nothing which the power is a power to do. To conceive of a sphere of impenetrability, we have to postulate some other type of space-occupant whose passage it is empowered to obstruct" (1982: 68).

Keith Campbell, no friend of idealism, had, six years earlier, advanced a similar argument in a discussion of Roger Boscovich's conception of the world as an arrangement of material points the intrinsic nature of which consists solely of a power to accelerate other points. Campbell wonders

"What is at a material point? What distinguishes a location in space where there is a point from one where there is no such thing? All we can say is: at a material point there is something which accelerates other somethings which in turn accelerate somethings (including the first) which in turn . . . But what an odd object this is. Its *only* feature is to have an effect on things which have an effect on things which have an effect on things which . . . We seem to be caught in a regress or circle, forever unable to say what these things *are* which have an effect on each other" (1976: 93).

If all there is to a material point is its power to accelerate other points, *what* is accelerated?

"When one point moves another, all that has been shifted is a power to shift powers to shift . . . But powers to shift *what*? To be coherent, I consider that Boscovich's points must be *somethings* which have the power to shift one another. They must have some intrinsic features which make them things in their own right, and they must in addition have the power to shift one another. Then, and only then, will there be something to move about. There must be some answer to the question What is at a point? independent of accelerative capacity" (1976: 93).

Note that it is not simply that Boscovich's material points or atoms must have 'intrinsic natures'. Boscovich's powers *are* intrinsic to their bearers. The idea rather is that bearers of powers must have some intrinsic *qualitative* nature.

The situation resembles what we encounter in attempts to think about purely relational worlds (see e.g. Dipert 1997; Heil 2003: 102–5). Consider a world in which objects are constituted by relations into which they enter. Richard Holton (1999) describes a world comprising four objects, A, B, C, and D, each wholly constituted by relations in which it stands to other objects:

A is directly to the left of B and directly above C;
B is directly to the right of A, and directly above D;
C is directly to the left of D, and directly below A;
D is directly to the right of C, and directly below B.

Holton's world might be represented this way:

A • B •

C • D •

The labeled points here are meant only as visual aids, however. "There really is nothing more to A, B, C, and D than that given by the descriptions"

(1999: 10). You get from this representation to the world itself by erasing the points (and labels) while leaving the relations intact. The result is a world evidently bereft of qualities and qualitied individuals.

This is an exciting prospect, especially when you couple it with the perennially seductive thought that everything is what it is owing to ways it is connected to everything else. The difficulty is to get a grip on the ontology. This could be due in part to its being natural to think of relations as dependent on relata in the sense that, without the relata, there is nothing to relate. Imagine the Myth Busters setting out to subtract the cat while keeping the smile.

One possibility is that the attraction of a purely relational world (or a world in which *relata* are constructed from relations) rests on an illicit move from the idea that a world could be given a purely relational *description*—via graph theory, for instance—to the much stronger thesis that this is *all there is* to the world. Such a move might be especially tempting to philosophers who start with scientific formalisms then attempt to 'read off' an ontology directly from these.

Think of functionalism in the philosophy of mind according to which all that matters are relations among 'nodes' in a system. The intrinsic qualitative nature of the nodes themselves is presumed irrelevant. Transistors could be swapped for neurons, provided only that the transistors preserve connections to other elements of the system implemented by neurons they replace. It is one thing, however, to allow that the qualitative nature of what occupies a system's nodes could vary, another matter altogether to imagine that nodes are qualitatively empty, wholly constituted by relations they bear to one another.

My tentative suggestion is that the giddy feeling accompanying thoughts of purely relational worlds, or worlds in which objects are wholly constituted by powers to affect other objects, springs from a common source. In the case of purely relational worlds, it is hard to see what could distinguish one relation from another. What distinguishes Holton's directly-to-the-right of relation from his directly-above relation? How are we to count instances of each relation? Purely relational worlds arguably lack sufficient individuative resources. The same problem bedevils pure powers worlds. The real difficulty lies not in the threat of a regress, but in the fact that qualities play a central role in the individuation of powers. Strip away the qualities, and it is no longer clear what we are talking about.

Before turning to considerations favoring this diagnosis, let me note that proponents of qualitatively empty worlds sometimes appear to reason from the fact that science is silent about the *F*'s to the conclusion that science tells us there are no *F*'s. The line of thought calls to mind David Armstrong's 'headless woman': we move from a lack of awareness of a woman's head (the woman is a magician's assistant with black felt draped over her head) to the conclusion that we are aware of the woman's lacking a head (Armstrong 1968). The question we face is whether we can make sense of the idea that the physical world is bereft of qualities, a realm of pure powers. Suppose we grant that science is interested exclusively in powers: scientific descriptions of objects concern only what those objects do or would do. The issue is not whether we should accept what science tells us, but whether we should take this to be the end of the story.

Science is characterized by abstraction, what Locke calls 'partial consideration'. You might think of Newton's laws of motion, for instance, as concerning the behavior of objects in so far as they are massy. The laws provide a precise account of the contribution an object's mass makes to its overall complement of dispositionalities. Abstraction of this kind lies at the heart of scientific theorizing and indeed of much ordinary thought about the world. The mistake is to imagine that abstraction gives us a complete picture.

One way to begin getting at this point is by considering an example deployed by Unger in his assault on scientiphicalism and 'The Mystery of the Physical'. Unger, unselfconsciously invoking Berkeley, Campbell, Foster, Martin and others, contends that we can form no 'adequate' notion of a world of material bodies lacking qualities. Any humanly graspable conception of material bodies endows those bodies with 'extensible colors'.[8] We can conceive of translucent 'extensibly red' spheres, for instance, occupying successive regions of space and interacting in various ways. Subtract the qualities—sphericity and 'extensible redness'—and nothing remains of our conception.

Unger drives the point home by inviting us to envision worlds populated by mobile, extensibly colored spherical particles juxtaposed with worlds made up of bubble-filled extensibly colored 'plena' in which motions of bubbles mimic particle motions. Because particle worlds differ from bubble worlds only qualitatively, scientiphicalism is unable to distinguish the one from the other. The alternative is to reject the 'Denial of Qualities':

> "Against those who've assumed the Denial to hold, I've argued that, without conceiving a concrete reality that's Qualitatively endowed, we humans, at least, can't conceive at all adequately, any physical reality at all. . . . Once we reject the Denial, we may resolve our Mystery of the Physical. . . . [thereby removing] an obstacle to our having a tolerably clear conception of a World that's the way Scientiphicalism claims our actual world to be" (2006: 137).

Only by endowing scientifically specified objects with spatially extensible qualities can we frame a 'Humanly Realistic Metaphysic'.[9]

RECIPROCITY

Unger's 'Humanly Realistic Metaphysic' includes objects 'variously qualitied and propensitied'. But how are propensities—powers—and qualities related? Most of us have been conditioned to think it obvious that powers and qualities are distinct kinds of property: powers endow their possessors with capacities to inflict or suffer various changes; qualities are impotent. A conception of this kind would be natural for anyone accustomed to distinguishing dispositional and categorical properties.

The idea that qualities and powers are distinct kinds of property fits nicely with the view that powers and qualities covary contingently. In our world spherical objects roll, but in other worlds they need not. The ease with which we imagine such worlds leads Unger to describe in excruciating detail dozens imaginary worlds populated by dynamic, extensibly colored objects (typically translucent spheres) endowed with powers of attraction and repulsion. One such world might comprise red, blue, and yellow spheres moving about in a three-dimensional space. Blue spheres attract yellow spheres, but not red spheres. Here, the power to attract yellow spheres covaries with extensible blueness. Blue spheres could, in other worlds lack this power, possessing, instead, other powers or no powers at all.[10]

Notice that, if blue spheres are equipped with a power to attract yellow spheres, yellow spheres must, of necessity, possess a reciprocal power, the power to be attracted by blue spheres. So in any world in which blue spheres *contingently* possess the power to attract yellow spheres, yellow spheres in that world *must* harbor the reciprocal attractive power. The result, unremarked by Unger, presents us with an odd kind of necessary correlation. Although it is contingent that blue things have the power to attract yellow things and contingent that yellow things have the power to be attracted by blue things, in any world in which blue things have the power to attract yellow things, yellow things could not fail have the reciprocal power to be attracted by blue things (and *vice versa*).

You can see the prima facie oddness of such a view by thinking of it this way. Suppose God creates a world containing blue spheres and elects to endow these blue spheres with a power to attract yellow things. If God subsequently creates yellow things, God could not fail to give these yellow things the power to be attracted by blue things, a power they could have lacked otherwise.

You might be skeptical that powers have the reciprocal character I have attributed to them. Maybe all it takes is that blue spheres have an attractive power; yellow spheres passively cooperate. What, then, distinguishes the power possessed by blue spheres from other powers? It is a power to attract yellow things, a power to attract yellow spheres, not in virtue of their size or their sphericity, but in virtue of their yellowness. Blue things are 'yellow attractors'. We have a qualitative mode of individuation for a power. This, I think, is how Unger sees it. A qualitatively individuated power is contingently possessed by our imagined blue spheres, but it is a power blue spheres could have lacked, a power that could have been possessed, instead, by red spheres.

A magnetic bar has the power to attract iron filings. One way to think about such cases is to ascribe an *active* power to the bar, and *passive* powers to the filings, a distinction familiar to readers of Locke.[11] Let me suggest that

this asymmetrical picture is inappropriate, a product of our explanatory practices and contingencies of experimental manipulation. A magnetic bar attracts
iron filings in virtue of some feature of those iron filings. The attractive event
is a manifestation of reciprocal powers possessed by the bar and by the filings.
Similarly, in our imagined world, blue spheres attract yellow spheres in virtue
of reciprocal powers possessed by blue spheres and yellow spheres.

One source of difficulty facing anyone trying to move from consideration of extensibly colored spheres to serious ontology arises from the fact
that we are looking at toy worlds in which objects' powers are whimsi-
cally stipulated. In such worlds anything goes. Consider an actual power,
however, the power possessed by a billiard ball to roll (in a particular way)
down an inclined plane. In this case it seems obvious that the ball's manifesting this power is a mutual manifestation of reciprocal powers possessed
by both the ball, the inclined plane, the gravitational field in which they
are located, and assorted other factors. You would want to think about
powers in this way if you thought, as I do think, that one and the same
power could manifest itself differently with different kinds of reciprocal
disposition partner.[12] Suppose the billiard ball possesses the power to roll
in virtue of being spherical. In virtue of being spherical, the ball would
make a concave circular imprint in soft clay, would reflect light so as to
look spherical, would cast a particular sort of shadow. A ball's powers are
intrinsic to it, but how these powers manifest themselves depends on their
manifestation partners.

When you think of powers this way, you will be thinking of them as
reciprocal. In virtue of being as it is, each power would manifest itself in
a particular way with particular kinds of reciprocal partner.[13] Suppose we
accept reciprocity and see where it leads.

CONTINGENCY

Unger individuates powers qualitatively, but insists that the relation between
qualities and powers is contingent. Consider again our imagined Unger-style
world featuring red, blue, and yellow spheres, and assume, as before, that
blue spheres have the power to attract yellow things—blue spheres are yellow
attractors—and yellow spheres possess a reciprocal power to be attracted by
blue things. The contingency thesis requires that these powers be only contingently related to qualities possessed by their bearers. On Unger's view there
is nothing about blueness itself that connects blueness to the power to attract
yellow things. Similarly for yellowness: there is nothing about being yellow
that ensures that its possessors would be attracted by blue things.

It is time to ask how all this is supposed to work, however. Blue spheres
have the power to attract yellow things and yellow things a reciprocal power
to be attracted by blue things, but these powers are only contingently related
to blueness and yellowness, respectively. This means that the power possessed

by blue spheres could not be a power to attract yellow spheres in virtue of their *yellowness*. To think otherwise would be to turn yellowness itself into a power: in virtue of *being yellow* a sphere would be attracted to blue spheres. It must be that yellow things possess some reciprocal power that contingently covaries with yellowness. This power, and not the spheres' yellowness, is, so to speak, the target of the attractive power possessed by blue spheres. Parallel reasoning establishes that the power possessed by yellow spheres to be attracted by blue things is a power to be attracted by something with the right power, a power that contingently covaries with blueness.[14]

Does this maneuver help make sense of contingency? Consider the powers just described. What exactly are these powers *for*? Each is a power to attract or be attracted by objects possessing the other. If contingency holds, the powers are swappable. The power possessed by blue things might be possessed in some worlds by yellow things, and the power possessed by yellow things might be possessed elsewhere by blue things. Indeed the powers might belong to red and green things respectively: there are worlds in which red and green things possessed these powers and yellow and blue things possessed some *other* pair of attractive powers.

My sense is that such possibilities amount to distinctions without a difference. Unger's initial thought was right: qualities figure ineliminably in the individuation of powers. A blue sphere that possesses a power to attract yellow things, what we began by calling a yellow attractor, possesses a power to attract objects in virtue of their yellowness. Yellow things possess, by virtue of being yellow, a reciprocal power to be attracted by blue spheres in virtue of their blueness. It would seem to follow that the connection between 'extensible yellowness', a quality, and a power, the power to be attracted by yellow attractors is not contingent. Indeed it appears that this power is inseparable from the nature of the quality. More generally, in so far as we appeal to qualities in individuating powers, it appears that the pertinent reciprocal powers are powers possessed by objects in virtue of their possession of the pertinent quality.

If this sounds far fetched, it does so partly because we are dealing with stipulated powers. We have no reason at all to think that blueness must be bound up with the attraction of yellow things, or that yellowness has a special affinity for blueness. The point I want to make could be framed conditionally, however. *Were* the world as Unger describes it, *were* the world such that blue spheres were yellow attractors and yellow spheres were subject to attraction by blue things, blueness would not be contingently associated with the power to attract yellow things in virtue of their yellowness, yellowness would not be contingently subject to blue attraction.

POWERFUL QUALITIES

I believe that the widespread presumption that qualities and powers, at best, contingently covary springs from a latent Humean undercurrent evident in so much contemporary metaphysics. It begins with a basic confusion of powers themselves with *manifestations* of powers. In general, a power or disposition requires for its manifestation, a suite of reciprocal disposition partners. *How* a disposition manifests itself depends both on its nature and on the nature of its reciprocal disposition partners. A billiard ball's sphericity is responsible for the ball's rolling, but only on a solid sloping surface situated in a gravitational field. This same sphericity is responsible for the ball's reflecting light so as to look spherical and for the ball's making a concave impression of a distinctive sort in soft clay.

This feature of dispositions—one disposition, many kinds of manifestation with many kinds of reciprocal disposition partner—is easily missed if you imagine that conditionals used to pick out dispositions provide exhaustive characterizations or analyses of the dispositions they pick out. Distinct conditionals are presumed to pick out distinct dispositions. In identifying dispositions solely by reference to their manifestations, we are naturally led to suppose that different kinds of manifestation signal different dispositions.

Suppose I am right about this. Now think about Humean considerations apparently favoring contingency. We can easily imagine a ball closely resembling a billiard ball that does not roll down an inclined plane. One reason we can do this is that balls (and inclined planes) are complex objects. Two balls made of very different materials might nevertheless *look* just alike. A magnetized steel billiard ball would not roll down an inclined plane made of iron. It is however, rather more of a challenge to imagine a ball intrinsically indiscernible from this regulation billiard ball that does not roll, but tumbles down an inclined plane; reflects light so as to look cubical rather than spherical; makes a square-shaped impression in soft clay. If you grant that one and the same power could manifest itself differently with different kinds of disposition partner, it is much harder to hold the qualities constant while varying the powers.

Let me mention one more, related, difficulty for Unger, and indeed for anyone who regards qualities and powers as distinguishable, contingently related features of objects. Suppose perception of something involves a causal connection between what is perceived and the perceiver.[15] If qualities and powers are distinct, how could we perceive qualities? Suppose that red spheres are equipped with assorted powers, one of which covaries with redness. It is not the sphere's redness that causes you to perceive something red, but a power accompanying redness. You don't perceive the redness of a sphere, then, but only—what?—some power contingently possessed by red things. This turns on its head the idea that qualities are observable, powers unobservable!

The moment we divorce qualities and powers, we have little use for qualities. I have suggested that there are good reasons to think that qualities are required for the individuation of powers. Given the reciprocity of manifestations this, perhaps surprisingly, encourages the view that powers and qualities are not merely contingently associated. But if powers and qualities are associated of necessity, what is the nature of this necessity? Is it a brute necessary correlation? That would be hard to swallow. It would, in addition, take qualities out of the causal picture. This, I have suggested, is a source of unwelcome difficulties. We can accommodate the necessity and resolve the difficulties by identifying powers and qualities, turning properties into powerful qualities.

Philosophers are apt to regard such a view with disdain, but I suspect that nonphilosophers regard it as too obvious to bear mention. Things do what they do because they are as they are, and ways things *are* are qualities. When we cite qualities in causal explanations, when we say that the bull charged because the matador's cape was red, we are not citing features of objects we take to be correlated with their powers. The cape's redness, we think, sparked the bull's anger.

This natural way of thinking of qualities as themselves powers has been compromised by a strain of Humeanism that runs through so much contemporary philosophy and by accounts of powers that distinguish powers from their 'categorical bases': powers are 'higher-level', 'multiply realized' properties (see Prior, Pargetter and Jackson 1982). I have argued at length elsewhere against the idea that powers are 'higher-level' properties (see, e.g. Heil 2003; 2005; Heil and Robb 2003). 'Higher-level' properties collapse into their realizers. What of Humeanism?

Twentieth-century analytic philosophy inculcated a Humean picture of the world as a default. The world is characterized by what Santayana (1930: 110) called "radical contingency". We take it as obvious that contingencies can simply be eye-balled. However intimately related the *F*'s and *G*'s are in our experience, it seems easy to conceive of their not being so related. The burden of proof falls to those who would deny contingency. Unless you can show that the *F*'s and *G*'s are related of necessity, it is reasonable to suppose that their relation is contingent. The situation resembles the heavyweight boxing crown: to be dethroned, the champ must be decisively defeated.

It is time we recognized that, in philosophy, there are no default views, no heavyweight champs. Substantive claims of contingency, no less than claims of necessity, as Charlie Martin used to put it, need to earn their keep. Spinoza might be right: apparent contingencies could turn out to be merely apparent. Telling a story according to which the *F*'s and *G*'s are related of necessity, then, need not oblige us first to provide a definitive refutation of Humeanism. The story's plausibility depends on how well it does what we want such stories to do: provide an illuminating ontological picture that makes sense of the world and our place in it. Against this background, I believe a conception of properties as powerful qualities has much to recommend it.

POSTSCRIPT: PRIMARY AND SECONDARY QUALITIES

Berkeley attacked materialists who held that secondary qualities (tastes, sounds, colors, smells) were mind-dependent. When we try to conceive of a material object altogether lacking in such qualities, we find ourselves brought up short. If secondary qualities are mind-dependent, then, and if we cannot conceive of objects lacking in such qualities, objects must be mind-dependent.

Whatever you might think of this argument, it is worth noting that the underlying assumption is that primary and secondary qualities alike are *qualities*. Berkeley, following Galileo, takes the secondary qualities to be mental. Let me propose another way to think about the distinction.

Assume that the primary qualities are qualities possessed by the fundamental things. Assume, as well, that these qualities are powers—powerful qualities. The fundamental things possess shape, mass, and size, for instance. And, in virtue of their possession of these qualities they do and would do various things. What about the secondaries? Think of secondary qualities as arrangements of the primaries. If you arrange the corpuscles in a particular way, the result is something red—something that looks red in virtue of reflecting light in a particular way. When God creates the fundamental things and arranges them in a particular way, God has *thereby* created all the secondary qualities. The secondary qualities are secondary by virtue of being no addition of being.

If something like this is right, we can agree with Berkeley. In depicting to ourselves any object we depict it as possessing various secondary qualities. This is because we depict medium-sized objects, and medium-sized objects are complex. When we imagine viewing a simple corpuscle, we imagine it as it appears on a photographic plate or a monitor, and images on photographic plates and monitors are complex entities possessing secondary qualities. More fundamentally, when we imagine what something—a corpuscle, for instance—might look like, we are conjuring a visual appearance, an experience of a complex entity. The corpuscle is not red, or any color at all. But our image is as of something red, something billiard-ball like. None of this implies that secondary qualities are mind-dependent, none of it yields an argument for idealism.

ACKNOWLEDGMENTS

This paper was presented at the conference 'Powers: Their Grounding and their Realization/held at Oxford in July 2008. Here I develop arguments initially sketched in Heil (2003) and in a critical study of Peter Unger's *All the Power in the World* (Heil 2008a).

NOTES

1. My conception of powers owes much to C. B. Martin (see Martin 2008). Its roots go back to my Enlightenment heroes, especially Locke and Spinoza.
2. This might be put in terms of causal completeness or 'closure', the idea that the physical world is causally autonomous. If you accept scientiphicalism,

however, you are more likely to regard the thought that mental qualities, or indeed qualities of any kind, could make a causal difference as something akin to a category mistake: no need to appeal to a contentious closure thesis.

3. On Davidson, see Heil 2008b. Although he describes himself as a physicalist, Galen Strawson should probably be added to the list; see Strawson in Freeman 2006.

4. David Chalmers, a contemporary exponent of scientiphicalism, regards the reconciliation of mental qualities with the scientiphicalist picture as the last remaining 'hard problem' (see Chalmers 1996). The options, he suggests, are 'something like epiphenomenalism' and panpsychism.

5. Versions of the argument not aimed at a defense of idealism can be found in Armstrong (1961, chap. 15; 1999); Smart (1963: 73–5); Campbell (1972: 93–4); Martin (1997: 213–17; 2008: 61–9); Blackburn (1990); and Heil (2003: 97–110).

6. Foster (1982: 67–8). Foster cites Leibniz, Boscovich, Kant, Priestley, and Faraday as among those who have defended this kind of view. See Harré and Madden (1975), chap. 9.

7. Cited in Harré and Madden (1975: 172).

8. 'Spatially extensible color' (2006: 158) is a central feature of Unger's 'humanly realistic' conception of material reality. 'Spatially extensible colors' need not be actual *colors*, however, but only objects' qualitative clothing, Foster's spatial 'filling'.

9. Unger assumes what Foster denies: that spatiality is a paradigmatic physical characteristic.

10. If blue spheres could have different powers in different worlds, might there be 'mixed' worlds in which some otherwise identical blue spheres have one power, others another? If not, why not? (See Blackburn 1984: 186.)

11. Shoemaker (1980, 1998) follows suit in speaking of 'forward-looking' and 'backward-looking' powers.

12. This is not to deny that some powers might manifest themselves spontaneously. Manifestations of such powers would appear to be uncaused. Many powers, however, evidently manifest themselves as they do only with the right kinds of reciprocal partner.

13. This way of thinking about powers has long been advocated by C. B. Martin; see his *The Mind in* Nature (2008).

14. Unger distinguishes quality-directed powers ('Propensities [that] *concern only something as to the Quality of disposition partners*') from power-directed powers (212–13), but it is difficult to see how, given contingency, a power could be anything *but* power-directed.

15. If you accept an ontology of powers, you will want to say that perceiving is a mutual manifestation of dispositions of us—our perceptual systems—and of perceptual stimuli. In the case of visual perception, this might be structured light radiation (which is in turn a mutual manifestation of dispositions present in ambient light and those present in objects seen).

5 Manifestations as Effects

Jennifer McKitrick

INTRODUCTION

According to a standard characterization of dispositions, when a disposition is activated by a stimulus, a manifestation of that disposition typically occurs. For example, when flammable gasoline encounters a spark in an oxygen-rich environment, the manifestation of flammability—combustion—occurs. In the dispositions/powers literature, it is common to assume that a manifestation is *an effect* of a disposition being activated. (I use "disposition" and "power" interchangeably). I address two questions in this chapter: Could all manifestations be effects that involve things acquiring only dispositional properties? And, is thinking of manifestations as *contributions* to effects preferable to thinking of them as effects? I defend negative responses to both questions.

If all properties are dispositional, as the pandispositionalists claim, then any time the activation of a disposition results is something acquiring a new property, it results in something acquiring another disposition. Some worry that a vicious regress ensues (Swinburne, 1980; Bird, 2007a, 2007b: 132–46). While I believe that regress arguments can be addressed, my worry is that, on the pandispositionalist view, manifestations become unobservable.

Thinking of manifestations as effects is problematic in cases where what actually occurs is not the kind of effect that the power is a power *for*, but rather a complex interaction of various powers. Because of this, some prefer to think of manifestations as contributions to effects (Molnar, 2003: 194–8; Mumford, 2009). I argue against this proposal on the ground that it introduces mysterious new entities into our ontology. In the end, the most plausible view is that a single kind of power can have different kinds of effects, some of which involve the instantiation of non-dispositional properties.

I proceed as follows. In the first section of this chapter, I show that the philosophical concept of a manifestation is the concept of an effect. In the second section, I argue against the claim that all manifestations involve instantiations of only dispositional properties. In the third section, I argue against the view that manifestations are contributions rather than effects.

MANIFESTATIONS

Examples of manifestations in the philosophical dispositions/powers literature include events such as "breaking, dissolving, stretching" (Crane 1996: 1). A manifestation is sometimes characterized as a change (Crane, 1996: 1), "behavior," or an "outcome" (Molnar, 2003: 57). More often than not, manifestations are said to *occur* (Crane, 1996: 38). So, the philosophical concept of a manifestation is, minimally, that of an event—either an event-type, or a particular event which occurs at a particular place and time.

Sometimes philosophers say that a disposed object *exhibits* or *displays* its manifestation (Hüttemann, 1998: 129). This is in accordance with ordinary English, according to which the term "manifestation" refers to an outward or perceptible indication, a public demonstration, an exhibition, display, or revelation. While colloquial usage and the term "manifestation" itself suggest something that is "manifest"—obvious or at least observable, philosophical use of the term does not adhere to this restriction (Molnar, 2003: 60). Though I argue that some manifestations must be directly observable, not all manifestations are. For example, manifestations of charge in subatomic particles is not observable in any obvious or direct way.

Manifestations are said to be caused, brought about, produced, or triggered (Molnar, 2003: 86; Mumford, 2009: 102). This suggests that they are effects. What it means to say that manifestations are effects depends in part on what one means by "effect". I think it is sufficient for my purposes to say an effect is an event that has a cause, and that an effect involves something instantiating properties, typically acquiring new properties. The assumption that manifestations are effects lies behind the debates over whether dispositions are causally relevant to their manifestations (McKitrick 2005; Block 1990; Kim 1988; Prior, Pargetter, and Jackson 1982). While some argue that dispositions cause their manifestations and others argue that it is the causal bases of those dispositions that cause their manifestations, all parties to these debates implicitly agree that manifestations are events that are caused by something or other.

Often, when an object manifests a disposition, a new property or properties are acquired, either by the disposed object, some other object(s), or both. For examples of each: the elastic band takes on a new shape; the provocative cape changes the bull's mood; and the water-soluble tablet dissolves and the surrounding liquid approaches saturation. Perhaps an object can manifest a disposition without any change occurring. Suppose, for example, a structure is stable since its creation. Stability seems dispositional since calling something "stable" speaks to what it would do in certain circumstances. In the face of various forces, a structure manifests its stability by remaining upright and intact. While circumstances may change, the manifestation of stability does not seem to involve anything acquiring a new property. However, that is not to say the manifestation is not an event in this case. On some views, an event just is a particular instantiating a property at a time (Kim 1976).

So far, I haven't provided an argument for the claim that states manifestations are effects as much as I've tried to be convincing in that that is what we've been assuming all along, and that its part of our concept. Incidentally, in claiming that manifestations are effects, I'm not claiming the converse, that all effects are manifestations of dispositions. That might be true, given a dispositional account of causation. But perhaps random or improbable events are effects, but not manifestations of dispositions. If it is ever the case that something does something it is not disposed to do, perhaps that behavior is not the manifestation of a disposition, but that is not to say that it is an uncaused event.

MANIFESTATIONS AS ACQUISITIONS OF DISPOSITIONAL PROPERTIES

If a manifestation involves a particular acquiring a property, could that property be a disposition? Certainly. Something can be disposed to acquire a disposition. For example, metals are magnetizable, that is, they are disposed to become magnetic.[1] English doesn't have many words for such dispositions, but the basic idea can be generalized. Many things that are not fragile could be said to be "fragilizable"—disposed to become fragile when dried or frozen, for example.

But could *all* manifestations consist of acquisitions of *nothing but* dispositions (as the pandispositionalist must maintain, given our understanding of manifestations)? Many philosophers worry that this would lead to a vicious regress, giving them reason to resist pandispositionalism. According to Molnar and Armstrong:

> "Pan-dispositionalism combined with the plausible view that all manifestations are changes in the properties of objects, evidently gives rise to a regress" (Molnar, 2003: 172).
> "Given a purely Dispostionalist account of properties, particulars would seem to be always re-packing their bags as they change their properties, yet never taking a journey from potency to act" (Armstrong, 1997: 80).

But is this regress vicious? One might think a disposition to produce a disposition to produce a disposition is no worse than a cause which produces an effect which is itself a cause for a further effect. This sounds less like regress and more like progress. If there's anything to the objection, there must be an important difference between the regress and a causal chain. So, what is supposed to be problematic about this regress?

It is sometimes argued that, if all properties were dispositions, nothing would occupy space, nothing would happen, or nothing would be actual. I think that adequate replies to such arguments have been made: There's no good reason to think that objects that instantiate only dispositional properties cannot occupy space; There's no good reason to think that an object acquiring a disposition is not an event, or "something happening"; And finally, there's no good reason to think that nothing would be actual, since dispositions are actual, even when their manifestations aren't (Martin, 1994: 1; Molnar, 2003: 173–7). Furthermore, these explanations are puzzling qua explanations of the viciousness of the regress. According to the claims previously stated, at any instant of a pandispositionalist world, nothing occupies space, nothing happens, and nothing is actual. If this were problematic, it would be so independently of the idea that dispositions beget further dispositions.

A more plausible interpretation of the regress worry involves an understanding of disposition claims in terms of counterfactuals. On this view, to have a power is just to have a certain counterfactual true of you, and which counterfactuals are true depends on similarities among possible worlds. If all properties are powers, what is true at a world depends on what is true at nearby possible worlds, and what is true at those worlds depends on what is true at other worlds, and so on (Blackburn, 1990: 64). However, this version of the regress worry is no stronger than a counterfactual analysis of dispositions. Indeed, it may be weaker, if as Holton suggests, certain arrangements of worlds could support all the needed counterfactuals and, consequently, disposition claims (Holton, 1999).

I suspect that there is something problematic about the regress, and I suspect that it has something to do with the fact that dispositions can fail to manifest, or be latent. One way to formulate a regress argument in a way that exploits this feature of dispositions proceeds as follows:

1. Manifestations involve particulars instantiating properties.
2. If all properties are dispositions, then manifestations involve particulars instantiating dispositions (1).
3. A disposition is either manifest or latent.
4. If all properties are dispositions, then every manifestation involves either
   a. a particular instantiating a latent disposition, or
   b. a particular instantiating a disposition that manifests by giving something a latent disposition, or
   c. a particular instantiating a disposition that manifests by giving something a disposition, which manifests by giving something a latent disposition, or
   . . .
   d. a particular instantiating a disposition that gives something a disposition, which gives something a disposition, and so on infinitely (2, 3).

5. It is not plausible that every manifestation consists of either a, b, c, or ... n.
6. Therefore, not all properties are dispositions (4, 5).

The strength of this argument depends on premise (5). Intuitively, the consequent of (4) is not attractive, but what's wrong with it? It is hard to say without repeating the objections we've already replied to, that nothing happens, nothing is actual, and so on. However, this argument has done nothing to make those objections more powerful.

Maybe what's wrong with the scenario described in the consequent of premise (4) is that, if all manifestations are acquisitions of latent dispositions, or chains of acquisitions of dispositions on into the future, it is not clear that any manifestation is ever really *displayed*. It is not clear that we could ever *observe* a manifestation. For example, it is hard to tell when magnetizability is manifest, because it is hard to tell that something is magnetic, unless we observe a manifestation of magnetism, such as the movement of a metal pin towards the magnet. If the manifestation of being magnetic were a matter of something acquiring yet another disposition, it is not clear how we could observe the manifestation of magnetism. So, perhaps the problem with the pandispositionalist world is not that nothing happens or is actual, but as Swinburne suggests, that nothing is observable (1980).

Granted, we sometimes observe *that* an object has a disposition. But how do we do that? Sometimes, we observe that something has a disposition by observing it manifesting that disposition. When I see the rubber band stretch I judge that it is elastic. But what if the object is not manifesting that disposition? We can still justifiably judge that it has the disposition if it has manifested the disposition in the past, and it doesn't seem to have changed. When I stop stretching the rubber band and it resumes its former shape, I reasonably believe that it is still elastic. Or, sometimes we judge that something has a disposition because it seems to be just like something else that is displaying or has displayed the manifestation. So, while I haven't seen all of the rubber bands in the box get stretched, they appear to be indistinguishable, and I reasonably believe they are all elastic like the first one was. These thoughts inspire the following argument that I will call the Observability argument:

1. The only chance that one has of observing that an object has a disposition is to observe that object displaying a manifestation of that disposition, or by observing other properties of the object (such as properties similar to those of other objects which display or have displayed the manifestation).
2. To observe that an object has some property by observing that it has some other property is to *indirectly* observe the first property.
3. Therefore, dispositions are, at best, indirectly observable (1, 2).

4. Therefore, if all properties are dispositions, no properties are directly observable (3).
5. In order to *indirectly* observe any property, one must *directly* observe some other property.
6. Therefore, if all properties are dispositions, all properties are unobservable (4, 5).
7. Some properties are observable.
8. Therefore, not all properties are dispositions (6, 7).

The extent to which the Observability argument still counts as a "regress" argument is unclear, but how one characterizes it is perhaps less important than how the pandispositionalist responds.

One possible pandispositionalist reply to the Observability argument is to deny premise (1) and instead claim that some dispositions are directly observable. For example, it seems that you observe power when you walk in a strong windstorm, try to push two magnets together (with like poles facing), or stand dangerously close to a large explosion.

Such a reply provokes the following question: If a disposition is directly observable, does that mean that the disposition is observable when it is not manifesting? That sounds incoherent. While being observable may not be necessary for a disposition to be manifest, it does seem sufficient; if a disposition is observable, it's manifest. And arguably, what one observes is not the power itself, but the manifestation, just as premise (1) claims. In the case of the powers of wind, magnets, and bombs, one observes the movement, pressure, resistance, heat, and light. Of course, the pandispositionalist must say that moving, pressing, resisting, etc., are themselves powers. But even if that were true, it would not serve to explain how the magnetism, the explosiveness, or any other power, is observed. Hume may be *persona non grata* in this discussion, but perhaps he is right to suggest that, while one observes causes and effects, one never directly observes the power of a cause to cause its effect (1888: 77).

Another possible pandispositionalist reply is to say that some things have dispositions to cause observation-experiences, such as visual or tactile experiences, and therefore, those dispositions are observable. For example, we observe that something has a disposition to cause a warm sensation because we experience feeling that sensation. But it seems that, while we do experience warm sensations, in doing so were are observing the sensation, not the disposition to cause that sensation. Could the warm sensation itself be disposition? Perhaps one might think so, if one thought that the nature of mental properties is exhausted by their causal powers, or functional role. However, if one has a view of mental properties according to which some of them have an intrinsic, occurrent, qualitative character, then the manifestations of dispositions to cause such experiences cannot consist solely of acquisitions of further dispositions.

A similar pandispositionalist response appears in Bird's reply to Swinburne's epistemic regress argument (1980: 134). Bird's argues that what stops Swinburne's epistemic regress is the fact that some manifestations of dispositions involve agents acquiring epistemic properties, such as being aware that something in one's environment has a certain property. These epistemic properties would themselves be dispositional, but their instantiations count as observations or knowledge of the dispositions that they are manifestations of. For example, suppose a red thing in the environment causes, by some chain of events, an observer in the appropriate circumstances to have a certain mental property—an awareness of redness. According to the pandispositionalist, the redness is a disposition, as is the awareness. But regardless, the redness is observed. Since one can observe without observing that one is observing, having the observation stops the regress. As a response to my Observability argument, Bird's reply would amount to a rejection of premise (1), which says:

> "The only chance one has of observing that an object has a disposition is to observe that object displaying a manifestation of that disposition, or by observing other properties of the object".

Bird's response to Swinburne suggests that he would say that sometimes we observe that an object has a disposition, not by observing a manifestation, but by the manifestation *being* an observation.

To respond, consider what powers we could observe, according to this view. Suppose that a power causes an observation and is thereby observable. The observation that one has is presumably an observation of that power. So the observable power is a power to cause an observation of itself. If the essence of any power is to be a power for a particular manifestation, then all of the observable powers are just powers to cause observations of themselves. Consequently, if all properties are powers, the only properties we observe are powers to cause observations of themselves. Note that this would exhaust the content of the observation; it would not include any awareness of any qualitative aspect of the property, nor any other manifestation it may have. The content of the epistemic state would be nothing more than "something has the power to cause my awareness of it". But surely, our vast and varied range of observations has more content than that. It is not clear how we would even distinguish different properties, on this view. In fact, it is not clear that there would even be distinct observable properties on this view.

In light of Bird's response to Swinburne, perhaps the Observability argument needs to be dialed back a bit. It is not that pandispositionalism entails that no properties are observable. Rather, it entails that, at most, one property is observable, and that property is the power to cause awareness of itself. This still strikes me as a *reductio* of the view.

MANIFESTATIONS AS CONTRIBUTIONS

Even if, contrary to the arguments of the previous section, all manifestations were acquisitions of dispositional properties, manifestations would still be effects. Notable detractors of this view include Mumford and Molnar, who say:

> "we must sharply distinguish between *effects* and *manifestations*" (Molnar, 2003: 195);
> "[P]owers manifests themselves in contributions to events, rather than straightforwardly in events themselves" (Mumford, 2009: 104).

On Molnar's view, a power's characteristic manifestation makes it the power that it is. A power always has the same manifestation. However, an exercise of a power does not always have the same *effect*. That's because powers don't act in isolation. An effect is an occurrence that is the result of the interaction of several powers. One power can contribute to different effects, but it always makes the same contribution. On this view, a manifestation is a contribution to an effect, and an effect is a combination of contributory manifestations.[2] A favorite example of this phenomenon is the case of the horses pulling the barge down the canal (Molnar, 2003: 195). While one horse exerts a south-westerly force and the other exerts a south-easterly force, the effect is not a manifestation of either of those forces, but a southward movement that is the result of their combination.

While the horse-drawn barge is a persuasive example, note that the term "manifestation" is being used in a new way. Suppose an apple falls to earth. It falls a little more slowly than it would in a vacuum, and maybe the wind is blowing, so the precise way it falls is affected by multiple forces. We would normally say that the apple's fall is a manifestation of the gravitational attraction of the earth. But according to the Molnar/Mumford view, the apple's fall cannot be a manifestation of the earth's gravity. Likewise, events such as breaking, dissolving, or stretching aren't manifestations either. That constitutes a substantial revision of the application of the term.

One might think that, in the case of the apple falling, the other interacting forces are so minor that the actual effect is very similar to what the pure manifestation would be, and that explains why it may sound odd to say that the fall is not a manifestation of gravity. However, the moon's orbit around the earth is also an effect of the earth's gravity. If the earth's orbit is also very similar to a pure manifestation of the earth's gravity, then the apple falling and the earth's orbit must be very similar to each other. But these phenomena seem so dissimilar that the idea that they are both effects of the same power was a remarkable discovery. If a power must always have the same manifestation, then either we need a story about how the moon's orbit and the apple's fall count as the same manifestation, or we must deny that they are both manifestations of the earth's gravity.

There is nothing inherently wrong with making the terminological choice not to call an effect a "manifestation". What is more important is the reason for the choice. On the Molnar/Mumford view, an effect is not called a "manifestation" because that term is reserved for a newly postulated kind of entity—something that exists in addition to the power and the effect. Lest we multiply entities beyond necessity, we should question whether we have good reasons, empirical or otherwise, to postulate "manifestations" so understood.

Molnar talks as if manifestations are not observable, since effects never consist of the manifestations of just a single power (Molnar, 2003: 12, 15, 60). Similarly, Mumford says manifestations are observable only in rare laboratory conditions (Mumford, 2009: 104). We have already noted that one cannot directly observe an object's powers. Anyone worried about the empirical rigor of a powers ontology should note that the "manifestations as contributions" view introduces another type of unobservable entity into the causal story.

Suppose you observe an object in the circumstances of manifestation for a certain power. You might observe an effect, which is, on this view, the combination of various manifestations of various powers. But you don't directly observe the manifestations of those powers. Perhaps you can subtract an object from an interaction in question, and attribute any difference in effect to the loss of a manifestation of that object's power. But suppose you had a magnet hovering over a pin that was standings on its head. When you remove the magnet, the pin falls. You observe the pin, the magnet, and their movements. It seems reasonable to infer that the magnet was exerting some sort of power over the pin. However, is there any reason to think that, in addition to the magnet, the pin on its head and the magnet's power to attract the pin, there's another distinct entity in this scenario—the manifestation of that power?

In addition to wondering what kind of empirical evidence we could have for manifestations on this view, it seems fair to ask: What kind of thing is a manifestation? It is called "a contribution" but if that just means something that is contributed, we are still left wondering, what kind of thing? The view is not that the manifestation is an intermediary event that occurs between the power and the effect. If it were, it would be an intermediary effect, and so not an alternative to the claim that manifestations are not effects. Furthermore, Mumford explicitly says manifestations aren't events, and that they are simultaneous with effects. So perhaps a manifestation is part of the effect, a property of the effect, or a force. Let's examine each of these suggestions.

The expression "contribution" to an effect might suggest a manifestation is part of an effect. But what type of part? Perhaps it is a spatiotemporal region of the effect. But it's not clear how this suggestion would work with the paradigm examples of effects that aren't supposed to be manifestations. Consider the barge going down the canal. According to the previous suggestion, the manifestation of one of the horse's power would be a spatiotemporal part of this effect. What part could that be? If it is wrong to say that the manifestation is the barge moving, then it must also be wrong to say that the manifestation is some portion of the barge moving. Like the over-all effect, any part of the effect will be the way it is as a consequence of various powers. If there is reason to think that events aren't manifestations, these same reasons would seem to count against spatiotemporal parts of events being manifestations.

If a manifestation is not an effect, but a contribution to an effect that is simultaneous with that effect, another possibility is that the manifestation is a property of the effect. However, this suggestion faces the same difficulties as the previous one. It is not clear that there is any property of the barge going down the canal that could plausibly count as the manifestation of the southwestern horse's power. Furthermore, if acquiring or instantiating a property counts as an event, then this suggestion might not be an alternative to the view that manifestations are effects.

A third suggestion is that a manifestation is a force. On this view, when a power is triggered, it produces a force that contributes to an effect. For example, earth's gravitational power produces a manifestation that contributes to an apple moving in a certain way. The manifestation of the earth's gravitational power is not the apple falling, but rather the force of gravity that contributes to the falling. One problem with this suggestion is that forces seem very much like powers. It is not clear how to differentiate gravitational power from gravitational force. It seems like the right thing to say is not that gravitational power produces gravitational force, but that gravitational power just is gravitational force.

But suppose one wanted to distinguish the power from the force, with the force being the manifestation of the power.[3] Even if we make this distinction, the force seems no less power-like. It seems that we are distinguishing between two powers, with the second power being the manifestation of the first power. As we have already seen, that is acceptable in some cases. But the problem is that, if the manifestation of a power is itself a power that contributes to an effect, we have yet another entity in the process. Arguably, a latent power cannot contribute to an effect, so the power must be manifest. If the power must be manifest, then when the first power is triggered, it produces a second power which produces a manifestation which contributes to an effect.

Consider how complex the process of activating a power has become. Traditionally, the manifestation process was described in terms of a power, an activation condition, and a manifestation. On the current scenario, even in the simplest cases of a power manifesting, we have not only a power, a trigger, a manifestation, but also a second manifestation, and a then distinct effect. What's worse, whatever reason we have to call the first manifestation a force must be a reason to call the second manifestation a force, too. And if the second manifestation is also a force, and that force must also be manifest, then it looks like we have another sort regress in the making, reminiscent of Zenon's paradox: Infinitely many manifestations/forces must exist before the triggering of a power can result in an effect.

Another possible view is that the manifestation is a force, but not distinct from the original power. This would certain be more ontologically economical and avoid the sort of regress discussed previously. On this view, to say that the *manifestation* of gravitational power contributes to an effect is just to say that *gravitational power* contributes to that effect. In other words, the power is its own manifestation. The view that powers contribute to effects is plausible, and has been defended elsewhere (Hüttemann, forthcoming). However, if we want to call anything a "manifestation" in this scenario, it is not clear why we should say it is the power rather the effect.

Furthermore, holding that all dispositions are their own manifestations would force one to relinquish the idea that dispositions can be latent, that is, possessed without manifesting. If the proposal that a power is its own manifestation is plausible, it only works for dispositions that constantly exhibit their manifestations. Even in the case of constantly manifesting dispositions, one might want to distinguish between the power and its manifestation: being stable is one thing; remaining intact is another. More problematically, if there are any dispositions which only exhibit their manifestations when they are activated, the nature of their manifestations remains a mystery.

If manifestations aren't effects, it is not clear what they are. The preceding arguments suggest that manifestations are not spatiotemporal parts of effects, properties of effects, nor forces. Thinking of manifestations as "I know not what" is not a preferable alternative to the common view that manifestations are effects, despite some apparent difficulties of the common view.

If manifestations are effects, admittedly identifying dispositions via their manifestations is more complicated. One could retain Molnar's view that each power has a unique manifestation. However, if we say that actual, specific effects are the manifestations, we will have to suppose that each object has many more powers than we may have originally thought. For example, the earth would not have gravitational attraction *simpliciter*, but a different power for every possible object in every possible circumstance. The other possibility is to abandon Molnar's identity criterion and say that the same power can manifest in different ways. I favor the second approach, though I am not adverse to the idea that things have a multitude of specific powers as well.

NOTES

1. Example due to Broad (1933: 266–7).
2. This view should be distinguished from that of Hüttemann (forthcoming), who argues that dispositions, not their manifestations, are contributions to effects.
3. This appear to be Nancy Cartwright's view (2007, 2009).

6 Puzzling Powers
The Problem of Fit

Neil E. Williams

INTRODUCTION

There is a growing interest in powers (or dispositions as they are often called), and a growing number of realist theories of powers appearing in the philosophical literature. What such theories have in common is a treatment of the metaphysical aspects of causation in terms of an ontology of irreducibly causal properties—properties whose causal nature is their (primary) essence. Ontologies that admit irreducible causal powers are to be contrasted with ontologies that take all properties to be inherently non-causal, properties whose causal capacities come after the fact through the addition of some independent causal-cum-modal feature, such as a law of nature.

My concern here is with a problem that arises for those ontologies that countenance irreducible causal powers.[1] The problem I consider is one that concerns the way those powers work together to produce their manifestations. Powers must (typically) act in conjunction with one another to produce manifestations; a requirement of their working together is that they have the appropriate 'fit' for one another. If the salt is to manifest its solubility in the water, the water must likewise manifest its power to have the salt go into solution; there is no space for disagreement. However, as powers are intrinsic, and the manifestations they are capable of producing are set and incapable of change, their managing to line up is a matter of great mystery. Somehow the powers must be engineered such that they have the appropriate fit for one another. I call this 'the problem of fit.'

As far as I can tell, the problem of fit arises for any powers-based metaphysic that includes real but non-reduced powers, and endorses the following three theses: (i) powers are intrinsic properties, (ii) the set of manifestations a power is for is essential to it, and (iii) manifestations are produced reciprocally through mutual interaction. In presenting the problem I am not targeting any power-based metaphysic in particular. The three theses that give rise to the problem appear to a greater or lesser extent within most accounts in which powers play the primary causal role, but the problem is avoided where the three theses in question are not all part of the account.

Additionally, despite this looking like an attack on powers, it is not my intention to argue that a powers-based metaphysic is undesirable or untenable, or even that one of the three theses needs dropping. In fact, my conclusion is not intended to cast a negative light on power-based metaphysics at all. The problem I consider is not a problem without a solution; it is simply not a solution that resides where one would expect. It is not the case that an inconsistency can be derived from the conjunction of the three theses, but their combination raises an unpleasant difficulty. Each of the three theses is such that it is independently plausible, and the fact that they jointly give rise to a problem need not undermine that initial plausibility. All things considered, an ontology of causal powers is generally better off with these three theses than without them; dare I say, I am mildly skeptical about viability of any powers-based metaphysic that does not endorse all three of the theses.

The solution, I suggest, must come from *beyond* this characterization of the powers, through further specification of their nature and as part of the fuller metaphysic in which the powers are situated. No serious metaphysic stops at the postulation of certain ontological features alone. An account must given of how these features operate, how these features explain what it is they are employed to explain, and even what might explain their being as they are. It is within this wider account that I suggest we look for solutions to the problem of fit. To that end, I shall argue that powers are best thought of holistically, such that their individual natures are collectively determined.

The order of presentation is as follows: I begin with a brief presentation of the three theses. Though each of the three theses could easily be the topic of its own chapter, limited space precludes a full defense of each. This is followed by a discussion of the problem of fit. Having presented the problem, I return to a discussion of the three theses in order to show that the best response to the problem is not to be found by abandoning one or all of the three theses, and that a view is better off with them than without. Once I have argued that the problem of fit is not to be solved by rejecting one of the three theses, I propose a potential solution to the problem, which I call 'power holism'. Finally, following the presentation of power holism, I consider a number of suggestions as to what kind of larger metaphysic would permit this power holism.

THREE THESES ABOUT POWERS

The problem of fit arises from the conjunction of three plausible theses about the nature of powers. The theses are: the Intrinsicality Thesis, the Essentialist Thesis, and the Reciprocity Thesis. I shall present each in turn.

1. Intrinsicality Thesis: Powers are Intrinsic Properties

The first thesis is that powers are intrinsic properties. According to it, the instantiation of a power by a given object depends on that object alone, and not what properties may or may not be instantiated by any other contingent objects.[2] This means that an object's instantiating a power property is independent of: what other objects happen to be present in the world, the locations of other objects and the object in question, whether or not a power is ever manifested, and perhaps most important to the discussion at hand, what powers happen to be instantiated by other contingent objects (should there be any). An object will have numerous powers, most of which will never be manifested due to contingent facts about the locations and distribution of other powers, but this lack of manifestation has no bearing on what powers an object has. This is what it is for powers to be intrinsic.

2. Essentialist Thesis: The Set of Manifestations a Power is Capable of Producing is Essential to it

The second thesis concerns the identity of powers. According to it, the identity of a power is given by the set of manifestations it is for—this is its essence.[3]

We commonly think of a power as the ability of an object to bring about some *specific* manifestation when met with the appropriate stimulus—the sort of thing that roughly corresponds to a subjunctive conditional—but this is only half the story.[4] The other half of the story is the power property that underlies this ability, that property in virtue of which the associated subjunctive conditionals are true. These are really just the same thing viewed from two different perspectives. The former perspective focuses on the effects of the power, and individuates powers according to a single manifestation type. The latter perspective sees powers in terms of the underlying property that supports the powers in the first sense, and is individuated according to the range of potential manifestations it supports.[5] What we have is a hub-and-spoke model, where the power property is the hub, and the spokes are the many different types of manifestations the hub is capable of bringing about for each different type of stimulus.[6]

The set of spokes supported by the hub gives the essence of the power. This means that in any world we find a power of type P (type may be a matter of identity or exact similarity depending on whether the properties are tropes or universals) it will provide its possessor with the same set of abilities; the power is *for* precisely that set potential manifestations.[7] As the identity of the property is determined according to the abilities it supports, it follows from the essentialist thesis that the manifestations of a power will be necessary. If they were contingent, then the set of manifestations a power is capable of producing would vary from world to world—which is incompatible with the essentialist thesis. This means that *anywhere* we find a power property of the type P, it has the abilities supported by P, even if P supports abilities that will not be manifested due to the lack of appropriate stimulus.

3. Reciprocity Thesis: Manifestations are Often the Mutual Product of Powers in Distinct Objects or Parts of Objects Working Together[8]

The third thesis describes what it takes for a power to be exercised. As we have noted, specific abilities are often thought of roughly in terms of subjunctive conditionals, such that to have this or that ability is to be such as to produce manifestation M when met with stimulus S. Though frequently overlooked, for the great majority of cases we are interested in the stimulus S that is required for M is the presence and absence of other powers.[9]

> "I have been talking as if a disposition exists unmanifested until a set of background conditions is met, resulting in manifestation. This picture is misleading, however, because so-called background conditions are every bit as operative as the identified dispositional entity. A more accurate view is one of a huge group of disposition entities or properties which, when they come together, *mutually manifest* the property in question; talk of background conditions ceases" (Martin 2008: 50).

The basic idea behind the reciprocity thesis is that manifestations are a mutual affair. Producing manifestations requires the *co-operation* of two or more powers, where these powers complement one another. Consider the smashing of a martini glass by a rock. It takes more than just a rock— you need a martini glass too. This is not just to say that the breaking of the glass is a manifestation that requires both objects to be present (though that should not be ignored), both objects must have the appropriate powers. If the two objects are not appropriately powered, or lack the powers for that kind of manifestation, then some other manifestation would occur.

It perhaps goes without saying that if either the rock or the glass has different powers, then a different manifestation will result. But this is no threat to reciprocity, it merely recognizes that objects can vary in the mutual manifestations they are capable of producing. Whatever manifestation the rock and glass give rise to is a product of the powers of the rock *and* the glass, powers that work together to produce what they do—it is not simply up to one object or the other. This is the case if their mutual manifestation is the shattering of the glass, the rock's bouncing off, or even the shattering of the rock.

Let us be clear exactly what is being claimed here. I am *not* saying that the manifestation two (or more) objects produce cannot be surprising or unexpected: that is simply an epistemic matter and easily explained. What I am saying is that when manifestations are produced that involve two or more objects, the powers of the objects involved must cohere. Each must manifest powers that are for an identical manifestation. Consider what the alternative would mean: the glass manifests its power to shatter, and the rock manifests, what, some power for which the manifestation is *not* the glass's shattering? No sense can be made of this. The only power the rock can manifest is that which matches that of the glass. This is not a matter of you turning left and me right, this is *me* turning *both* left *and* right simultaneously. It cannot be permitted—powers will always be reciprocally matched.

The mutuality of causal action—whether it results from powers or not—is not an unfamiliar notion. Recall Mill's lesson that when looking at causation we need to consider the total cause (Mill 1967: Bk 3 ch. 5).[10] When considering causation we tend to focus on a single salient feature of the cause, treating it as *the* cause, thereby downgrading the importance of the other factors involved.[11] And yet without those other factors 'the' cause could not have produced the effect. We say that it is the rock that broke the glass. The rock is the *subject*, it is the one we are interested in; the glass is merely the object of the rock's action. But when powers are the source of causal action, the rock does not act *upon* the glass, the two act *together*. It follows that it was a mistake to single out a single feature and treat it as *the* cause in the first place. All aspects of the cause are involved. This is the essence of mutuality.

Perhaps the worst offenders of singling out causes are those who speak in terms of 'active' and 'passive' powers, where the 'active' powers are the causal 'doers', and the 'passive' powers idly acquiesce. Similar connotations follow from distinctions like 'agent' versus 'patient', and 'triggering conditions' versus 'standing conditions'. In as much as these distinctions are intended to be epistemic, they are reasonably innocuous. It is as metaphysical distinctions they become dangerous. They suggest that some feature of the cause has causal dominance over the other. This bias is most obvious in the case of agent/patient; it conjures up images of human agents acting freely as prime movers and forcing the surrounding world to comply. But this implication of causal inequality cannot be permitted. The water contributes as much to the salt's going into solution as the salt—there is no sense in which any power involved is any less than any other.

What if the so called 'patient' is categorical—would this not require that the 'agent' power alone is the lone causal actor? Contrary to what is suggested, because the purportedly passive categorical property contributes to the manifestation, it cannot be categorical after all. In order to influence the 'agent', it too must be powerful—there is no halfway house for powers. If they contribute nothing, then they cease to be causally relevant and fall out of the equation. A property either contributes causally, which means that the property has the power for whatever manifestation is produced, or it plays no causal role whatsoever.[12] Perhaps the only good that comes from thinking of powers as active and passive is that it recognizes the need for powers on the part of all objects involved. We might think of this as an implicit endorsement of the claim that all parties involved have reciprocal powers. This is the only sense in which the active/passive distinction is even close to getting it right; it otherwise skews the picture of the causally egalitarian powers.

Nor can it be the case that one or the other object has no relevant powers at all. If the glass has no powers at all (*vis-à-vis* the incoming rock), the result is not a passive smashing or a passive rebounding, it is an impossibility. If causal effects are just the manifestations of powers, then how can powerless glasses participate in manifestations? We need powers all around; reciprocity abounds.

THE PROBLEM OF FIT

Having described the three theses that set up the problem of fit, I turn now to the problem itself. Stated briefly, the problem is that powers have to work together when they produce manifestations (reciprocity), but as they are not relations (intrinsicality), and they cannot change with the circumstances (essentialism), the fact that they are causally harmonious is without explanation. Powers 'fit' together for the production of mutual manifestations. To fail to have the correct fit is to describe an impossible situation: the operations of the powers cannot permit anything less than perfect congruence. But the fact that powers have the appropriate fit for one another is not something that is yet accounted for. The very possibility of reciprocal power based causation demands nothing short of perfect harmony on the part of the interacting powers, but their intrinsicality and necessity are insufficient for the manufacture of that harmony. That is the problem of fit.

Let us consider the problem more closely. Central to the intrinsicality thesis is a kind of independence. As per our working definition of 'intrinsic', for a property to be intrinsic is for its instantiation to be independent of the presence or absence of other objects. This sets up part of the problem, as it makes clear that the having of powers—as intrinsic properties—in no way depends on any other contingent objects. The having of powers is also independent of whether or not those powers should happen to be manifested. Each power is the locus of many potential manifestations, but its instantiation in no way depends on those manifestations ever being realized.

However, though the having of some specific power is independent of its being manifested, it is nevertheless individuated in terms of the set of potential manifestation types it supports. Fragility is the ability to shatter, flammability the ability to combust, elasticity the ability to stretch without damage. And this connection between the power and what manifestations it is for is necessary. This is the essentialist thesis. Its importance in developing our problem is that what the intrinsic powers are *for* (that is, the manifestations they are capable of producing) is some specific set of determinate manifestations. Their potential effects are written into them; it is their nature to produce certain prescribed manifestations (when met with the appropriate circumstances).

This would not be problematic were it not the case that powers produce manifestations (when they do) in causal partnerships. The final feature of the problem then comes from the reciprocal nature of power-based causation. In all instances of transeunt causation, causation is a matter of the power properties of distinct objects working together to create manifestations: it is a mutual affair. And even when not interacting, powers must line up with one another in order that transeunt causation be possible at all. They must be built for mutual and harmonious interaction, even if interaction should never occur.

Powers are intrinsic properties, and what they are for is necessary and determined, but the production of manifestations is co-operative. This is where the problem arises. If causation was always non-interactive—or conversely if powers were relational or indeterminate, there would be no problem of fit. It is precisely because the having of the properties and what they are 'for' is independent of their causal interactions that the question of fit arises. The problem is explaining the fit. A proper fit is the only option, yet nothing about the intrinsicality or necessity of the powers prepares the properties to fit together.

An analogy might prove useful. Consider a jigsaw puzzle. The primary task when working on a jigsaw puzzle is to position the pieces so that they form a united whole—typically some image or other. The matter of jigsaw puzzle completion is literally one of fit. The pieces need to be fitted together. Except for a few anomalous jigsaw puzzles, each piece can only be fitted into the puzzle in one way. The completed puzzle is the perfect example of fit—the image of the completed puzzle only emerges if the pieces admit of what we might call a 'harmony of shape', and that is exploited in their being joined. The harmony that jigsaw puzzle pieces enjoy mirrors that of the reciprocal powers. Like the puzzle pieces, they too must admit of the appropriate fit for one another in order to produce manifestations. They must stand in the right kind of relation to one another—that of being *for* the same manifestation.

Now, let us recall how it is that jigsaw puzzles are made (that is 'made' in the sense of created by toy companies, not put together). That is to say let us reflect on what allows for, or even provides for, this fit in the case of jigsaw puzzle pieces. That is simple enough: they are created by cutting up some picture. You start with a complete and whole image which is then cut into pieces, and it is no surprise that the pieces consequently admit of the right kind of fit for one another. But imagine what would happen if jigsaw puzzles were not made that way. Imagine, for instance, what would happen if jigsaw puzzle manufacturers divided the task of creating jigsaw puzzles amongst a variety of different laborers, without providing each with any indication of what the final image was to be, and without allowing for any collaboration. What are the odds that such a jigsaw puzzle could ever be put together? I have seen some mighty hard jigsaw puzzles in my day, but this one takes the cake! Even if a puzzle was as simple as those intended for the youngest of children, consisting of only four or five large pieces, the odds that our puzzle makers could get their pieces to coincide are astronomically low. You simply cannot build a jigsaw puzzle that way. And yet that is exactly the case with our powers: they are intrinsic, so do not enjoy the ease of collaborating that relations might afford, they have their effects necessarily, so what they are 'for' cannot vary or be assigned on the occasion of interaction, and yet the theory has it that they must come together harmoniously for the production of mutual manifestations. That any manifestation should occur is like the completion of a most improbable jigsaw puzzle—but anything less than completion is unthinkable. Worse yet, any world where the puzzle does not come together is an impossible world.

It is in this last regard that the analogy between fit for puzzles and fit for powers breaks down. In the case of puzzles one can imagine getting lucky and having the pieces fit, but any world without the fit for powers is an impossible world, and it cannot be luck that divides the possible from the impossible. Might it be the case that fit is a local phenomenon, such that despite a lack of total fit, on those occasions that token powers line up a manifestation results? (By analogy, the puzzle cannot be completed, but this and that piece fit together.) The short answer is that a lack of fit for powers is impossible in the token case, so local fit fares no better. Imagine a heavy rock with the power to smash a particular martini glass. The powers of the rock (r) are such that when it impacts on the martini glass (m) with a certain high velocity (v) it will result in a state of affairs that is or includes m's being smashed. However, m's powers are such that if struck by r at v, m emits a loud 'ping' but does not break. Now imagine that we strike m with r at v. What happens? Does m shatter—as was r's power, does m remain in tact, and emit a loud ping sound—as was m's power, or does nothing occur, because the two powers do not fit? The answer: none of the above.

The suspicion that a lack of fit could simply mean no manifestation is produced comes from the mistaken thought that when things do not change there is no causation involved. One point of defending a metaphysic of irreducible powers is to have the *powers* serve as the causal basis. As almost all token events are causally connected to some other event(s) that precede and follow them, the need for fit is paramount. There are many scenarios (most even) that produce rather boring 'static' manifestations that do little more than maintain the status quo, but even then it is still the case that all the concrete particulars involved have powers with the right fit for one another.[13] Nor does the unnoticed work of the powers end with the static abilities. C. B. Martin notes that powers are often hard at work producing manifestations that are nothing more than the prevention of other manifestations by other powers.[14] This is not to mention that the frequency of 'successful' manifestations is far too common to be a purely random occurrence. Causation is ubiquitous; holding out for luck in any shape or form simply will not do. We cannot have a world in which such a lack of fit occurs. The need for fit cannot be marginalized.

That is the problem of fit. As I have claimed, the problem demands some sort of explanation on the part of the theory. Unlike many problems raised in the philosophical literature, I do not pose this problem as if it is incapable of solution. I think it can be solved, and will consider a number of proposals below. The point to keep in mind, however, is not whether or not the problem can be solved, but how elegant the solution happens to be. If you can only solve a problem by taking on board some highly dubious claims or mechanisms, then the overall attractiveness of an ontology of causal powers suffers. And when it comes to systematic metaphysics, the attractiveness of the theory counts for a lot. Ontological proposals are typically judged according to a kind of cost/benefit analysis that weighs their problem solving ability and intuitiveness against their theoretical simplicity and economy (of ontological categories). The greater the number of implausible claims an ontology requires, the weaker the theory becomes (all else being equal). However, before turning to solutions, we must first examine why the problem of fit cannot simply be avoided by dropping one or all of the theses that give rise to it.

REJECT ONE OF THE THREE THESES?

Met with a problem that arises from the conjunction of three theses, a natural first response is to question the theses themselves. That is what I shall do next. However, I hope to show that we should look elsewhere for a solution, as an account of irreducible causal powers is better off with the three theses than without.

1. Deny Intrinsicality?

The intrinsicality thesis is endorsed by virtually every proponent of a powers-based metaphysic. In fact, it is all but universally agreed that the right account or analysis of 'power' and its synonyms (whether ultimately realist or reductive) must treat them as intrinsic.[15] That makes rejecting the intrinsicality thesis a pragmatic non-starter. The only (public) dissenter of the intrinsicness thesis is Jennifer McKitrick, but even she admits that many powers will be intrinsic, she merely rejects the claim that they are all that way (McKitrick 2003).[16] Though I am largely unmoved by her arguments (McKitrick has a very catholic approach to properties that makes room for properties that others—myself included—see no need for), very little is lost should it turn out that some powers are extrinsic. At worst, should it turn out that only *some* powers are intrinsic, the problem of fit would still make for a considerable problem. Hence, if we are to avoid the problem of fit, nothing short of wholesale dismissal of intrinsicness will suffice, and that is not something the proponent of powers is willing to endorse.[17]

2. Deny Essentialism?

With little chance of the intrinsicality thesis being rejected, what ground might be gained by rejecting the essentialist thesis? For starters, nothing can be gained by *only* denying that the set of manifestations a power is for are essential to it. All one would get is a treatment of powers according to which the same power was for different sets of manifestations in different worlds, but within each world it would still be for a specific set of manifestations, and so the problem of fit would remain.[18] What must be added is that even within a world, powers are not directed at some *specific* set of manifestations, but instead embody a kind of 'raw' and directionless causal center—with its various abilities still *to be determined*. Call these contingently specified powers 'TBD powers'. Only if powers are TBD powers could they avoid worries about fit, as fit would, presumably, arise at times of manifestation, determined somehow in accordance with the other partnering powers. However, despite initial appearances, we cannot usefully think of the power properties as being TBD powers while holding the rest of the power metaphysic constant.

The problem with the idea of a TBD power is the question of what eventually determines what the power is for. It cannot be the case that the manifestation is determined in conjunction with the various power partners, as there would still have to be something in the powers that determines their joint nature. What could that be if not something in the property already? In other words, if the manifestation is determined in conjunction with the various partners, we still have to postulate an intrinsic structure within the powers that makes them such that they create said manifestation with said partners. In order that the TBD powers result in determinate manifestations, there must be some causal *mechanism* by which the TBD powers go from to-be-determined to determined—this is itself a power.[19] If this is just the process of some other (perhaps more basic) power operating within the power, then we have the same problem all over again and we are back to square one. On the other hand, if this role is played by anything but a power, then some other causal-cum-modal feature is doing the work, and despite appearing to be a power-based metaphysic, we have some other sort of metaphysic in place. And that is the real problem here: the contingency we gain by rejecting the essentialist thesis does not remove the need to determine what the power is for, it just moves it elsewhere. And there is nowhere it can be moved that can help us with the problem of fit.

3. Deny Reciprocity?

Central to the problem of fit is the reciprocal nature of the manifestations. At first blush it seems that if we remove this feature—or at least amend it somewhat—we can avoid the problem. However, this proposal fares no better than the previous two.

We have already seen that any non-egalitarian system of powers quickly breaks down into an egalitarian one, so we cannot hope to escape reciprocity by claiming that only one of the interacting objects carries the power, such that it *imposes* the manifestation of that power on the other objects involved. Regardless of what we might think about the 'passenger' objects, if they play any role in the production of the manifestation in question, they must have the power to do so. That leaves with just one option: the denial of interactive (transeunt) causation.

The rejection of *interactive* causation would not mean the end of causation altogether, as we could still have immanent causation, but it would mean that none of the standard examples of causation (rocks shattering martini glasses; billiard balls colliding; wrenches turning nuts) would be causal *in the way we took them to be.* What we would end up with is a power-based version of Leibniz's metaphysic—the apparent causal interactions being nothing more than an intricate series of changes and shifts in position carried out in accordance with each individual object's internal plan. And that is where the biggest problem with this solution comes in: rejecting interactive causation avoids the problem of fit, but introduces in its place a parallel problem regarding the harmonious states of the non-interacting objects. This is a kind of internally-driven harmony, but is no less problematic than the original problem. Where the problem of fit asks how it is that the intrinsic powers line up in the right way so as to produce mutual manifestations, its non-interactive counterpart problem asks how it is that the powers of the objects that direct their individual paths can be such as to line up in the right way so as to *appear* to produce mutual manifestations; we are no better off.

As it happens, I think rejecting interactive causation is a solution worse than the problem: it defies common sense and undermines the very phenomena it was developed to explain. But even for those who do not agree, that the problem of fit resurfaces in another form is reason enough to look elsewhere.

POWER HOLISM

With the problem of fit before us, I shall now consider one way that the problem might be resolved. I do not suggest that this is the only solution—or even that it is the best—but it is one that I think a number of proponents of a powers-based metaphysic will find reasonably attractive, and is worthy of exploration.[20] The solution comes into two parts: the first part concerns the nature of powers, offering one way they could be that would provide for fit; the second part is somewhat more speculative, and considers three ways the world could be that would allow for the powers to be the way the first part of the solution suggests. The core of the first part is that powers are properties whose natures are determined *holistically*—powers are structured in terms of each other. The second part considers ways in which this holism can arise. Let us start with the first part.

As per the working definition for intrinsicality, a property is intrinsic just in case its being *instantiated* is a matter of the way that object is itself, independent of the presence or absence of any other wholly contingent object. Intrinsicality concerns the *having* of the property, not what the property itself is like. Hence, the intrinsicality thesis contributes to the problem of fit by placing one sort of restriction on the powers (concerning their instantiation), but does not otherwise limit us in terms of the nature of powers. Including the other theses we know that powers must work with one another, and that their causal profile is essential to them. What all three leave ample room for is an account of how the powers are engineered.

In order to provide the fit of powers, we must set up the powers so that they always match. How can this be done? One way is to cram all the information about every other property into the power, thereby 'building' powers according to a plan—a plan that includes what kind of manifestation would result from each and every possible set of reciprocal partners. In keeping with our jigsaw analogy, this is nothing more than having our individual laborers building their particular puzzle piece from a blueprint. With a blueprint to work from, it is hardly surprising that the puzzle pieces should fit together, even if they are constructed separately. If each laborer knows the shape of the other puzzle pieces and the shape her own puzzle piece should have, then getting them to line up afterwards presents no difficulty at all.

Returning to the power properties, the result of packing in all this information is that each property contains within it a blueprint for the entire universe. Fit then, is to be explained by the internal blueprint each carries. Each power property is intrinsic, but contains within it organized plans for every possible circumstance in which it might find itself. These plans constitute instructions for what manifestation (if any) is to be produced in each circumstance. However, in order to generate the 'blueprint' that the power follows, it would have to be the case that the other powers on the blueprint were *already* set, but as their nature must be determined in the same fashion, we face the same problem again—we have nowhere to start (and a vicious regress looms large). We can avoid this problem if the determination of powers is not engineered piecemeal, and instead they are all set up *at once*. What we need is power holism.

In order to get clear what I mean by 'power holism', we will first need to get clear about what 'holism' means. As the term has seen a great many a philosophical applications (perhaps far too many), I will start by stating what I do *not* mean by 'holism'. 'Holism' is often understood in terms of the somewhat clumsy and trivial aphorism that the whole is more than the sum of its parts. This can be refined in any number of ways, but in each we find the familiar thought that either features of the whole are emergent, do not reduce to, or cannot be explained by, features of the constituent parts, or instead that features (or even the existence of) the parts would not obtain in the absence of the other parts that make up the whole. For instance, in the philosophy of physics, 'holism' is sometimes taken to be the thesis that the properties of position or spin can only (properly) be attributed to a system and not to those particles that make it up (Healey 1991); and in moral theory 'holism' can mean the anti-particularist claim that reasons are altered by their context (Dancy 2000). What these interpretations have in common—and therefore what makes them of no use in the present case—is that they concern the sort of features that can be instantiated by the individuals that make up a system or whole. But our interest is in the nature of certain properties themselves, not the individuals that have them. Similarly useless are versions of holism that understand it as an explanatory or purely epistemic notion; what we require is an ontological conception, but not one that takes the existence of constituents to depend on that of others, or where the holism results in relational properties (because powers are intrinsic). What we need is a notion of holism according to which constituents of the whole determine their natures collaboratively, through a sort of collective engineering.

Of the range of extant holisms, what is sometimes called 'semantic holism' comes closest to the meaning that I have in mind. Here is one version of semantic holism: "the specific, determinate meaning of each belief depends on the specific, determinate meaning of all other beliefs with which it is arranged in a system of beliefs: if the meaning of one constituent of a system of belief changes, the meaning of all the other constituents changes as well" (Esfeld 1998: 374). This has all the features I want to replicate: first, there is no suggestion that this or that belief depends for its existence on any of the other beliefs in the system; second, the determinate meaning of a belief depends on *all* other beliefs in the system; third, changes to any belief result in changes to all beliefs; and fourth, there is no suggestion that beliefs are relational in virtue of gaining their determinate meanings this way. *Mutatis mutandis*, this is the model of holism to be applied to the powers in power holism. No power depends for its existence on any other power, and powers are not relations, but all powers within a system contribute to the nature of all other powers, such that each is set up for the appropriate fit with one another. Powers are capable of fit for one another because they are determined collectively.

> *Power Holism:* The specific, determinate nature of each power (that is, the set of manifestations a power is for and the precise partners required for those manifestations) depends on the specific, determinate nature of other powers with which it is arranged in a system of powers.

Given the way I have constructed the problem of fit, it makes sense that the powers that make up a system of powers—and therefore that collectively determine each other's natures—are the powers that combine to produce manifestations (if or when they do). That is how I envision power holism, and as far as resolving the problem of fit is concerned, this is enough. Nonetheless, depending on how one thinks of manifestations, we might have additional lines of determination within a system of powers. It is an open question what ontological category manifestations belong to. As the (potential or actual) effects of reciprocal powers there is some reason to think of manifestations as events, and though I am prone to treat them as states of affairs, a common suggestion is that manifestations are properties, and that these properties are powers.[21] If one adopts this last suggestion, there is no need to amend the thesis of power holism, but one finds additional connections between the powers. A power's nature would then be determined *via* connections to its power partners *as well as* to the powers that are its potential manifestations.

A system of powers is a set of powers such that every power in the set has at least one other power as a reciprocal partner. On one model of powers, *every* power has *every other* power as a reciprocal partner.[22] In that case, there is no power that falls outside the system, and the system is highly inter-related. But we could also have a model of powers that is far less inter-related. For instance, Alexander Bird prefers a picture of powers according to which each power has just one ability associated with it (think of one spoke for every hub), and many powers are not connected with each other in any way at all. Is this conception of powers a threat to power holism?

The short answer is no—but it does give rise to two slightly different forms of power holism. On the first conception of powers, every power is connected to every other; by analogy we might think of all the powers in that large system as forming a ring.[23] Call this 'strong' power holism. On the second conception of powers, groups of powers have natures that are inter-related, but we have multiple systems, and no system shares any power with any other system. We have multiple rings, rather like the Olympic rings (only no ring contacts any other). Call this 'weak' power holism. As ought to be clear, weak power holism is as much a form of holism as strong power holism, only the latter is more inclusive. Within each of the smaller rings of weak power holism we still find a series of powers that has its nature determined by its power partners, only the rings of one color have no contact or connection with the rings of any other color.[24] This makes for a strange view of reality, as the different color rings would be like ghosts to one another—causal systems that pass through each other without any possible contact or awareness—but strange is not impossible. And just as with the strong version, the weak version provides a response to the problem of fit. Of course, if weak power holism is the response, then what needed to fit was not every power with every other, but smaller sets of powers, but the difference is only one of degree.[25] Regardless of the number of systems involved, the problem of fit arises, and a version of power holism comes to the rescue.

As a final word on power holism, the suggestion of holism for powers is not entirely new to the literature. In addition to the occasional vague murmurings in the direction of holism made by other authors, Stephen Mumford has an account of powers that is explicitly holistic, and, if I am interpreting him correctly, it bears most of the features of power holism as I have described it.[26] Mumford proposes that we understand properties as "clusters" of abilities that both exhaust the nature of properties and "fix the identity of the property;" consequently "a property's causal roles are necessary to it" (Mumford 2004: 171).[27] And though these properties are intrinsic, he claims that "[t]he world is a single whole, composed of properties whose essence and identity are determined by their place in that whole" (Mumford 2004: 184). He even adds that a "world comes with a whole, connected system of properties," where the identity of each property "is fixed by relations to other properties," such that "change one property and we change all the properties" (Mumford 2004: 182, 171, 215n3). This looks like power holism to me.

BEYOND POWER HOLISM

As I noted before, power holism is only half the response to the problem of fit. The other half involves the greater metaphysic in which the holism is situated. Power holism gives powers the right sort of fit for one another, but it does nothing to help explain how this holism is afforded. We now need to ask what kind of world *allows for* the fit that power holism bestows?

Let me start by noting that there is a sense—a very natural sense—in which power holism is an 'after-the-fact' metaphysic. What I mean is that in order to have a system of powers that can determine the natures of the individual powers, you first need to have the powers 'available'. There needs to be, metaphorically speaking, opportunity for the powers to 'communicate' with one another in order to sort them out. Recall the near impossible task of manufacturing jigsaw puzzles by constructing the pieces in isolation. That task becomes quite easy if we permit collaboration between the individual piece-makers. There are plenty of ways of doing this—you could put them together in a room, or draw up plans for the completed puzzle and pass them around—but whatever the strategy it will require the right sort of temporal or spatial proximity. They cannot collaborate if every piece-maker cannot communicate (directly or indirectly) with the makers of the adjacent pieces. But what counts as collaboration when it comes to powers; how do *they* convene? I will consider three answers that might be given, all which relate to the sort of world we might have that could contain holistic powers.

Brute Force

For some, taking the investigation any further is to go well beyond what we need or properly understand. Looking beyond power holism is undoubtedly to engage in big-picture, and highly speculative, metaphysics. Why not just recognize that there are necessary relations that hold between powers that determine their natures, and be done with it? That is, why not just accept power holism as a brute metaphysical fact?

As with much metaphysical reasoning, the suggestion of bruteness is always at hand and ever ready to step in as a would-be solution to prevent further investigation. There is nothing wrong—in the sense of inconsistency or error—about invoking a 'those are just the facts' answer as to how power holism might arise. Nor does it fail to be a genuine option in the present scenario. But as with all claims of bruteness, it fails to provide the philosophical quiet which drives so much of our investigation. If we were satisfied by bruteness, scientists would be largely unemployable and we would have long since abandoned our metaphysical quests.

That is not to deny that bruteness can—and must—be present in any substantial metaphysic. There must be an end point to all investigation; whatever entities reside at the fundamental level are incapable of full explication, as this would require another level, more basic than that it explains. Nonetheless, it is one thing to recognize the place of bruteness, and yet another to concede that the entities, features or facts at hand constitute the end point. Bruteness has its place, but it would be a mistake to decide that we have reached the end until we have seen the alternatives. With that in mind, I suggest we continue the search, and only resort to bruteness if the alternatives are unsavory. Even then it will be unable to provide the security and warmth we are after, but it will have to do.

Platonism

With the right picture of properties one can provide opportunity for collaboration. The Platonist has such a picture. According to the Platonist, all properties are necessary existents that enjoy a supernatural permanence outside of whatever instantiations may or may not obtain. Unlike their Aristotelian counterparts, they are not tied to the spatiotemporal realm, and do not stand or fall according to their place in it. Regardless of how the details of Platonism get fleshed out, all powers are always available to collaborate in such a way as to holistically determine the nature of each. It may be an open question whether the best metaphor in this case is that of all the powers being together in the same room (Platonic heaven?), or that of a Platonic blueprint each power follows when instantiated, but either neatly affords the holism we are after. Hence there is one potential way to lay the foundation for power holism: be a Platonist about properties.[28]

Naturalism and Monism

What if Platonism is not to your liking, and brute facts leave a nasty taste in your mouth? One account of properties (and existence generally) goes by the name 'naturalism'. According to this view, all things that exist do so within space and time; there are no 'supernatural' entities that exist outside the spatiotemporal realm.[29] Nothing about this picture demands that properties are not collaborative, but under naturalism there is a tendency to think of properties as existing when and where they do, freely popping into existence and out of existence as a matter of mere happenstance, (somewhat) randomly distributed about the universe. Can naturalism permit the collaboration that power holism requires?

Though the initial response looks like it ought to be 'no' (there can be no supernatural blueprint, and the apparent contingency of instantiation does not look amenable to a convention), naturalism is not without its means. First of all, one could simply append a brute fact power holism to one's naturalism. That would do the job. But even without the brute response, there is another way. All one needs is to have the powers arranged in the right way, and this can be achieved if one adopts a (substantial) form of *monism*.

Just like 'holism', 'monism' has a range of meanings, but all point in roughly the same direction: singularity. Jonathan Schaffer has identified two historically central versions of monism—existence monism and priority monism—and either serves our purposes (Schaffer forthcoming). According to existence monism, the universe has exactly one (enormous) object in it: the one whole. It has no (proper) parts; all properties are properties of the one object, the 'blobject'.[30] Existence monism is monism of the sort frequently attributed to Spinoza and Hegel.[31] According to priority monism, exactly one object is ultimately prior: it has discernible parts (and those parts have properties), but they are all dependent on the whole which is their foundation. The world is not a collection of discrete particulars from which we can derive the 'whole world', the world is the primary particular, and we get the common particulars derivatively. On both views it is purportedly the case that monism is compatible with our perceptual experience, commonsense belief, and our best science.[32] For present purposes, we have no need to assess whether that claim is true—my only interest is in positing a potential way a naturalist might find room for power holism.

So what can monism do for holism? The though that all of existence is one big object, or that the whole that is everything is prior to any parts it might have, appear to provide a sufficient framework from which power holism could arise—even if naturalism is true. The properties had by the 'one' are all instantiated within the spatiotemporal realm, so naturalism is satisfied, but it also seems that the stage is set for the collaboration of the powers in virtue of their all being properties of the same particular. There is no need for a supernatural blueprint, if, so to speak, monism allows us to get all the properties in the same room.

As long as we can account for the apparent variety, nothing about monism is that odd or unusual. It just means that as a matter of fact everything is part of the same large concrete particular. Spinoza was happy enough with this picture of the world, and excepting the special place of mind, Descartes was too. I cannot see what has changed in the last three hundred and some years to make us think that we know anything better about the nature of reality at such an abstract level that would have us contradict them, so why not follow their lead? I think once one gets past the initial sense of implausibility regarding monism, it looks to have as much in its favor as any pluralistic alternative.

Nonetheless, some might find the thought of monism less attractive than the brute or Platonic alternatives. To them I offer a highly speculative suggestion. If we can make sense of something like existence monism *at a specific time*, nothing seems to rule out that universe later being pluralistic, if the parts of the one were to later become objects in their own right (priority monism already affords this in a derivative way, this would be non-derivative). This is a form of pluralism that grows out of monism. Imagine a great pane of glass as representing our monistic starting point. Now that great pane is shattered, and our single entity is divided into thousands of entities—some of which are similar to one another, but many of which are unique. Following the shattering, what were powers had by *parts* of the pane (for interaction with other parts of the pane) are now intrinsic powers of the many distinct shards. And the fit they have for one another is explained by the holism afforded by their common ancestry. This 'ancestral' monism boasts the additional plausibility of echoing the jigsaw puzzle example described before. Real jigsaw puzzles—the ones that are manufactured and admit of perfect fit—are cut from a single picture. The many pieces are the pluralistic ancestors of a single object, and they owe their perfect fit to their common starting place: they fit together because they were once *one*. Perhaps the universe is like this too.

CONCLUSION

I have proposed that one way to deal with the problem of fit is to have the nature of powers determined collectively. Whether this power holism comes about as a brute fact of nature, or relies on Platonism or monism, we have a picture of the world that is very close-knit. This result stands at the opposite pole to the loose and particularist picture of reality as given in Humean supervenience, and depending on one's account of properties, the unity inherent in a power-based metaphysic might extend to the oneness of the world.[33] The task now is to determine how costly this unity proves to be, if it is in fact costly at all.

ACKNOWLEDGEMENTS

My thanks to Michael McGlone and Jonathan Schaffer for comments on previous drafts of this chapter, and to audiences in Bristol (UK) and Tampere (Finland) where earlier versions were presented.

NOTES

1. I shall not be concerned with distinguishing between views that take all properties to be powers and those that take some or most properties to be powers, as long as there is no introduction of some other causal-cum-modal feature that would duplicate or replace the work of the powers.
2. It is a matter of much debate how best to define 'intrinsic', and it might well be the case that no entirely satisfying definition is to be found, but that is a discussion best had elsewhere. For present purposes I opt for the definition found in Lewis and Langton (1998), which states that for a property to be intrinsic its instantiation should be independent of both loneliness and accompaniment, but nothing I claim hangs on this definition in particular.
3. The manifestations here are best thought of as manifestation-types, as certain powers can be manifested more than once (for example, elasticity).
4. This is not to suggest that powers are analyzable in terms of subjunctive conditionals, just that there is some connection between them, and we tend to pick them out in that way. See Martin (1994) and Bird (1998) for more on the failure of the conditional analysis of powers.
5. From this point on I will use the term 'power' to refer to power properties, and 'ability' to refer to manifestation-specific ways powers can be exercised. A number of the authors quoted in this chapter use 'disposition' where I would use 'power' or 'ability'; unless the use is ambiguous, I have left the quotations as they appear.
6. To be clear, when I say that the power 'supports' many abilities, I do not mean to suggest that the two are distinct or that the supporting property is not powerful. A power is capable of bringing about numerous manifestations—it is by focusing on a single manifestation type within that set that we get the single manifestation conception (an ability). Hence, for a power property that is capable of producing (among other things) shatterings, we might speak of the fragility that the power supports, but this is really just to consider one aspect of the power. Alexander Bird (2007b: 21–4) seems to have the opposite intuition. He claims that we have no need for complex powers where conjunctions of simpler powers could do the same job. If he is right, hubs typically have only one spoke. However, I suspect that Bird is clinging too closely to a treatment of powers in terms of subjunctive conditionals. Although he played an important part in showing the failure of the conditional analysis of powers (Bird 1998), he seems to be suffering from a conditional analysis hangover, and is thinking of powers less as naturally occurring properties (hubs) and more as conveniently packaged and neatly individuated law-like subjunctive conditionals (spokes). Despite our differing intuitions, reducing the number of spokes per hub does not avoid the problem of fit, so we can ignore it for now. However, it will make a slight difference to the solution (as we shall see in the section 'Power Holism') giving us two slightly different forms of power holism.
7. Defining essentialism this way—in terms of the identity of the power in possible worlds—is far from ideal. On at least one view of properties (see the section 'Naturalism and Monism' in this chapter), a difference in what properties are instantiated at a world means that all properties in that world will differ. It follows on such a view that no property of type P exists in more than one world.
8. The terminology here, that of 'reciprocity' and 'mutuality' as applied to the causal action of powers, is due to C.B. Martin—I follow him in my understanding and application of these concepts. He writes that reciprocity holds

"between properties of different things or parts of things for the manifestation that is their common product—for example, the soluble salt and solvent water for the solution of the salt in the water," and later that the "important point remains that the manifestation of a given dispositional state will require the cooperation of some other dispositional states amongst its reciprocating partners" (1993: 82). Following Martin's lead, Heil says of a salt crystal's manifesting its power to dissolve in water that "this manifestation is a manifestation of both the salt crystal's disposition to dissolve in water and the water's complementary disposition to dissolve salt" (2003: 198).

9. Many instances where powers produce manifestations are reciprocal, but a small set are not. This difference corresponds to the difference between *transeunt causation*—causation *between* objects, and *immanent causation*—causation *within* objects (Lotze 1884, Johnson 1924, Zimmerman 1997). Putative cases of immanent causation include such occurrences as object persistence, locomotion, and particle decay. For the purposes of the present discussion, keep in mind that the reciprocity thesis is intended for cases when objects interact causally with other objects.

10. The lesson is repeated by Mackie (1965).

11. For instance, Lewis states that "we allow a cause to be only one indispensable part, not the whole, of the total situation that is followed by the effect in accordance with a law" (1973: 159).

12. I am uncertain that this second disjunct offers a live possibility. If a property neither produces nor prevents a manifestation, then its promoting that manifestation might still be a causal contribution, even if its doing so is counterfactually irrelevant.

13. For more on the notion of 'static' powers see Williams (2005). Though many static manifestations will arise without reciprocal partners, just as many will not.

14. "The life of most honest dispositional states is spent mostly in the presence of other dispositional states whose manifestation is the prevention of those former states from having *their* manifestation. Any particular set of manifestation conditions for a kind of manifestation must exclude other sets of manifestation conditions and so prevent the dispositional state from manifesting manifestations suited to the excluded conditions. It is a busy world" Martin (1993: 181).

15. For instance, Lewis—who defends a functional account of dispositions—says straightforwardly that "dispositions are an intrinsic matter" (1997: 138). And Armstrong, who identifies dispositions with certain categorical properties plus the laws of nature, says that "a disposition entails the presence (or absence) of non-relational properties of the object" (1973: 12). Representative of the realist side we find Molnar claiming that "[p]owers are intrinsic properties of their bearers. This is one of the prima facie basic features of powers that have to be saved by any analysis" (2003: 129).

16. McKitrick endorses an 'abundant' theory of properties, according to which any class of things, however gerrymandered, miscellaneous, and superfluous, is a property. She allows that many (perhaps all) of the non-intrinsic powers she defends may supervene on intrinsic powers.

17. Despite being hugely unpopular, if powers were relations, they would still be intrinsic to the collections of reciprocally partnered objects. And since there is nothing stopping those objects from interacting with other such collections (for manifestations that result from mutual production, prevention or permittance), we soon find that the only powers are powers of the entire world. Again, not an entirely untenable thesis, but a far cry from the picture of powers most defenders envision, and not something many are likely to

jump at. On the other hand, though it is hard to know just what to make of Karl Popper's account of 'propensities', in as much as they resemble powers, they come awfully close to being powers of a whole system, and not of the particulars that make it up (1990).

18. Not to mention that this would require a very different account of how powers are individuated; for the sake of argument I shall assume this account can be achieved, though I cannot claim to know what it would be.

19. Might the TBD power be determined entirely randomly? Perhaps, but this would be a far cry from what we find in the world. Most often, similar objects have similar powers, and similar sets of powers go together.

20. In conceding that this is not the only solution I do not mean to suggest that I am aware of others that I am failing to mention, I merely suspect that other solutions may be possible.

21. Regarding the nature of manifestations, Molnar (2003) speaks of them as events; Williams and Borghini (2008) treat them as states of affairs, Mumford (2004) and Bird (2007b) opt for powers, and Handfield (2008a, and in this volume) speaks of process types.

22. Most of the potential manifestations of such partnerings would be rather dull manifestations. Our tendency is to focus only on exciting manifestations, but though many are for such exciting things as change, other less exciting ones include prevention of other manifestations or having things remain as they are—but these are as genuine as any other. See Williams (2005).

23. This is not to suggest that a ring has anything like the appropriate architecture to map this type of holism; its application here is just for contrast with weak holism.

24. A related discussion can be found in Bostock (2003), though he rejects the possibility I consider.

25. Weak power realism also faces a second problem of fit, as each potential manifestation must be such that it does not coincide with, rule out, or come into contact or conflict in any way with, the potential manifestations of any other system of powers. This may be a reason to prefer thinking of powers as forming a comprehensive system.

26. The vague murmurings include Martin's inclination to speak of the range of powers and how they interact with partners as forming "lines" or "nets" (1993), which he says form "holistic nets" (2008: 46), and Heil's suggestion that the world be viewed "as a network of power" (2003: 97). Unfortunately, neither sees fit to elaborate on these remarks.

27. So as not to misrepresent Mumford's position, note that Mumford's preferred terminology is to speak of properties as clusters of 'powers', by which he intends what I mean by 'abilities'. To avoid confusion I have switched his terminology to keep it in line with what I have been using.

28. The general version of Platonism I describe would *allow for* power holism, but would not (without further details) *provide for* power holism. I leave it as an exercise to the reader to decide how those further details might be filled in.

29. Armstrong (1997) endorses this form of naturalism.

30. 'Blobject' is Horgan and Potrc's (2008) name for the one object of existence monism. They contend that 'blobjectivism' (the thesis that only the blobject exists) is compatible with the (indirect) truth of all our standard claims about the world and its inhabitants.

31. Schaffer (forthcoming) argues that this attribution is mistaken; he argues they are better interpreted as priority monists.

32. The compatibility requires certain revisions: under monism the claims of commonsense perception and science would not be strictly speaking true,

but either some appropriate paraphrase would be (Hawthorne and Cortens 1995), or they would have an 'indirect correspondence' with the world (Horgan and Potrc 2000 and 2008). How easily the revisions can be made will have a significant impact on the 'cost' of adopting monism.

33. According to the doctrine of Humean Supervenience "all there is to the world is a vast mosaic of local matters of particular fact" on which all else supervenes (Lewis 1986: *ix*).

7   Dispositions, Manifestations, and Causal Structure

Toby Handfield

INTRODUCTION

Typically—perhaps always—the manifestation of a disposition involves a causal process. That thought is fairly unexceptional. More interesting is the further thought that the process must be of a certain type for it to be a manifestation of a particular disposition. When salt manifests its disposition to dissolve, for instance, it seems not merely to involve an initial state in which the salt is solid, and a final state in which it is dissolved. Rather, it is important that salt undergo a distinctive kind of causal process. If the salt solution came about by a deviant process, we might say the salt was not manifesting its disposition to dissolve. For example, if we had a host of tiny nano-machines that pulled the individual ions out of the crystalline structure of sodium chloride, and the machines then built new water molecules around those ions, the deviancy of this process makes it look like the manifestation of a rather different disposition.[1]

If this claim about the link between the manifestation of dispositions and particular kinds of causal processes is correct, it suggests that causal processes form *natural kinds*.

Natural kinds are typically thought to (*i*) have real essences, and (*ii*) to facilitate scientific investigation—prediction and inference go better when it is prediction and inference about a kind. For my purposes in this chapter, I will be exclusively interested in the first claim about kinds: that they have real essences. This is because it is only the first idea about natural kinds that is directly relevant to my broader metaphysical project. In the next section, I will describe that project and how it motivates inquiry into the possibility of natural kinds of causal processes—but it should be stressed that even if you are not interested in pursuing my particular metaphysical project, there might still be good reason to find it of interest whether causal processes can be members of natural kinds.

Ultimately, I will argue that there are grounds for optimism: that there may be natural kinds of causal processes, and that these natural kinds might be used to explain the relation between a disposition and its possible manifestation. However, this optimism will be tempered with caution. The sorts of causal process kinds that would be compatible with current science appear not to have all the features we might have expected, a priori.

MOTIVATION: HUMEAN DISPOSITIONALISM

Why am I interested in looking for natural kinds of causal processes? Principally, because I am unimpressed by neo-Humean ontology, and I think that an ontology of causal powers is more attractive in some ways.[2] However, I think that such an ontology of causal powers could turn out to be more congenial to Humeans than most have thought. A crucial element in demonstrating this congeniality is to establish that there are natural kinds of causal processes, in terms of which causal powers might be *explained*. Let me explain this idea a little further.

I understand there to be two especially important parts of the neo-Humean position. The first is the idea that there are no necessary connections between distinct existences—in Lewis's framework, this is the principle of *Recombination*. The second is the idea that everything is loose and separate—in other words, that there are *lots* of distinct existences. In Lewis's framework, this is the thesis of *Humean supervenience*: the idea that all the ontologically fundamental properties are properties of spatiotemporal points and the only ontologically fundamental relations are spatiotemporal. All else supervenes on this 'Humean mosaic'.[3]

Humean supervenience is almost certainly false. In light of quantum entanglement, and possibly also in light of fundamentally stochastic processes, it appears that the world is not anywhere near as loose and separate as Humean supervenience requires.[4] But to concede that Humean supervenience is false in no way impugns the truth of Recombination. Indeed, Recombination appears a deeply attractive principle. It might even be thought that Recombination is an analytic truth; definitive of the very meaning of the term "distinct existence".[5] Whatever the case, I think it is hard to provide clear empirical evidence that this principle is false. Any time someone attempts to demonstrate a necessary connection between distinct things, it seems open to us to reinterpret the evidence as a scenario in which the putatively distinct things are not really distinct: the world is less loose and separate than you thought.

So, if you are a naturalistically minded metaphysician, and you want to propose a substantive account of causation, laws of nature, and dispositions, what is one to do? I don't think you should reject both the Humean doctrines simultaneously. We should try a more cautious approach, attempting to retain Recombination, while ditching the far less important—and most likely false—Humean supervenience.[6]

Retaining Recombination, then, we ask: What account can we give of the apparent necessary connections in nature—the connections between cause and effect, between laws and the phenomena they appear to govern, and between disposition, stimulus, and manifestation? These are, after all, apparently necessary connections between distinct existences.

The neo-Humean response is to deny that the connections are necessary. Rather, they are widespread connections; they are connections which it is particularly useful to know about. But for all that, there is no extra metaphysical glue holding these sorts of events together.

In particular, a neo-Humean explains the fact that a particular property confers a particular causal power by pointing to the global pattern of property instantiations that the property is involved in (the Humean mosaic). If *being solid sodium chloride* is instantiated in a global pattern such that most of its instances, when co-instantiated with *is wet* are followed by instances of *being dissolved sodium chloride*, then this very pattern of property instances is what explains the power to dissolve that is conferred by being sodium chloride. This is the feature of neo-Humeanism that I am most determined to avoid. It seems to get the order of explanation entirely the wrong way around. It is—I maintain—because of the intrinsic nature of the property *being sodium chloride* that it confers the power to dissolve.

So can we—consistent with Recombination—explain causal powers as *intrinsic* to the natural properties: as things which are conferred by the intrinsic nature of the properties, as opposed to things which are conferred by the global pattern of property instances? Note that, by retaining Recombination, I am opposed to traditional dispositional essentialists, who say that the natural properties are essentially such as to confer certain powers on their bearers, *without further explanation.*[7] At least for deterministic causal powers, this position involves a rejection of Recombination. For instance, suppose positive charge is essentially such as to confer the power to attract negatively charged things. Then two atoms, one of each charge, *must* be accompanied by a distinct existence—at least in time. Either they must be accompanied by a later change in velocity, or they must be accompanied by some sort of interfering factor that prevents the acceleration.

It is rather more difficult to show that dispositional essentialists must reject Recombination if they employ only probabilistic causal powers. If the stimulus condition for a probabilistic power is met, it can no longer be said that such a circumstance *necessitates* a distinct existence. But clearly there is a non-trivial constraint on what can happen, and this constraint is not obviously susceptible of further analysis. An alternative approach, which gives some *explanatory* account of such modal constraints, compatible with Recombination, is obviously preferable, in my view.

THE HUMEAN DISPOSITIONALIST PROGRAM

Working with dispositions in particular, I think that the following idea holds out some hope of explaining at least *some* of the modal nature of dispositions:

1. Identify the manifestation of a power as a natural kind of causal process.
2. Investigate the essential structure of such processes.
3. Attempt to identify internal relations between dispositional properties and such process structures.

The sort of internal relation that I have in mind at stage (3) is like that between the property "being hydrogen" and the structural property "being a molecule of H_2O". There is an internal relation between these, such that necessarily, anything which instantiates the latter has two parts which instantiate the former.

I won't try to say here just exactly how to account for this necessary connection. But it seems that this is the sort of connection that Humeans should not be chary of. Cowardly types will perhaps try to assimilate it to some sort of analytic truth, but I think we may happily admit it as an a posteriori necessity.

The sort of structure I have in mind at stage (2), though, is not the structure of a molecule—it is the structure of a causal process. So I am hoping for internal relations between a property such as *is a process of salt dissolving in water* and *is sodium chloride*. An internal relation like that would go some way towards *explaining* why being sodium chloride confers the power to dissolve in water. It would, moreover, explain why being sodium chloride is *essentially* such as to confer that power. Given the nature of sodium chloride, and given the nature of the process-kind, they would not be the things that they are if they did not stand in the internal relation that explains the power.

Moreover, if we start to understand the structure of natural kinds of causal processes, I speculate that we may see why not every conceivable process is possible. For instance, there presumably is no natural kind of process whereby oil dissolves in water. It is because there is no such possible process that *being oil* does not confer upon its bearers the power to dissolve in water.

So in effect, this would amount to an explanation of what has been called the 'Meinongian' feature of causal powers or dispositions: that they seem to 'point' to their potential manifestations, even where these are mere possibilia.[8] The explanation is that this 'pointing' is no more sinister than the fact that the property *being hydrogen* is essentially such that it is compatible with the structure of water.

Another reason to think that this approach to an ontology of powers is attractive is because it appears to handle Neil Williams's "problem of fit" (this volume) without requiring one to commit to a holistic account of powers.[9]

The problem of fit is to explain how it is that the many and diverse powers can be intrinsically powerful, and yet have mutually interrelated powers. A glass, for example, has a power to shatter when hit by a rock; and a rock has a complementary power to shatter the glass. If these properties are *intrinsically* such as to confer these powers, then it seems a remarkable fluke that they happen to confer these mutually complementary powers.

But by the same token, it seems metaphysically impossible that they could fail to confer mutually complementary powers.

If there are natural kinds of causal process however, which can be identified with power-manifestations, then it is possible to give a straightforward explanation of this. The explanation for why the rock and the glass have these two mutually complementary powers is that there is *one* manifestation kind—the shattering of a rock by a glass—in which both *being a rock* and *being a glass* are constituent properties.[10]

That, at any rate, is the program. I have called it "Humean dispositionalism".[11] Note that it by no means promises to explain *all* of the modal phenomena associated with dispositional properties.[12] For instance, it does nothing to explain why some manifestations might be *more probable* than others. All it appears to do is to explain why some manifestations are possible and others are not.

Still, I believe it is a promising start. And with that project as background, in this chapter I examine the key empirical claim that the project needs to sustain in order to be viable: the claim that manifestations of dispositions are causal processes that form natural kinds.

NATURAL KINDS WITH CAUSAL STRUCTURE

1. Visualizing Causal Structure

Suppose that manifestations of a disposition indeed form natural kinds. As I indicated before, the crucial feature of natural kinds that is of interest for my purposes is that they possess some sort of essential structure. For natural kinds of *processes*, such structure is presumably, in some sense, *causal structure*. It is something to do with the causal roles of the various factors in play, and how they interact.

In order to work out whether or not there exist causal processes with such causal structure, I could simply enumerate some examples of causal processes of manifestation, and attempt to determine by armchair reflection whether or not there is any essential causal structure in such processes. But this is not very easy, because it remains quite unclear what such causal structure would consist in.

I suggest that part of our difficulty in clarifying our ideas about causal structure is that we find it hard to *visualize* processes. We don't have any obvious mental picture that goes with the idea of a process, in the way that a Lewis diagram is such a convenient mental image when thinking about the structure of a chemical compound. That said, we do use visual representations—in both science and philosophy—to depict processes. This suggests an indirect way of determining whether or not the desired causal structure exists in the world. We can ask: do any of these representations capture the sort of structure that could plausibly be thought to be the essential structure of a natural kind of process?

Accordingly, in the remainder of this chapter I shall consider a variety of ways we actually represent causal processes, and discuss their prospects for representing the 'causal structure'—if there is such a thing—of those processes. By seeing what sorts of representations are suited to depicting causal structure, we shall get a better grasp on what such causal structure might be like, and whether such causal structure is likely to exist. Although the strategy is relatively indirect, I believe it will prove to have clear heuristic value. When I tell someone that the truth of an interesting philosophical claim hangs on the question of whether or not the manifestation of a typical disposition has something like an essential causal structure, I have come to expect a blank look. But if I can say, pointing at a diagram, that the truth of the philosophical claim hangs on whether or not this sort of diagram is a good representation of typical disposition manifestations, then there is a much better prospect of understanding.

Employing this approach, I will argue that the prospects are promising for Humean dispositionalism. That is, there are methods of representing causal processes that seem to capture—or at least help us to develop a grasp of—what sort of structure might be essential to those process-kinds. Moreover, these types of representation are drawn directly from areas of empirical science which we have good reason to regard as roughly true. So we have some reason to be optimistic that the empirical nature of the world is at least compatible with the existence of natural kinds of causal processes.

2. Criteria for Kindhood

Before examining those methods of representation, I wish to prescribe some conditions on what the hoped-for kinds must be like. These criteria are not intended to be platitudes about natural kinds, but are crafted with an eye to the Humean dispositionalist project, of grounding facts about causal powers in internal relations between process kinds and natural properties.

First, the sorts of processes that get identified as members of these kinds must at least roughly match our intuitive ideas about what is involved in the manifestation of a disposition. Call this the *identity requirement*. If a candidate account of causal processes tells us that every time a match is ignited, it actually involves a process entirely located more than 100 years in the future, then this is a good sign that the account is inadequate. Similarly, if a candidate account entails wildly implausible identity conditions for the kinds of process, then this is reason to reject it. Whether or not Barack Obama is president of the US at the time a match is lit, for instance, should not make any difference to what kind of lighting process is instantiated.

Second (and related to the identity requirement), I suggest an *intrinsicness requirement*: natural kinds of causal process must be characterized exclusively in terms of intrinsic structure. This is not because I think it inconceivable for there to be natural kinds with essential extrinsic structure, but simply because I suspect it will prove to be conceptually convenient.[13]

To illustrate: consider a process of some salt dissolving in water. This process has many extrinsic properties. Some of them seem obviously irrelevant to the causal process. That the dissolution is being watched by a class of high-school students, for instance, is surely not very interesting. However, there are other properties which might appear extrinsic and yet also be relevant. Imagine that the dissolution is taking place in an extremely strong magnetic field, and further that this might make a difference to how rapidly the dissolution occurs. In such cases, it seems to me that we can accept the requirement that the crucial structure of the process is intrinsic—we merely need to liberalize our conception of what is *included* in the process. A region of the magnetic field, for instance, seems to be part of the process of dissolution, in such a case.

(Generally, this second requirement will mesh with the first, identity requirement. But it is possible that, in light of empirical science, attempting to meet this requirement will lead us to realize that many processes are much "bigger" than we thought they were. And that will pull *against* the identity requirement—that the processes identified roughly fit our intuitive ideas about process-identity.)

A third requirement—also derived from the first—is that it should be possible to identify the difference between a process of non-manifestation of a disposition as opposed to the *masking* of a disposition.[14] A rat is given some poison. Having ingested the poison, the rat is disposed to die in a couple of hours. But the rat then eats some ryegrass, and that happens to act as an antidote to the poison. The rat survives because the disposition to die was interfered with—or masked—by the antidote. This process is importantly different from the process by which the rat's sibling—which never consumed poison in the first place—survives over the same period of time. The sibling never had the same disposition to die in the relevant period of time. If a natural kinds account of causal processes is going to be plausible, then, it should enable us to distinguish these two types of scenario as involving distinct kinds of process.

This *masking requirement*, however, is defeasible. It may not be necessary, for all sorts of physical system, to distinguish masking cases from other cases. This might be because no sensible physical distinction between masking and non-masking can be drawn. As I will discuss, there are indeed some physical systems which appear to be like this.

With these requirements in place, I now turn to examine some methods of depicting processes.

NEURON DIAGRAMS AND CAUSAL MODELS

Neuron diagrams have been used for some time in philosophical discussion about causation. The conventions of a neuron diagram are appealingly straightforward:

- Circles ("neurons") represent possible events. When shaded, they represent events that occur. When empty, they represent events that do not occur.
- Arrows represent "stimulatory signals" between neurons. A stimulatory signal is sent if and only if the neuron at the base of the arrow is shaded.
- Arrows with blobs on the end represent "inhibitory signals" between neurons. Similarly to stimulatory signals, an inhibitory signal is sent if and only if the neuron at the base of the arrow is shaded.
- The temporal order of events is from left-to-right.

In a diagram such as Figure 7.1 below, it is fairly clear what causes what. It is partly for this reason that neuron diagrams are so useful in the now rather baroque literature attempting to provide an adequate analysis of token causation.

An alternative approach to representing causal phenomena that has found recent favor is to use causal models.[15] Causal models consist of a set of structural equations. Such equations encode in a fairly straightforward way the relevant counterfactual dependencies in play.

I will omit discussing the technical details of how causal models are used to analyze causation because, for my purposes, it suffices to note that they are similar to neuron diagrams: both methods of causal representation

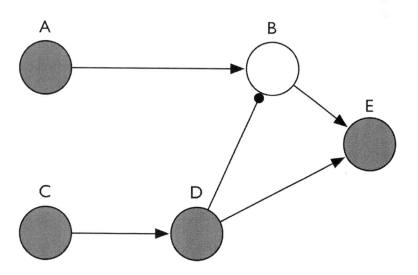

Figure 7.1   This sort of neuron diagram represents a scenario where one cause preempts another potential cause. C, rather than A, is the cause of E. But had C not occurred, E still would have occurred.

relatively directly encode information about counterfactual relations between possible events.

Does either of these approaches represent causal processes in a fashion compatible with the three constraints identified previously? Apparently not: they fail the intrinsicness requirement. The reason for this is that both these methods of representing causal structure are concerned with relations of counterfactual dependence between "nodes" in the structure. And relations of counterfactual dependence are not intrinsic to their relata.[16] Consequently, the structure that is represented by neuron diagrams appears not to be intrinsic structure.

To illustrate, suppose that Figure 7.1 represents the notorious causal scenario by which Suzy throws a rock (*C*) which then strikes a bottle (*D*), causing it to break (*E*). Billy throws a rock (*A*) at the same time as Suzy, and his rock would have hit (*B*) if it hadn't been for Suzy's throw—Suzy throws faster. Now suppose we modify the scenario somewhat. All the same events happen, and all the *local*, intrinsic features of the scenario are the same.[17] Billy throws, Suzy throws. Suzy's rock hits. Billy's throw does not. Bottle smashes. What is *different* is that there is a robot watching Suzy's throw. If Suzy does not throw, the robot will fire a laser (*R*), destroying Billy's rock. So now, if Suzy does not throw, the bottle won't break. This necessitates a change in the diagram (see Figure 7.2 next page). We need to insert additional neurons, to represent the robot, and the way in which the robot acts as a further inhibitor on the possible event of Billy's rock hitting the bottle (*B*). Even if we wanted to leave out the robot from the diagram, we would at least need to change the relations of counterfactual dependence between the neurons that we already have. The original diagram, as a representation of this new scenario, falsely implies that the bottle would have smashed if Suzy had not thrown. To rectify this, the arrow between *A* and *B*, in particular, should be removed or the description of *B* should otherwise be changed.

Notice, though, that this change in the causal structure of the scenario does not involve any change in anything like the "intrinsic structure" of the original set-up.

In response, we could expand our understanding of the *location* of the process, so as to include the presence or absence of the robot explicitly. But the resulting conception of processes seems to get the identity conditions for processes wrong, thus failing the identity requirement. It is very strange to think that *whether or not the robot is present* changes the kind of process. The robot does not *do* anything! Admittedly, in a very limited way, the robot's presence makes a difference because it would exert minute gravitational and radiation effects on the flying rocks, thus changing their trajectories very slightly. But it is not for that sort of reason that neuron diagrams push us to pay heed to the robot. Rather, the robot is included because it poses a merely counterfactual threat to the process by which the bottle smashes. This is not the sort of factor that warrants a distinct process kind for our purposes. Our aim is to identify process kinds that are

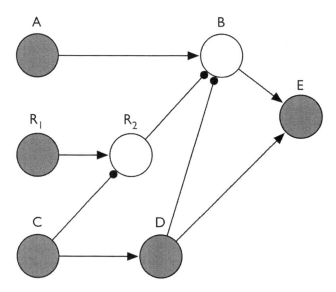

Figure 7.2 The modified Billy-Suzy scenario, with a watchful robot, waiting to zap Billy's rock (R), in case Suzy does not throw.

essential to the manifestation of dispositions. And although it makes some difference to precisely what occurs, the robot's presence apparently makes no difference to what bottle-smashing dispositions are manifested.

This sort of phenomenon—whereby a network of counterfactual dependence can be disrupted by adding in various "threats" or other potential interveners, is completely general, and in no way relies upon eccentricities of the Billy and Suzy story. So we can generally expect that a counterfactual structure approach will fail either the intrinsicness requirement or the identity requirement. Consequently, I suggest that we reject the neuron diagram and causal model approaches as ways to identify natural kinds of causal processes.

SPACE–TIME DIAGRAMS

Another possibility is that causal structure can be represented by space time diagrams. An obvious benefit to these diagrams, in contrast to neuron diagrams, is that they focus on what actually happens, rather than merely counterfactual possibilities of interaction.

Consider first, a very simple example of how one might identify causal structure in a space time diagram depiction of a Newtonian world. Take the disposition of two masses to gravitate towards one another. As a space time diagram, the manifestation of this disposition would look like Figure 7.3 next page. The mark of causal *interaction*, in such a diagram,

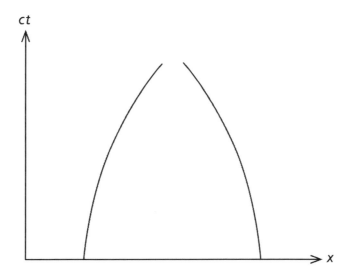

Figure 7.3   A space time diagram of two Newtonian objects accelerating toward each other.

is the curvature of trajectories. Inertial motion—unaffected by any causal influence—is represented by a straight trajectory.

So, using examples like this, will it be possible to identify process-structure that is intrinsic, that at least roughly matches our intuitions about the identity conditions for processes, and that accounts for the distinction between masking and non-masking cases?

There are two principal difficulties with space time diagrams for this purpose. First, a world-line reflects, in its curvature, the *net* forces acting upon the object. So how would one identify the structure of the process of the Earth revolving around the Sun, and distinguish that from the process of the moon revolving around the Earth, for instance?

Perhaps this is a difficulty that we should simply live with, however. Both processes are happening at the same time, and a certain amount of idealization would be necessary to represent the 'pure' version of each process. Given that the world involves a great deal of causal interaction, it might be naive to hope for a representation that has easily disentanglable components relating to the different causal processes. Moreover, there may be no physical basis for separating the world into any particular number of causal processes. So for now, I propose to gloss over this difficulty. I will return to discuss it in more detail in the following section' Demarcating Causal Processes'.

The second problem with space time diagrams, however, is that they will conflate the difference between various types of *masking* and cases of non-interaction. Consider Figure 7.4 at the bottom of the page. This could be a case of two positively charged particles—A and C—that are disposed to repel, but this process is being *masked* by the negatively charged particle B in between. Or it could be a case of three uncharged particles that have no disposition to repel. A space time diagram seems incapable of capturing this sort of difference—and this is a crucial difference if we are interested in the distinction between the masking of a disposition versus the sheer absence of the disposition.

For purely gravitational interactions, space time diagrams do not have this difficulty, because gravitational attractions cannot be masked by other gravitational attractions. So it remains possible that space-time diagrams are appropriate ways of representing the causal structure of some sorts of interaction, but not all. (Indeed, it seems far from coincidental that we do not typically use space time diagrams to represent electro-dynamic phenomena—where masking is possible—but we do use them to represent gravitational phenomena.[18])

But this simplistic use of space time diagrams suggests another, richer approach that shares some common roots: the idea that causal processes are space time trajectories, characterized by the sorts of physical quantities that they instantiate.

CONSERVED QUANTITY APPROACHES

Wesley Salmon (1984; 1998) and Phil Dowe (1992; 2000) have both made important contributions to the literature on causation by developing an

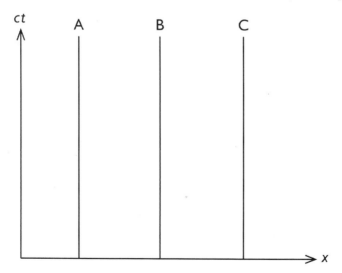

Figure 7.4 Three bodies moving through space time without undergoing acceleration. Whether this is the result of masking or simply due to non-interaction is not resolved.

idea that emerges naturally from the use of space time diagrams: that causal processes are 'world-lines'; objects which can be represented by space time trajectories. Not any trajectory will do, however. The space time trajectory of a cricket ball is just the right sort of object to be a causal process. It is not a gerrymandered object, and it is clearly capable of effecting causal influences on things (one may readily test this claim by throwing a cricket ball at a window, for instance). A roving spot of light on a wall, however, is not a causal process, even though it describes a continuous trajectory in space time. Although the light is interacting with the wall, causing it to radiate energy, it is not the moving spot that brings this about: it is the beam of light coming from the source that is the relevant process. World-lines such as that of the spot are known as 'pseudo-processes'. Subsequently, I review the main attempts that Salmon and Dowe have made to distinguish causal- and pseudo-processes.

In his earlier work, which is perhaps the best known account of causal processes, Salmon claimed that the spot of light on the wall is not a causal process because it is not *able to transmit a mark* (1984: 142). That is, no local modification can be made to the spot which would endure in subsequent stages of the process. You can't, for instance, paint a polka-dot on the spot and have it propagate to the subsequent stages of the spot's history.

This account, by appealing to an *ability*, seems to invoke a basic sort of disposition (or at least a counterfactual consideration) to characterize the essence of a causal process. This is obviously not congenial to my project of grounding causal powers (which are surely a sub-species of disposition) in causal processes.[19]

Salmon abandoned this account, precisely because it contained unanalyzed counterfactual concepts, and instead adopted a proposal of Dowe's (1992), that a causal process is one which transmits *a conserved quantity* (1998: 257–58). For Salmon, a process 'transmits' a conserved quantity between two points *A* and *B*, if and only if the process possesses the quantity at *A*, at *B*, and at every stage in between. Moreover, it must do this *without* interacting with anything else. The roving patch of wall that is illuminated by the spotlight may well possess a quantity of energy that is invariant at every stage of its history, but it does not—and cannot—do this, without interacting with anything else. Rather, it must be engaged in constant interactions with incoming photons from the light source in order to possess this invariant quantity.

Dowe complains that this account has a number of deficiencies, the details of which need not concern us here (see Dowe 2000: 114–19). In turn, Dowe suggests that the roving patch of wall, even though it may possess a conserved quantity, fails to be a causal process because it is a *time-wise gerrymandered* object: it lacks genuine identity through time (98–101).

For our purposes, it is not necessary to adjudicate between Salmon's later account and Dowe's account of causal processes. Rather, what is crucial is that we establish that some sort of account of causal processes can be developed, along broadly similar lines, which preserves the idea that causal processes have the sort of structure which meets the three requirements indicated before: the requirements of intrinsicness, identity, and masking.

1. Immediate Problems in the Dowe–Salmon Account

There are three evident obstacles to employing a Dowe- or Salmon-style account to the end of identifying causal structure suited for natural kinds.

First, the very idea of a *conserved quantity* might be tacitly dispositional. It is plausible to think that a conserved quantity is not merely one which *happens* to be conserved, but one which *would be* conserved under a variety of counterfactual circumstances. Consequently, conserved quantity accounts of causal processes might be uncongenial in much the way that Salmon's earlier, mark-transmission theory, was uncongenial for the purposes of giving an account that grounds facts about dispositions.

But there is no reason to insist that conservation be understood in this way. Conservation might be explained in terms of some other nomic concept, or it might be explained in purely actualist terms, as a brute accident.[20] Even if conservation is a modal phenomenon, and its modal nature has to be appealed to in the explanation of dispositions, it still constitutes significant progress, in my view, to have explained modal features of dispositions in terms of a more narrowly delimited modal phenomenon: the conservation of certain physical quantities.

A second concern arises with respect to Salmon's account. By defining a process in terms of an "absence of interaction", it may appear to breach the intrinsicness requirement. That is, whether or not something is a causal process, for Salmon, depends not only on how that process itself intrinsically is, at every stage of its history, but also on whether or not it is interacting with another process.

This concern, however, seems to be misplaced. A causal interaction—for both Dowe and Salmon—is defined as "an intersection of world-lines which involves exchange of a conserved quantity" (Dowe 2000: 90; Salmon 1998: 253). Interaction is therefore something that cannot happen at a distance. Whether a region is an intersection of world-lines may not be strictly intrinsic to that region: one might need to look just outside the intersection to region to see if there are multiple processes leaving or entering. But even if this concession must be made, it is plausible that this is a *local* property, in the sense that it supervenes on any infinitesimally small neighborhood of space time surrounding the region of intersection.[21]

(So I am, at this point, suggesting that the intrinsicness requirement might best be relaxed to a requirement of *locality*. Notice that the putative causal structure that was captured by a neuron diagram failed, not only to be intrinsic, but also failed to meet this requirement of locality.)

A third concern affects Dowe's account. Recall that Dowe invokes the idea of a 'time-wise gerrymandered' object, and explicates this as one which does not have constant identity through time. So an object (call it *Nikita*) defined as the mereological sum of (*i*) the Sphinx during the year 1801; (*ii*) Freud's pipe during the year 1901; and (*iii*) the Sun during the year 2001—would be a time-wise gerrymander. It is to be distinguished from a space-wise gerrymandered object, such as: the Sphinx, Freud's pipe, and the Sun, all during the year 1901. This latter object, though rather strange and unfamiliar, at least has the same identity conditions through its life, and so is eligible to be a causal process, says Dowe.

One could, of course, create a new predicate—*is ertnog*—which denotes the property of being the Sphinx in 1801, *or* Freud's pipe in 1901, *or* the Sun in 2001, and insist that the time-wise gerrymandered object Nikita does have consistent identity conditions: it is always ertnog. Exactly how Dowe might respond to such moves, I will not address here.[22] What I will address is the broader concern, that *however* we spell out the required concept of identity over time, it is essential that the account not rely upon extrinsic properties, lest the intrinsicness requirement be breached. (The remainder of this subsection may well be skipped, for those who are happy enough to take it on faith that an intrinsicalist account of identity through time can be given.)

Dowe considers there to be two ways in which identity through time might be explicated, consistent with his overall approach. The first is to insist that identity through time is strict numerical identity. In the jargon that has become popular, objects involved in causal processes *endure* through time, by being wholly present at many times, rather than *perduring* by having different temporal parts located at different times. The surprising implication of an endurance account, however, is that any properties of an enduring thing which are possessed only temporarily turn out to be relational, by the following sort of argument:

Suppose, for *reductio*, that a property P is possessed temporarily by an enduring object, a at t_1. Later, at t_2, a lacks P. So:

(1) Pa at t_1.
(2) $\neg Pa$ at t_2.
(3) a at $t_1 = a$ at t_2.

By the indiscernibility of identicals, a at t_2 must be P. But we have already established that it is not-P. Contradiction.

We can most easily avoid this absurdity by denying that "is P at t_1" denotes having the same property as "is P at t_2". Rather, what is involved in each case is a relation between the object and the time. The object a is P-wise related to t_1 and it is not P-wise related to t_2. No contradiction arises from this, but it comes at a serious cost: what we thought were intrinsic properties have turned out to be relations to times. In particular, this means our account has profoundly violated the intrinsicness requirement, for properties of causal processes, such as possessing a certain quantity of mass-energy, will turn out not to be intrinsic. Consequently, it would appear that the relevant structure of a causal process is doomed to be extrinsic.

However, again, I think that this variety of extrinsicalism is much less threatening than the sort of extrinsicalism which motivated us to reject the neuron diagrams considered earlier. Here, the sorts of relations involved are relations to the space time region in which the process is located. That is at least a *local* phenomenon, even if it is not strictly intrinsic.[23]

The second approach to analyzing identity through time which Dowe identifies as compatible with his theory is a broadly Humean perdurance account in terms of similarity and continuity. On this approach, the different stages of a thing's history are distinct parts of a larger, temporally extended whole. Different temporal parts may have different intrinsic properties, in the same way that different spatial parts of a spatially extended whole can have different properties.

This second approach may be more problematic for the purposes of identifying causal structure, however, because it sometimes relies upon relatively global judgments about similarity and continuity, in order to find the most highly eligible candidate to be the future 'continuant' of the original entity.

To illustrate, consider a version of the famous thought experiment concerning the Parthenon.[24] A stone thief gradually removes the stones of the Parthenon, over a period of several years, until all have been removed. However, whenever a stone is taken, it is soon replaced by the caretakers of the Parthenon, so that, even after all the original stones have been removed, the structure that is on the site is extremely similar to that which was there before the thefts began. Is the structure that is present after all the stones have been stolen identical to the Parthenon, or is it merely a fake? Arguably, this depends upon what has happened to the original stones. If they have been shipped by the thief overseas, and reassembled into a Parthenon-like structure in San Francisco, then common-sense ontology would judge that the Parthenon has been moved to San Francisco. If the stones have been broken down to make gravel, typical intuitions are that the Parthenon survives on the original site. Therefore, whether or not the structure on the original site is identical to the original Parthenon depends on facts that are remote from that spatiotemporal region.

The Parthenon, being an artifact, may not be the sort of object that is particularly important for the purposes of a metaphysics of science. So these concerns may be somewhat out of place. For present purposes, I merely wish to register the danger that Dowe's account of causal processes, wedded to a continuity/similarity-style account of identity through time, is likely to run afoul of my project. Other perdurantist accounts may work, but they will have to ground facts about identity through time in considerations intrinsic to—or at least local to—the object in question.

So, depending upon how we characterize the notion of a causal process, it looks like we are likely to have to breach the intrinsicness requirement.

But this has led us to a more moderate requirement of *locality*: the structure of a causal process must supervene at least on the spatiotemporal neighborhood of the process. It appears that, on both Salmon's later account and on Dowe's account, this requirement can be met.

2. Causation by Disconnection

The Dowe–Salmon approach to causation is notorious for having difficulty in dealing with certain sorts of causation: causation involving "disconnection" is not going to show up as a continuous world-line, nor as a series of world-lines linked by interactions. Consider the claim that my plant died because I failed to water it. There is no world-line leading from my "non-watering" to the death of the plant. There are world-line processes that occur in the plant that lead to its death, and these processes would not have occurred if watering had taken place. But there is no actual physical connection between non-watering and death.[25]

This is clearly a problem if you think that causal processes must serve the role of underwriting an analysis of token causal claims such as '*A* is a cause of *B*'. But I am not interested in that purpose. That is, I am not attempting to give an analysis of token causal claims—indeed, for such claims, I suspect a counterfactual approach will be necessary. Rather, I want to know if a world-line account of a causal process can be used to capture the causal structure of a disposition's manifestation, and if it can do so in a way compatible with the three requirements I listed previously.

3. Causal Structure in Dowe–Salmon Processes

Having warded off these initial concerns, it seems clear that Dowe–Salmon processes are highly suited to capture the sort of structure that is of interest to us. To briefly review the two key problem cases that we have considered so far:

Billy and Suzy. Whether or not the robot is present will make—as we have noted—some very small difference to the causal process of Suzy's flying rock. But if we allow ourselves some sort of abstraction away from minor details like that, there is surely going to be some common causal structure to the case where Suzy smashes the bottle in the presence of the robot and the case where she smashes the bottle in the absence of the robot. In both cases, what is crucial is that the rock-process reach the bottle with a certain momentum, and that it then participate in a causal interaction in which much of that momentum is transferred to the bottle, which then splits into a large number of fragmentary processes. This case does not naturally fit talk of dispositions, but if we allow ourselves to describe it in such unnatural terms, this seems to be a good approximation of what we might think essential to the manifestation of the rock's "disposition" to smash the bottle.

Masking versus non-interaction. The three particles in Figure 7.4 do not indicate, from their trajectories alone, whether or not they are interacting in such a way as to mask their dispositions to attract or repel, or if they are in fact not disposed to interact at all. A Dowe-Salmon account of the masking case would presumably involve appealing to interactions with the *fields* generated by the charged particles. The non-interaction case would not involve such interactions. So there would be a clear difference in causal structure.

The previous discussion of Dowe-Salmon processes is already enough, I suggest, to give us grounds for optimism about the prospects for identifying essential causal structure in the processes by which dispositions are manifested. But the reader might reasonably wonder whether such essential causal structure can be found in quantum phenomena. Although I lack the expertise to give a comprehensive answer to this question, I will, in the next section, attempt to show that the use of Feynman diagrams in quantum field theory is highly apposite for the purposes of representing causal structure.

FEYNMAN DIAGRAMS

Feynman diagrams are an appealingly intuitive method of representing interactions in quantum field theory. What is particularly striking about them is that they seem to provide precisely the sort of structure that we have been looking for. They appear to represent interactions as discrete and local events, hence giving rise to high hopes that they will capture some sort of intrinsic or local structure. In momentum space, they do not merely represent inputs and outputs to a causal interaction, they also represent different *ways* that the output can come about. Hence they appear to be able to distinguish between cases of masking as opposed to cases of non-interaction.

As it turns out, however, what I have just said about Feynman diagrams might be a little misleading. What exactly are Feynman diagrams? They are devices to assist in calculating the probability of an outcome, given an initial state, in quantum field theory. Each line and vertex in the diagram is associated with a term or step in the calculation. So they serve a remarkable dual purpose of giving an iconic representation of an interaction, while also facilitating calculation of the probability of that interaction.

A few words on how to interpret Feynman diagrams: first, the temporal order of events is from the bottom to the top. Though, strictly speaking, it is only the events at the *upper boundary* of the diagram that are taken to be in a definite temporal order relative to those at the *lower bound-ary* of the diagram. Any apparent ordering of events in between these extremes is merely an artifact of the representation. This is because—apart from the upper and lower boundaries—Feynman diagrams are just graphs. They are defined by *topological structure* alone.

Arrows pointing up represent electrons. Arrows pointing down represent positrons. Each straight section of arrow represents an electron moving at constant momentum for a period of time. Wiggly lines represent photons. Junctions of lines (i.e. vertices) represent absorptions/emissions of photons, positrons and electrons. That's it, for our purposes.

So a diagram like Figure 7.5 below represents a positron and an electron annihilating, and two photons being emitted. And in Figure 7.6 below, the sort of process described would be the repulsion of two electrons. The change in momentum of the electrons is mediated by the exchange of the photon.

Because of conservation constraints, every emission or absorption of a particle is accompanied by a change in momentum. So the exchange of particles is associated with changes of state. This looks like a strikingly *discrete, local, and intrinsic* account of causal interaction. An extremely attractive thought, then, is that a Feynman diagram could indeed represent the degree of causal structure we are looking for in trying to identify natural kinds of causal processes.

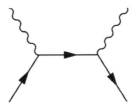

Figure 7.5 A Feynman diagram 'representing' positron-electron annihilation, resulting in the emission of two photons.

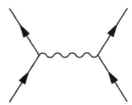

Figure 7.6 Two electrons exchange a photon. This is the sort of underlying process that might account for a repulsive interaction between two negatively charged particles.

1. Interpreting Feynman Diagrams

So what's the problem? The problem with this thought is that Feynman diagrams do not—at least in standard interpretations of QM—represent "what actually happens". Rather, they are an aid to the calculation of the probability of an outcome, given an initial state. Here is how you use Feynman diagrams in a calculation:

1. Take a given initial state—involving two electrons with given momenta, say.
2. Take a final state, in which they have different momenta.
3. Then draw *all possible* Feynman diagrams which have these initial and final states.

So to calculate the probability that two electrons will repel each other, in addition to a diagram such as that in Figure 7.6 on the previous page, it would also be necessary to consider diagrams like Figures 7.7a and b below. All of these—plus infinitely many more—represent "ways" that the particles can go from the initial state to the final state. And each of them contributes to the calculation of the probability of the final state, given the initial state. (More precisely, each represents a term in a perturbation series, which is used

(a) First way

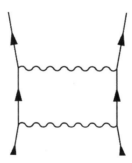

(b) Second way

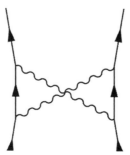

Figures 7.7a and 7.7b Two further ways for two electrons to manifest repulsion.

as a means to gain an accurate approximation to the actual calculation. For most purposes of approximation, only the first one or two terms in the series need to be calculated—but in principle, all are required.)

Feynman was wont to say—or at least imply—tantalizing things like: each diagram "represents a way" that the process can occur (Feynman 1985: 93). But if one is told an event can occur in one of N ways, and the event does occur, one would typically think it safe to infer that the event has occurred in one—*and only one*—of those N ways. But this sort of claim is not vindicated by the apparatus of QM. Rather, what can be said is that the state vector evolves in accord with the Schrödinger equation. The state vector's evolution is entirely deterministic, and there is no question of it evolving one way or another. The evolved state-vector yields a certain probability that we will observe a given outcome.

As far as orthodox QM is concerned, then, the individual diagrams in Figures 7.6 and 7.7 do not depict separate processes. They are merely devices we use to calculate the probability of a process that is specified in terms of:

• the initial particles' types and momenta, and
• the final particles' types and momenta.

In other words, processes are defined purely by input and output. Call any such process—specified in the previous terms—an "orthodox QM-process".[26]

2. Do Orthodox QM-processes Have Causal Structure?

So: could there be *natural kinds* of orthodox QM-processes? That is: does an orthodox QM-process possess intrinsic structure that might constitute the real essence of a natural kind?

I think we can hazard a positive answer to this question. Wheras it is unsettling that we cannot identify the causal structure of an orthodox QM-process with any single Feynman diagram, as we might have wished, we can at least say that the structure of an orthodox QM-process is approximately represented by a *set* of Feynman diagrams. (The very fact that this seems to undermine traditional ways of representing a process as a single way that things happen is perhaps apt, given the stochastic and/or indeterminate nature of QM phenomena.) Such a set has intrinsic structure. It has intrinsic properties such as 'contains diagram X as a member'. Moreover, each of the members have associated amplitudes—so there will be further intrinsic properties of the set, such as: 'has a member with amplitude n'; 'contains members whose amplitudes sum to p'; etc.

However, although orthodox QM-processes are quite rich in structure in the above sense, they lack the sort of structure required to make the most rigorous sort of distinction between masking and non-interaction. Recall Figure 7.4, which was ambiguous as to whether it represented three uncharged particles undergoing non-interaction, or three charged particles whose repulsive and attractive forces cancel out. The two sorts of scenarios involved are different not only with respect to the causal interactions, but also in the *nature* of the participating particles. Only one of the cases involves charged particles.

Feynman diagrams—and the apparatus of QM in general—are perfectly capable of distinguishing cases of this sort, for the simple reason that orthodox QM-processes are defined, in part, by the types of particles in the initial and final states. So a process involving charged particles is ipso facto a different type of process from one involving uncharged particles.

But one might have thought it possible for there to be two distinct possible processes involving precisely the same final and initial conditions. In one case, the particles interact, but the interactions cancel out—giving rise to a case of masking. In the other, the particles simply do not interact. Although these two possibilities are incompatible with determinism, one might have thought they were genuine possibilities in light of the apparently indeterministic nature of quantum mechanics.

This distinction, however, is strictly not possible given the nature of orthodox QM processes. No two distinct QM-processes exist that have identical final and initial states.

So we cannot use the apparatus of Feynman diagrams to draw this more subtle distinction between masking and non-interaction. But as I noted in section 3, the requirement to distinguish masking from non-interaction is a defeasible one, and this may be precisely the sort of case where it is apt to be defeated.[27]

DEMARCATING CAUSAL PROCESSES

The previous reflections, both upon the use of Feynman diagrams in physics, and on the nature of Dowe–Salmon processes, are grounds for cautious optimism about the possibility that the world contains the sort of causal structure that could constitute the essences of natural kinds of causal processes.

But, as mentioned earlier, there is reason to be concerned that, even if the world contains the right sort of structure, the processes that we end up with will still not fit the *identity* requirement, which requires that the kinds have intuitively plausible identity conditions. For more intuitively familiar types of natural kind, it is generally quite clear where each distinct member of a natural kind is located, and consequently, it is clear how many members of the kind there are. One could take a sample of chemicals, for instance, and—worries about vagueness aside—there would be a determinate fact about how many atoms of each chemical kind are present in the sample. Causal processes, in contrast, seem less amenable to determinate facts, both about identity and about location.

With respect to the numerical identity of causal processes, any bit of space time that contains more than one or two fundamental particles will likely involve an enormous plurality of causal influences and phenomena. There seems to be no non-arbitrary manner of counting up the 'number' of causal processes that are present in that region. With respect to the location of processes, given the possibility of events in the past or future having an effect on a causal interaction, very distant phenomena might need to be included in our understanding of a causal process. Consequently, causal processes might be surprisingly large. If we have to take account of all the past influences, we might need to include the entire backwards light cone of the objects that are paradigmatically thought to be involved in the process.

Putting these two concerns together, it begins to look like the only non-arbitrary way of defining a causal process is simply to take the *entire universe* as a single process, and give up hope of finding smaller processes that are members of genuine natural kinds. This response would be an overreaction. The identity conditions for process kinds may not be as transparent to us as they are for other kinds, but that fact is not, in itself, grounds for despair that there could possibly be such conditions. Rather, there are at least four grounds for resisting the sorts of worries cited before.

In the first place, chemical compounds are often thought to be excellent examples of natural kinds, but chemical compounds are themselves subject to vague identity conditions. Consider two molecules of H_2O that are undergoing the process of converting into one molecule of H_3O^+ and one hydroxide ion (OH^-). This involves one of the hydrogen atoms being pulled out of its covalent bond, and forming a hydrogen-bond with one of the unbounded electron pairs on the oxygen atom of the other molecule. When this sequence of events is examined on the micro-scale, it is not the case that there is some single moment at which the hydrogen nucleus is unequivocally 'released' from its original covalent bond. Rather, we are confronted with the same problem we have in working out when we have stepped off a mountain, or when a man becomes bald, or when a collection of grains of sand constitutes a heap. There are numerous possible places at which we could equally plausibly draw the line, and no clear fact of the matter as to which is the correct one.[28]

Secondly, as the example of water illustrates, we are already reasonably familiar with the possibility that distinct kinds can 'overlap'. A molecule of water contains parts—such as protons, electrons, hydrogen atoms, and so on—that are themselves members of other natural kinds. So the fact that the world appears to contain numerous overlapping causal processes is not itself fatal to the possibility of there being distinct kinds involved.

In the case of causal processes, to accommodate such overlap, we cannot merely hope to distinguish the distinct processes by spatiotemporal means. A sphere of metal may be undergoing a process of rotation as well as a process of heating, for instance.[29]

The typical method by which we try to distinguish such intertwined processes is to use a degree of idealization—we can ask: what is the trajectory the relevant objects would take *in the absence of any other processes?*[30]

Where causal influences interact in complex, non-linear ways, we will have less reason to think that the answer to hypothetical questions like this will be of much use in identifying genuinely distinct processes. But in many cases it does seem that the multiple influences combine in a linear fashion, or in some other fashion that makes their independent reality seem plausible. Accordingly, we have some reason to think that there could be genuine kinds of causal process at play.[31]

Thirdly, anyone who wishes to believe in natural kinds will surely think that fundamental particles such as electrons are among the very best candidates for such status. But arguably we are beset with even greater difficulty in providing determinate identity conditions and determinate locations for electrons. The indeterminacy of an electron's location is a well-known phenomenon of quantum mechanics. Less well known is that there are some parts of quantum field theory in which the very number of electrons (and other particles) is indeterminate.[32] So if we are to have any natural kinds at all at the quantum level, it appears we must put up with a degree of indeterminacy in those kinds. That should make us more comfortable, in turn, with some more limited indeterminacy with respect to natural kinds of processes.

Finally, and most importantly, by adopting approaches such as the Dowe–Salmon account of a process, rather than a neuron diagram style approach, then we can analyze the causal structure of processes in terms of *actual influence* rather than merely counterfactual potential-to-influence. Consequently, we can legitimately restrict our attention to the influences *in a given space-time region.* In doing that, we are not required to take into account all of the possible threats and hypothetical interveners that could have influenced what happened in that space-time region. I suspect it is only when we assume that causal structure must include merely counterfactual influences that we will be forced to blow out the location of a causal process, with the eventual result being that we must include the entire backwards light-cone of an event in order to include all the causal structure that goes into the process. The conserved quantity approach forestalls this difficulty.

CONCLUSION

It is uncontroversial that the world contains causal processes. What is more doubtful is that those processes contain a sort of structure which might be suitable to serve the purpose of constituting *natural kinds* of causal processes. In particular, it seems doubtful that causal processes contain a suitably intrinsic structure.

However, if we relax our intuitive pre-conceptions about the nature of natural kinds, we can see that there may well be natural kinds of causal processes. In Dowe–Salmon accounts of causal processes, we have a relatively well-developed and empirically informed account that is compatible at least with highly localized causal structure, even if it is not strictly intrinsic. Moreover, in current physics, the use of Feynman diagrams is an example of a method of representation that, despite incorporating a fair degree of quantum ontological strangeness, is still sufficiently rich that it appears to represent sufficient causal structure to constitute natural kinds of causal process.

I have done nothing to address those who are skeptical that the world contains natural kinds of any sort whatever. In particular, I have done nothing to address skepticism with regard to the *de re* essential properties that are characteristic of such kinds. But on the basis of the aforementioned discussion of causal structure, I conclude that, if the world contains any natural kinds at all, it is quite plausible that it contains natural kinds of causal processes.

ACKNOWLEDGMENTS

I wish to thank Stephen Barker, John Bigelow, Alexander Bird, Richard Corry, Phil Dowe, Antony Eagle, Harry Perlman, Dean Rickles, Neil Williams, and Alastair Wilson for their valuable comments on earlier drafts of this chapter. Thanks also to the audience at the conference 'Powers: Their Grounding and Their Realization', held at Oxford in July 2008.

NOTES

1. Though, depending upon the details of the case, we might say that the nano-machines are merely catalyzing the process by which the salt manifests its ordinary disposition to dissolve.
2. For a paradigm example of neo-Humean ontology, see the works of David Lewis, perhaps best represented in Lewis 1999.
3. See the Introduction to Lewis 1986b for Lewis's principal statement of this idea.
4. For a recent and forceful expression of this point, see Maudlin 2007: 53–61. See also Oppy 2000.
5. Or perhaps not. For further discussion of plausible formulations of this idea, see Wilson Forthcoming.
6. Lewis himself only wished to defend the a priori tenability of Humean supervenience (1986b). And in that enterprise, it comes down to a show of confidence in one's philosophical intuitions about the above concepts. If one is prepared to bite a few bullets, Humean Supervenience can come out looking quite tenable indeed—perhaps we can say it is a priori surprising, but not a priori untenable (Oppy 2000: 96).
7. I consider this to be a feature of the views of Ellis, Bird, and Mumford, for instance—though there are significant differences in the precise nature of the

ontologies these theorists advocate, they all appeal to brute modal facts of some variety.

8. Armstrong 1997: 79.

9. Moreover, the concern that a powers-ontology is afflicted by some sort of vicious regress seems to be motivated by holism (see, e.g. the contributions of Lowe, Marmodoro, and McKitrick to this volume). So by avoiding holism, my preferred approach promises to avoid any such regress.

10. This is not to say that there can be *only* one manifestation kind in which these properties are constituents. Being a glass confers the power to emit a 'ping' noise when struck gently by a rock. This power, and the complementary power of the rock are explained by the existence of a different manifestation kind.

11. Handfield 2008a.

12. So my program is less ambitious than Brian Ellis's 'Scientific Essentialism' (2001), which tries to explain all natural necessity in terms of essences of natural kinds. That said, Ellis's ideas are obviously closely related to mine, and I was moved to think more about the structure of causal processes by his paper with Caroline Lierse (Ellis and Lierse 1994), where he explicitly claims that there is a necessary connection between a disposition and the causal process in which it is manifested.

13. Thanks to Alexander Bird and Jennifer McKitrick for pressing me to clarify my justification on this point.

14. See Bird 1998; Choi 2003; Fara 2001; Johnston 1992 for discussion of masks and antidotes.

15. Pearl 2000. For a relatively accessible discussion of the philosophical application of causal models see Hitchcock 2001.

16. This point has been made by Lewis (2004) and also Peter Menzies (1999).

17. In this context, I am merely appealing to an intuitive sense of location: to a folk understanding of where the process is located. This is appropriate, given my stipulation of an intuitive *identity* requirement. I'll return to the idea of locality in the section 'Conserved quantity approaches'.

18. Thanks to Alastair Wilson for prompting this thought.

19. Though it would admittedly be an interesting result if all the many and varied causal powers are grounded in a single basic sort of disposition: the ability to transmit a mark.

20. Salmon notes this point of difficulty, and responds by explicitly embracing a mere regularity account of reconservation: a quantity is conserved just in case it is, for all time, unchanged. "[I]t makes no difference whether that true generalization is lawful; only its truth is at stake" (1998: 259). Dowe does not directly address the issue.

21. See Butterfield (2006: 714–6) for some brief discussion of locality and its relation to intrinsicness.

22. See Dowe (2000: 98–101), where Dowe manifests an awareness of these concerns, and elects simply to leave identity through time as a primitive, unanalyzed concept in his theory.

23. In related vein, Bradford Skow (2007) argues that on all viable accounts of space, shape properties—often taken as the very paradigm of intrinsic properties—are in fact extrinsic. However the sort of extrinsicness he identifies is often—to my mind at least—relatively 'unalarming'. It involves relations to the spatial region in which the shape-bearer is located, or to necessarily existent entities, such as numbers.

24. See Dauer 1972, responding to an earlier paper by Smart (1972).

25. See Dowe 2000, chapter 6 for Dowe's attempt to deal with this problem. See Schaffer 2004 for a spirited rebuttal.

26. By 'orthodox' I do not mean to invoke thoughts of the Copenhagen interpretation. I merely mean approaches that do not reify what is represented by Feynman diagrams—and this includes a wide variety of relatively standard approaches.

27. See Handfield 2008b: 304–5 for further discussion of the issue of finking and masking for the fundamental properties. Some dispositionalists have even suggested—on quite independent grounds—that fundamental causal powers may not be susceptible to finks or masks (Bird 2007: §§3.3.2–3.3.3). For such dispositionalists, this convergent argument might be quite welcome.

28. Even more unsettling to our comfortable view of water as involving a clearly defined, stable structure, recent results in physics suggest that, when observed on extremely short time-scales, water behaves like $H_{1.5}O$ (Schewe, Riordon, and Stein 2003). Whereas the interpretation of these results is still uncertain, it reminds us of what should be a familiar fact: that whatever traits we take to be essential to water, we may, in light of empirical discovery, have to live with various qualifications and hedges, to the effect that these are merely *typical* properties of water.

29. The example is due to Davidson, who was discussing the ontology of events (1980b: 178).

30. In defending his account of causal processes, Wesley Salmon had to tackle much the same issue, because his definition of a causal process requires the absence of interaction.

    "You'd want to say that the speeding bullet transmits energy-momentum from the gun to the victim, but what about its incessant, negligible interactions with ambient air and radiation?" Of course. In this and many similar sorts of situations, we would simply ignore such interactions because the energy-momentum exchanges are too small to matter. Pragmatic considerations determine whether a given 'process' is to be regarded as a single process or a complex network of processes and interactions". (Salmon 1998: 258).

31. For a recent discussion of the relation between the reality of component causal influences and the analytic method in science, see Corry (2009).

32. See Teller 1995: 110–13.

8 Causal Powers and Categorical Properties

Brian Ellis

INTRODUCTION

The aim of this chapter is to argue that there are categorical properties as well as causal powers, and that the world would not exist as we know it without them. For categorical properties are needed to define the powers—to locate them, and to specify their laws of action. These categorical properties, I shall argue, are not dispositional. For their identities do not depend on what they dispose their bearers to do. They are, as Alexander Bird would say, 'quiddities'. But there is nothing wrong with quiddities. And, in the second half of this chapter, I shall defend the thesis that all categorical properties are quiddities.

Causal powers are properties that are displayed in causal processes. Of these, there are two principal kinds: powers to act, and powers to resist. The powers to act are the drivers of causal processes, e.g. the forces of nature, the potential differences, the temperature differences, the pressure gradients, and so on. The powers to resist are the properties that tend to reduce the influence of the powers, e.g. inertial mass, electrical resistance, elasticity and so on. Whatever one's theory of causation, one must suppose that these causal powers are all dispositional, i.e. have identities that depend essentially on what they dispose their bearers to do. I do not think, as Shoemaker, Bird, and others do, that all properties are causal powers, or even that all dispositional properties are causal powers. There are propensities, such as decay probabilities, which are dispositional, but not causal, and categorical properties, which are neither dispositional nor causal.

I begin by developing the theory of physical causation on which I am relying. If you do not accept this, then you need not accept the theory of causal powers that I shall propose. Nor must you accept my conclusion that the categorical properties are all quiddities. So, a lot hinges on it.

PHYSICAL CAUSAL PROCESSES

Causal processes necessarily involve causally related states of affairs. For a causal realist, the important metaphysical question is: What is the nature of this relationship? But the prior question is: Why should one be a causal realist? The short answer to the second question is that the only plausible alternative to causal realism is causal phenomenalism. But causal phenomenalism leaves this relationship unexplained, as the critics of Hume's theory of causation have long been arguing. Hume's regularity theory is more or less faithful to the phenomenology of causation. For, it is an account of causation that would enable us to distinguish, in many cases, between states of affairs that are merely successive, and ones that are related as causes to effects. But it does nothing to explain the phenomena. Nor does it explain why causal laws normally apply strictly only in idealized circumstances, or how there can be such a thing as singular causation, or why genuine causal laws have nomic necessity. What is needed, and what every causal realist would insist upon, is a theory of causation that would tell us what causal processes really are. For, if we had such a theory, we should not only be able to explain the phenomena upon which our common beliefs about causes and effects are based, but also the recognized status of causal laws, and their acknowledged applicability to single cases.

In paradigm cases, causation involves energy transference from one thing to another. In Hume's billiard ball example some or all of the kinetic energy of the impacting ball is transferred to that of the ball impacted upon. In the act of warming oneself in front of the fire, the chemical energy stored in the wood is released as heat in the process of burning, and the heat energy is transferred radiantly to the person who is warmed. Such examples are obviously causal processes, and the mechanism of causation is no less obviously that of energy transfer. Therefore, it is initially plausible to suppose that this is the mechanism we are seeking. It is true that not all causal connections are quite like this. For in many cases, the causal process is two-way. Electrons, for example, repel each other, and gravitational masses attract each other. But in these cases there is, it is now believed, an exchange of virtual particles—photons in the first of these two cases, and gravitons in the second. So, these cases do not seriously undermine the initially plausible suggestion that causation is essentially an energy transfer process.

The most troublesome counter-examples to the energy transfer theory of causation derive from blockings, bluffings, and diversions. I might, for example, make the room darker by pulling the curtains. Or, Shane Warne might cause the ball to miss the bat and go through to the stumps by not spinning it as much as usual. There are certainly energy transfer processes involved in producing the desired outcomes in these cases. But they are not produced directly. I made the room darker by preventing the light from outside from getting in, and Warne got his wicket by not doing what he was pretending to do. So the thesis that causation is essentially an energy transfer process linking cause to effect is not strongly supported by our linguistic practices. Nevertheless, there does seem to be a good case for distinguishing between the direct effects of the energy transfer processes that are initiated by us, and the outcomes that we intended to achieve. There is also a good case for distinguishing between the effects of natural physical energy transfer processes, and the outcomes that we find sufficiently interesting to note. We are, after all, interested here in what causation really is, not in the realization of our wishes or intentions. Accordingly, I distinguish between physical causation, and causation more broadly construed. I define a physical causal process A $\Rightarrow$ B as an energy transference from one physical system S_1 in a state A to another physical system S_2 to effect a physical change B in that system (relative to what the state of S_2 would have been in the absence of this influence).

In the simplest kind of case, an energy transmission from one thing to another consists of a particle emission (e.g. a photon), its transmission as a Schrödinger wave, and its subsequent absorption (e.g. on a photographic plate, or any other particle-absorbing surface). I call all such processes 'elementary causal' ones, and postulate that all causal processes consist ultimately of such elementary ones. We know that these elementary causal processes are all temporally irreversible, because the process of particle-absorption is temporally irreversible. For, there is no such thing as the instantaneous, or near instantaneous, reflation of a Schrödinger wave. Therefore, it is reasonable to suppose that all physical causal processes are temporally irreversible, and that the temporal order is the physical causal order.

But this level of analysis, which we may call 'the base level', is not appropriate here. It establishes the temporal asymmetry and temporal direction of physical causation. But it is much too deep for the purposes of this chapter. At this level, even the physical objects that are the bearers of causal powers do not exist. However, physical objects capable of having causal powers manifestly do exist at what I shall call 'the object level', i.e. at the level of ontological reduction at which we may speak freely of physical objects and their properties. The question of how things at this level may ultimately be constituted by elementary events and processes will be set to one side for the time being—although I shall have something to say about this question towards the end of the chapter. The causal processes that are the displays of causal powers are presumably ones that belong to natural kinds. For, if they were not of natural kinds, the causal powers would not be natural properties. But this is not much of a restriction. Clearly, there are a great many natural kinds of causal processes in nature. For example, all of the chemical reactions described in chemistry books are processes that belong to natural kinds; and the equations that describe these reactions are presumably descriptive of their essential natures. There are also a great many natural kinds of physical causal processes occurring in other areas of science. Think of those of meiosis, meitosis, refraction, reflection, diffraction, crystallization, and so on.

CAUSAL POWERS

At the object level, there are apparently two very different kinds of properties, dispositional and categorical. The dispositional properties are those whose identities depend on what they dispose their bearers to do, and the categorical ones are those whose identities depend on what they are—but not, apparently, on what they do. The latter are the spatiotemporal and numerical relationships that are required to describe the structure of things. The causal powers, on the other hand, belong in the category of dispositional properties, along with propensities (see section 'Who's Afraid of Quiddities'), which, I shall argue, are not causal powers. What these active properties all have in common is their dispositionality. The categorical properties, in contrast, are essentially passive; since there is nothing that their bearers are necessarily disposed to do just in virtue of their having these properties. Nevertheless, I will argue, the categorical properties do have some vital causal roles. For these properties determine where the active properties of things may exist, or be distributed, and, consequently, where the effects of these activities can be felt.

Given this preamble, we may define a causal power as any quantitative property P that disposes its bearer S in certain circumstances C_0 to participate in a physical causal process $\Rightarrow$, which has the effect $E-E_0$ in circumstances C_0, where E is the actual outcome and E_0 is what the outcome would have been if P had not been operating. In general, the changes that P induces/prevents in the circumstances C_0 will depend on the measure of P. Let P_0 be the measure of P for S in the circumstances C_0. Then, since P is a causal power, P must have a law of action A that describes what it does when it acts. If there were no such law of action, there would be nothing to connect different exercises of the same causal power. Since, by hypothesis, the value of the causal power involved in transforming E_0 into E is P_0, the law of action A (P, x) for P must be one that has the effect $E-E_0$, where P = P_0, and x = C_0. That is, $E-E_0 = A (P_0, C_0)$.

This effect, it will be noted, is a function of two variables, P_0, which is the measure of the causal power in the circumstances, and C_0, which is the set of values of the relevant parameters describing the circumstances in which P is operating. (NB. E_0, which is the set of circumstances that would have obtained if P had not been operating, would often, but not always, be the same as C_0. In prevention cases, however, E_0 and C_0 would normally be different.)

To illustrate: a weight above ground level has causal powers just in virtue of the potential energy it possesses, e.g. it has the power to compress things and the power to stretch them or pull them down. Ultimately, this power is, of course, that of gravity. How the causal power of the weight affects other things depends on where it is, and how it is fixed in its position, e.g. on whether it is resting on something, or hanging from it. Suppose the weight is of magnitude W, and that this weight is hanging at the end of a wire S made of some elastic material M. An elastic material is, by definition, one that is, within limits, intrinsically disposed to resist distortion, and, if distorted, to revert back to its original shape. If a piece of such material is stretched, for example, then it will be disposed to resist being stretched, and to regain its original shape, once the stretching force is removed. Let S be of length l_0 before the weight is hung upon it. The action of hanging W from S then causes it to become extended, and (provided that the elastic limit is not exceeded) to acquire sufficient potential energy to return to its original length and cross-sectional area once the weight is removed. Let l be the extended length of S. Then the weight loses potential energy $(l-l_0)$ W, whereas the wire gains exactly this much elastic energy in the process. So, the process is a simple physical causal process, involving a direct energy transfer from the weight to the wire. And there are two causal powers involved in this process: the power to act (gravity) and the power to resist (elasticity).

The elasticity P_0 of the material of S of the wire is defined by the law of action for W on S. The effect, $(l-l_0)$, of hanging W on S and is proportional to initial length l_0, and inversely proportional to the cross-sectional area A of the wire. Thus, $(l-l_0) = W\, l_0/AP_0$

Like the laws of action of all causal powers, that for W on S is quantitative, depends on the magnitude and location of the power concerned, and involves one or more other categorical properties essentially. In this case, these other categorical properties are the original length l_0 of S, the amount $l-l_0$ by which S is extended, and the cross-sectional area A of S.

A CONJECTURE

There are two conditions that must be satisfied by all causal powers. Firstly, their instances must all have contingent locations. The active powers must act from somewhere, and the resistive ones must be properties of the object or medium that is doing the resisting. But where the things that are acting or being acted upon must always be a contingent matter. For nothing has its location necessarily. Secondly, the causal powers must all have defining laws of action—i.e. laws that spell out in detail what each causal power would dispose its bearer to do, and the circumstances in which it would be so disposed. For this is what it is to be a dispositional property. And, the causal powers are essentially dispositional.

It follows from this analysis that location is not a causal power. Firstly, the instances of location do not have contingent locations. They are locations, and where it is located, it is located necessarily. Locations are not where they are contingently, because you cannot move a location to anywhere else. Secondly, location does not have a defining law of action, i.e. a law that spells out in detail what it would dispose its bearers to do. But if location is not a causal power, plausibly the same must be true of any properties, such as spatial relations, on which the locations of things depend. I therefore speculate that what holds for locations also holds generally for all categorical properties, including all of the purely structural properties of things.

THE CASE AGAINST QUIDDITISM

The fundamentally Lockean position outlined here has been attacked on two fronts. There are strong categoricalists, who deny that there are any genuine causal powers, and strong dispositionalists, who deny that there are any real categorical properties. I have discussed the principal arguments for and against strong categoricalism elsewhere, and I shall not repeat this discussion here. The main objection to my position now appears to be coming from strong dispositionalists, who argue that (a) if the categorical properties of things had no causal powers, then we should not know about them, and (b) if the causal powers of the different categorical properties were not distinctive of them, then we should have no way of distinguishing between them. Therefore, they say, the categorical properties must all have or be distinctive causal powers, i.e. powers that would distinguish them essentially from one another. Otherwise, it is said, they would all be mere quiddities. I call this 'the argument from quidditism'.

The argument from quidditism is, at first sight, a very persuasive one. Nevertheless, it is unsound. For, as we shall see, the categorical properties of things can make a big difference, even though they neither are, nor have, any causal powers. For example, the locations of the causal powers can affect what actually occurs. One possibility, therefore, is that categorical properties are more like the locations of the instances of the causal powers than the causal powers themselves. This is the position I wish to defend.

Most of the properties we think of as categorical are ones that depend upon our being able to recognize common patterns of spatiotemporal relations. It is not my firm view that they are all dependent upon such patterns of relations. For I have no proof that this is so. But certainly a great many of them are: e.g. shape, size, orientation, speed, handedness, direction, angular separation, and so on. And, like the spatiotemporal relations upon which they depend, they are fairly clearly not causal powers. It could perhaps be argued that spatiotemporal relations are not causal powers because they are not properties. Hence, the fact that the dimension of spatiotemporality is not a causal dimension might easily be reconciled with a strong form of dispositionalism. All genuine properties, it might be said, are causal powers.

However, the properties I am calling 'categorical' are not out-of-the-way, *recherché* properties. Every law of action of every causal power refers to some of the categorical properties of the circumstances in which it may be effective, and the properties that I have listed previously are among those that are most often required to describe these circumstances. So anyone who uses the 'not really properties' defence would owe us an account of what they really are. And, to their credit, I do not know of any strong dispositionalist who has ever used this argument. The argument on which they seem to rely most heavily is the one from quidditism.

In his defence of Sydney Shoemaker's (1980) strong version of dispositional essentialism, Bird (2005) argued that what makes a property the property it is, i.e. what determines its identity, is its potential for contributing to the causal powers of the things that have it. Bird's case for this strong version was that anything weaker would condemn us to quidditism. For if there were any property whose identity did not depend on what it disposed its bearer to do, but only on what it was (quidditism), then we should, necessarily, be ignorant of it. So, Bird is evidently committed to arguing either (a) that location is a causal power, or (b) that a location has at least some causal powers essentially.

It is clear from what has already been said that location is a not causal power. It is not a causal power, because there are no laws of action of location, and the instances of location do not have locations. Nor do the specific instances of location have any causal powers essentially. If you remove all of the causal powers from any given location (and this would always seem to be a possibility), the location remains, but the causal powers do not. Therefore, it cannot be said truly that the locations of things have any causal powers essentially. Therefore, locations are all quiddities.

But, if locations are all quiddities, then so are relative locations. For the actual locations of things depend essentially on their locations relative to things whose actual locations are taken as given. That is how they are defined. And, if these relative locations had causal powers, then we could reasonably argue that the actual locations of things must also have causal powers. But we have already excluded this possibility. Therefore, relative locations neither are nor have any causal powers. Therefore, the shapes of things, which depend essentially on the relative locations of their parts, must all be quiddities too. And, if this is so, then, plausibly, the same must be true of all of the categorical properties. They must all be quiddities.

WHO'S AFRAID OF QUIDDITIES?

It is said that nowadays no one is afraid of Virginia Woolf. This may well be so. But there are plenty of people who are afraid of quiddities. They think that if the world contained any quiddities, then they would be unknown to us, and unknowable, and hence that any claim to knowledge of such things would have to be false. But this is not what follows from categorical quidditism. It just means that that the shapes, sizes, orientations etc. of things cannot be known without the mediation of the causal powers that are located within them. But since everything that we can or do know about does have causal powers, the quidditism of the categorical properties does not matter. In fact, the categorical properties have long been recognized by empiricists as being among the most directly observable of properties.

But, how could anything that does not have any effects essentially be observable? My answer is straightforward: easily. It could, like location, do so by determining where the causal powers act from, and so where their effects may be felt. The shape of an object has no effects essentially (since does not itself do anything), but it does partly determine the shape of the pattern of effects produced by the reflective powers of its surface material. For the shape of the object is one of the factors determining the spatial distribution of these powers. An unilluminated square has no visible effects. But an illuminated square does have such effects. It looks square. It is true that it does not have this effect essentially. For it is not essential to the squareness of an object that it should look square, or even that we should be capable of vision. The squareness of the object is not a source of the energy transfer processes that result in this perception. The lights that enable us to see, and the reflectivity of the various parts of the object's surface, are the sources of these. The shape only determines where the reflected light may come from. But, like location, the object's shape is inert. It is just a quiddity.

The causal powers of the lenses of our eyes produce images on our retinas of the shapes of things in our fields of vision, and the causal powers of the rod and cone cells in our retinas reproduce encoded versions of these retinal images in our occipital cortices, which, presumably, then ramify through the integrative circuits of our brains to produce conscious awareness of the shapes that we are observing. So, there is no great mystery about how we are able to know about the categorical properties of things in our environments. There would only be a mystery if there were no sources of power to illuminate the objects we see, or to reflect the light from their illumination, or if we ourselves lacked the visual or mental capacities to pass on or process the encoded information that we receive when we look at things.

There is no need, therefore, to be afraid of the categorical quiddities of nature. On the contrary, they are among the most direct objects of knowledge that we have of the world. They are not the only such objects. For the causal powers of things also give us direct knowledge of the world. They color the world that we see, provide taste to the world that we savor, material presence to the world that we feel, and so on. But this direct knowledge is much more ambiguous. The colors are normally mixtures of many different kinds of light, and the tastes are usually our overall responses to many different kinds of substances. There is no good reason, therefore, to think that all properties are causal powers. Indeed, the best explanation that we have of the content of our sense experience derives from the view that there are two kinds of properties, categorical ones, as well as causal powers.

Those who wish to say that all of the most basic properties in nature are causal powers have another reason, besides fear of quidditism, for holding their position. This is the worry they have that if any of the basic properties in the world are categorical, then many of the fundamental laws of nature, viz. those involving these properties, must be contingent—contrary to the theory of scientific essentialism. For the argument for the metaphysical necessity of the basic laws of nature derives from the thesis that the most fundamental kinds of things in nature all have dispositional properties essentially. Thus, if x is a thing of kind K, and P is an essential and dispositional property of things of this kind, then all things of the kind K must have P, and so must be intrinsically disposed to behave in the manner prescribed for things with this property in the circumstances in which P would be activated. But this argument only works, if the essential properties of the most fundamental natural kinds are all dispositional.

I used to think something like this myself. But I now see that the fundamental properties of things cannot all be dispositional, if by 'dispositional' properties we intend to refer only to causal powers. For causal powers must have categorical locations, and could not exist otherwise. Therefore, no monistic theory of properties could possibly be founded on causal powers alone.

Nevertheless, the fact that:

(a) instances of causal powers must have locations, and so are dependent on categorical properties, and

(b) the laws of action of the causal powers all involve categorical properties essentially,

does not entail that the laws of action of the causal powers are contingent. The laws do tell us how things having the various causal powers essentially must be disposed to act in circumstances of the kinds that would activate these powers. Hence, their obedience to these laws is not just a contingent matter of fact, but a metaphysical necessity.

PROPENSITIES AND MONISTIC DISPOSITIONAL ESSENTIALISM

Propensities are dispositional properties, i.e. properties whose identities depend on what they dispose their bearers to do. But, unlike the causal powers, they are unconditional, and the activities of their bearers do not depend on the circumstances of their existence. They are what might be called 'absolute' dispositional properties. Some examples are: half-lives, radioactive decay potentials, and excitation levels. These properties are certainly dispositional, but they are not causal powers, as causal powers are here defined. For the processes of radioactive decay and photo-emission are not causal processes. A substance that undergoes radioactive decay does so independently of the circumstances of its existence, and there is no describable energy transfer process that connects the radioactive particle to its decay products. At the moment of radioactive decay, an instantaneous change of state occurs, in which the decay products come immediately into being. But there are no temporally extended processes by which this change of state comes about. The gamma rays (if any) that are emitted, do not take time to get up to speed. Nor do the decay particles take time to form or be ejected once the process begins. The same is true of photo-emissions. The excited atom emits a photon and falls to a lower level of excitation. But there is no causal process by which this change of state comes about. It just happens.

Another process of this kind is that of Schrödinger wave absorption. There is a certain probability of an absorption event occurring—defined by the absolute value of the wave amplitude at the relevant point. But the change of state that occurs when a Schrödinger wave is absorbed is instantaneous, and the point of absorption is localizsed. But, as in the radio-active decay processes, there is no temporally extended process by which this change of state comes about. It just happens. According to quantum mechanical theory, the mechanism of energy transfer between systems, which is of the essence of causality, is the Schrödinger wave. Minimally, a causal process involves an emission event, an energy transference, and an absorption event. But the emission an absorption events are not themselves causal processes. They are the ingredients of such processes. Hence, the emission and absorption potentials of quantum mechanics are not causal powers, as causal powers are here understood, but something more primitive than causal powers.

In the previous section making a case against quidditism, it was argued that there cannot be a viable form of strong dispositionalism that is based on an ontology of primitive causal powers. All instances of such powers must be located, and their laws of action must depend on the categorical properties of the circumstances in which they would be active. But propensities are more primitive than causal powers, and their laws of action are independent of circumstances. Therefore, if there is a viable form of strong dispositionalism it must be one that is based somehow on an ontology of propensities. I do not see how to construct such an ontology. For, I do not see how to explain what the categorical properties might be, given such a basis. But, I cannot rule out the possibility of such a thesis one day being developed.

Meanwhile I think it is sensible to accept, at least provisionally, a less ambitious ontology that includes both causal powers and categorical properties. Strong categoricalists, such as Armstrong, imagine that they live in a world of quiddities. Their main problem is to explain what causal powers really are. For they certainly need them. Strong dispositionalists, such as Bird, imagine that they live in a world of causal powers. Their main problem is to explain how causal powers can be located. For they certainly need locations. Causal realists, like me, distinguish between categorical properties and causal powers, give a satisfactory account of both, and have the best of both worlds.

9 A Powerful Theory of Causation

Stephen Mumford and Rani Lill Anjum

THE DISPOSITIONALITY OF CAUSATION

When it comes to causation, we should think less of necessity and more of dispositionality. Others have already suggested that it should be possible to get a theory of causation from an ontology of real dispositions or powers (Harré and Madden 1975, Bhaskar 1975, Cartwright 1989, Ellis 2001, Molnar 2003: chap. 12, Martin 2007: chap. 5). Such a project is far from complete but even here we find that the key point of a dispositional theory of causation has been lacking. One of the key attractions of a dispositional theory of causation should be the claim that causes dispose towards their effects. This offers us something stronger than Humeanism, in which everything is loose and separate. Unlike many opponents of the old Hume, however, we do not want dispositionality to be reduced to necessity either for that too would be to overlook what is most important about dispositionalism. Causes do not necessitate their effects: they produce them but in an irreducibly dispositional way.

Many theories of causation assume that it must involve some kind of necessity, or that the cause must be entirely sufficient for the effect.[1] It is, however, not always clear what necessity means in this context. It is often accepted that causal processes can be prevented or interrupted and thus that any such necessity cannot be strict. In that case it is not clear what the alleged necessity adds to the notion of causation, nor how it deserves the name.

There is, though, already an older tradition that acknowledges the dispositional nature of causation. Aquinas's philosophy of nature, according to Geach (1961), is one in which causes only tend towards their effects rather than necessitating them and the view presented in this chapter is on that account neo-Aquinian.[2] Many contemporary treatments of causation follow from Hume, however, as he was traditionally understood prior to the 'New Hume' debate. Constant conjunction is there depicted as a necessary condition for causation having occurred. Dispositionalists have highlighted the weakness of constant conjunction, pointing out that there can be accidental cases that were not genuinely causal, and instead saw real dispositions as somehow imposing natural necessity on top of constant conjunction. We argue that a true dispositionalism, in contrast, is one in which a cause only tends towards its effect. For a general causal claim to be true, such as that smoking causes cancer, there need be no constant conjunction. And for particular causal claims, even if one cause indeed produced its effect, that doesn't mean it necessitated it. Something could have gotten in the way of the effect, even if it did not as a matter of fact.

CAUSAL PRODUCTION

How, one might wonder, can there be causal production unless there is necessitation? Isn't necessitation required for causation because a cause has to be sufficient for its effect; in other words, it must necessitate it? On the contrary, we maintain that the most natural account of causation is one that does not require necessitation. The issue of causal production should be seen as independent from the issue of causal necessitation for, as Collins, Hall and Paul (2004: 18) say, that would be "simply to confuse *guaranteeing* an outcome with *causing* that outcome". Perhaps some things can be guaranteed but, if that is the case, it is not causation alone that makes the guarantee: it is something more. A cause should be understood, therefore, as something that disposes towards a certain effect or manifestation. That will suffice for general causal claims. In many particular causal claims, however, there is typically also a factive element, which states that the effect actually did/does/will occur. The dispositional theory thus says in the case of particular causal claims that a cause is something that disposes towards an effect and succeeds in producing it (at least partially).

How, then, would causal production work? We offer what can be called a *threshold account* in which an effect occurs when its causes have accumulated to reach the requisite threshold. Our preference is to outline this account in terms of powers, which we believe to be the most plausible truth-makers of causal claims, but we note that other views of the truth-makers may be able to make use of the same idea. A threshold account is consistent with causes being events or facts though we think that causation has an essentially powerful nature that sits especially well with it being understood in terms of thresholds rather than necessity.[3]

Causation typically involves complexity. As Molnar says (2003: 194–98), different powers accumulate polygenically and pleiotropically to produce what we would recognize as the effect of a causal process (see Mumford 2009). That these effects are polygenic means that they are typically produced by more than one power acting together. That powers are pleiotropic means that they make the same contribution to any effect of which they are a cause. The same power always makes the same contribution, when it manifests, even though the final effect may vary according to what other powers it is operating with. Among other things, this would allow us to understand the composition of powers along the lines of vector addition, as shown in Figure 9.1 at the bottom of the page. Powers can be plotted as vectors on a one-dimensional quality space with F and G as two possible effects of the accumulated powers. F could be the property of being cold and G the property of being hot, for instance. Vectors are a useful way of modeling powers because, like powers, they have a direction—the possible manifestation the power is 'for'—and they have a strength or intensity, indicated by the length of the vector.

The threshold account of causal production states that an effect is produced when some local aggregation of operative powers reaches the requisite threshold for that effect. In other words, an effect is caused when powers have accumulated to reach the point at which that effect is triggered. However, in reaching that point, we cannot consider simply the addition of operative powers. Other powers might be subtracting from the accumulation and tending away from the requisite threshold. In striking a match, for instance, and aiming to light it, I am doing what I think needs doing for the threshold for lighting to be met. I am using a match that I already judge to be suitably empowered, with its flammable tip intact. I am trying to strike it in the right way, against a suitable surface and in the presence of oxygen. But I will also be conscious of the powers that could subtract from those I have accumulated. I will try, for example, to keep out of the wind precisely because I know that the wind could tend away from the match igniting. Powers compose additively and subtractively in the sort of way we would have to consider when calculating vectors. To calculate a final effect, we have to consider the strength and direction of each individual vector. The resultant vector *R* will be constituted by all the component vectors along the lines of vector addition (Figure 9.2, next page).[4]

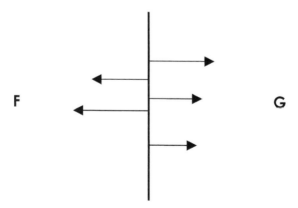

Figure 9.1 Powers modeled as vectors.

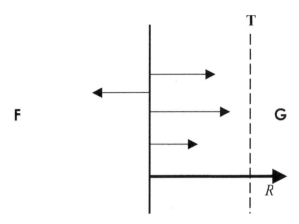

Figure 9.2   A resultant vector R that meets a threshold.

What, though, are these causal thresholds and how do they relate to effects? The threshold is not a real thing at all; it is only a way of understanding the point at which an effect occurs. Often thresholds are marked as particular points that interest us because they involve some significant or dramatic change. Water can become hotter and hotter, for instance, because of a variety of factors at work. There is, however, a significant threshold that can be passed when the water gets to 100°C because at that point the water turns from liquid to steam. In another case, pressure can be exerted on a vase and at some point the factors taken as a whole are enough to make the vase shatter. An effect need not be quite so dramatic, however. I may require simply that the water in my radiators reaches some point short of 100° but enough to keep my living room warm. The desired effect in this case is simply a comfortable room temperature.

The threshold idea of production, mixed with the idea of causes as polygenic, shows us why causal production does not require necessitation. Geach (1961: 102) provides a nice example that we can use in which the same room contains both a heating unit A, which can raise the room's temperature to 25° in an hour, but also a refrigerator unit B that can lower the room's temperature to 10° in an hour. On its own, the heater A would have enough power to raise the room temperature to 25°, and sometimes does so. But it doesn't necessitate it. It won't reach that temperature—won't reach the threshold—if the refrigerator is also on. If A alone is on, the room reaches 25° in an hour. But if A and B are both operating, the room reaches, let us suppose, only 15°. So even though the heater A in one context would have enough power for a certain effect, in another situation there is not overall enough for that same effect. Even though the unit A appears sufficient for this effect, because it actually succeeds in producing it in one situation, it cannot be the standard sufficiency as understood by philosophers because we can have another situation in which A operates but does not produce that effect. The example shows the way in which dispositionality, accumulation and subtraction are all in play when it comes to whether or not an effect is actually produced. The bare notions of necessity and causal sufficiency cannot do this justice.

CAUSES DO NOT NECESSITATE THEIR EFFECTS

What is the argument for the claim that, in general, causes do not necessitate their effects? In this section, the *argument against necessity* is advanced.

Let us call a group of polygenic causes $C_1, \ldots C_n$ and assume that there is a case in which together they produce the effect E, the match lights. Nevertheless, it can be claimed, had all of $C_1, \ldots C_n$ occurred but also some interfering condition I been present, such as a gust of wind, then E might not have occurred. We are taking I to be a real natural or physical possibility, rather than a mere logical one. This shows that $C_1, \ldots C_n$, although they caused E, were nevertheless consistent with E not occurring. Therefore, $C_1, \ldots C_n$ do not necessitate E, even if as a matter of fact they do cause E.[5]

It should be noted that the argument applies whether we are talking about the causes of an event as particulars or we are talking about type causal claims. We cannot say that causes of the types $C_1, \ldots C_n$ necessitate E if there are some instances of those types that fail to produce E. But also we cannot say that particular tokens of $C_1, \ldots C_n$ necessitated their token effect E if something could have prevented it.

The argument against necessity might immediately provoke objections. We anticipate four of them.

Objection 1

The first objection to the argument against necessity is that it works only by changing the original causal situation which, had it indeed been fully present, would after all have guaranteed the effect. Suppose, for instance, a simple case where we have just four causes of E, namely A, B, C, and D. A might be that a particular match is dry, B that it is flammable, C that there is oxygen present, and D that the match is struck. In this case A-D do in fact cause E: the match lights. But suppose I now allege that A-D might have occurred without E because, in some other situation, there is also the interference I—that the humidity is too high—which prevents E. An objection to this claim would be that this new factor, I, is really just the taking away of A because the match is no longer sufficiently dry when there is high humidity. We do not then, in this second situation, have all of A to D present because I is effectively just not-A by another name and we have thus failed to show that A to D are consistent with E not occurring.[6]

This could indeed be true in this particular instance but it does not establish that all such alleged cases of prevention are equally spurious, which is what would be needed for this objection to be successful. The genuine exception cases are those where all of the causes *A* to *D*, which in some cases succeed in producing *E*, are indeed present but *E* fails. Instead of high humidity, for instance, a strong wind might prevent the match from lightning. The wind is not a factor that is incompatible with *A-D*, that stops any of them happening or being the case, but still it interferes with *A-D* such that they fail to produce *E*. Another case that we think is clearly of this kind is that of a lumberjack felling a tree by cutting a wedge out of one side and then letting gravity take hold of it. Do the wedge and the gravity necessitate that the tree falls? Evidently not. The gravitational attraction to the Earth could still have been there, and the wedge cut out of the tree, but these are consistent with a cyclone appearing above the tree and sucking it off into the air.

Using the vector model, we can see that there is a clear distinction to be drawn between what we may call subtractive and additive interference (Figures 9.3 and 9.4). The argument against necessity is premised on the possibility of additive interference, which it seems hard to deny outright as a real possibility.

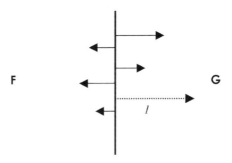

Figure 9.3   Subtractive interference (dotted vector is removed).

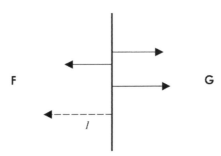

Figure 9.4   Additive interference (broken vector is added).

Objection 2

A second objection to the argument against necessity is that, as a matter of fact, there are some cases of causation where it is just absolutely impossible that there be any prevention because an effect follows a particular cause with absolute uniformity. Hume alleged a couple of causal examples of inviolable constant conjunction for instance.[7] One was that a flame would cause us to withdraw our hand. No man could "put his hand into the fire, and hold it there, till it be consumed". Another case he cites is that "A man who at noon leaves his purse full of gold on the pavement at Charing-Cross, may as well expect that it will fly away like a feather, as that he will find it untouched after an hour" (both examples 1748: VIII, 20). Contrary to Hume's claims, however, both these cases could be prevented. Some people have a condition in which they can feel no pain and would be capable of holding their hand in the flame. And even if, as a matter of fact, there were no such condition, its very possibility is enough for us to allow that such a causal claim admits the possibility of an exception. Again in the second case, there is at least the possibility that all those who pass by Charing Cross leave alone the purse for its owner's return.

An example from physics might be the case of gravitational attraction, which seems to be a universal phenomenon whose operation can never be prevented. Suppose one thought that gravity always resulted in a tendency to attract bodies. Gravity and this tendency are always conjoined with no possibility of prevention. Is this a counterexample to the claim that causes do not necessitate their effects? We argue not. It would be a misapprehension to think of gravity and the tendency as standing in a causal relation. On the contrary, gravity just is the tendency to attract bodies. What gravity, understood as such a tendency, actually causes (when it does) is the movement of bodies towards each other and whether it actually does so is obviously something that can be prevented by other powers and attractions. In the case of gravity, the constant conjunction between gravity and the tendency to attract is not indicative of causation at all but, it seems more plausible, identity.

In answer to objection 2, therefore, we argue that when we consider the world, it is clear that most causal cases admit the possibility of prevention. If there is a causal process for which there is no preventer, it seems the exception rather than the rule. And even then, it seems that we can countenance a possible preventer even if there is no actual one. To allow that is to accept that even this process does not involve necessity.

Objection 3

Might one be able to ensure the necessity of the effect by just including more? Might it be that as well as all the positive factors in the effect, all of C_1, ... C_n, part of the cause is also that all the possible interfering factors are ruled out? Burks made this move in defending the sufficiency of the cause for the effect, for example, stating that "By 'sufficient conditions' we mean a set of conditions, complete with respect to negative properties as well as positive ones (*i.e.*, counteracting causes must be explicitly mentioned)" (1951: 368). Hence, the cause, as well as C_1, ... C_n, includes $\neg I_1$, $\neg I_2$, and so on. Let us call this complete set of circumstances, both positive and negative, the set Σ. Is it the case, as Burks supposed, that Σ necessitates the effect in question, E? We can see immediately that it does not. The problem is that precisely the same argument can be applied to Σ. Although it may perfectly well produce E on any number of occasions, that does not mean that it necessitated E. There could have been Σ plus one other counteracting power, I_Σ, that prevents E. There is no reason to think that the possible interfering factors are of finite extent such that they could all be listed. And even if, as a matter of fact, interferers are of finite extent in actuality, to prove that Σ necessitates E requires that there is not even some physically *possible* I_Σ that can prevent E. There seems to be no plausible reason to rule out some such thing (though we will consider an attempt under the next objection). Rather, we should conclude from this that there is no Σ that could serve as a 'sufficient condition' for E even though Σ does indeed produce E.

It can also be noted here that if strictly there are no sufficient conditions for an effect then there are no INUS conditions either. Mackie famously characterized a cause as "an *insufficient* but *necessary* part of a condition which is itself *unnecessary* but *sufficient* for the result" (1965: 34). No matter how big and complex the total cause is, it would never be sufficient for its effect in the sense that it is impossible to have Σ without E.

Objection 4

Could it be said that attempting to mention all the causes of E in a finite list such as Σ is both misguided and not what we actually do when we pick out a cause of an effect? Isn't it the case that when we identify a cause of some effect, we automatically rule out any additional factors that might interfere with it?

There are a number of mechanisms for doing so. One would be idealized models where we abstract away from interfering factors and consider the causal process in isolation. But this, of course, can be no more than an abstraction and should not be mistaken for the actual causal scenarios as they play out in the world. There is, however, a real world correlate to abstraction, which is the case of 'screening off' (Cartwright 1999: chap. 3), where in some carefully controlled experiment we put up barriers to possible interferers. Armstrong's totality facts (2004: 57 ff.) would also serve this purpose as they are the higher-order facts that there are no more first-order facts. These could be used to stop the addition of anything further to Σ. Another suggestion might be that because we are surrounded by successful cases, where some particular set of causes does indeed produce an effect, we are able to refer to that cause, complex though it may be, ostensively. Employing externalist semantics, we might then always have this kind of causal situation in mind and thus as the reference of future causal attributions.[8] Finally, there would be a Lewisian kind of constraint (Lewis 1973a, 1986b) that in assessing causal claims we should consider only the closest possible worlds, which are worlds in which interferers such as I are ruled out as gratuitous differences from the actual world. All these solutions would purportedly work by picking out an exact kind of total circumstance, to which nothing could be added, that is successful for the production of E and thus, it would seem, sufficient for E. Let us call such a total circumstance, Σ^*.

If this kind of proposal is to add any more to those already discussed and dismissed, it is because it would have some automatic exclusion of any further preventers such as I_Σ. But then would the proposal really have established that Σ^* necessitates E? We should be skeptical of that. How would we know that circumstances of type Σ^* necessitate E? That would have to mean at least that every case of Σ^*, both actual and possible, is followed by E. How would we know that E always does follow? To say so is to assume the very thesis that we deny, that Σ^* necessitates E, and would thus be begging the question. Σ^* thus has no power to defeat the argument against necessity. It merely denies it.

The major reason this approach ultimately fails is that it 'works' by excluding one of the few things that could convince us of the presence of necessity. The 'solution' tries to automatically rule out anything being added to the successful causal set up of Σ that might block E. But then it automatically excludes one of the most reliable, this-worldly tests we have of necessity, namely, antecedent strengthening. When we want to know whether A necessitates B, where B on its own is not already necessary, one plausible test is to consider whether B would still be the case, given A, no matter what else happens. So if A is followed by B, *even if* C, D, and no matter what else, then that is a good reason to believe that A necessitates B. For example, we might think it necessary that 'if x is human, then x is mortal' because we could strengthen the antecedent in any way we wanted and we would still get a true conditional. 'If x is human and ϕ, then x is mortal' remains true for any ϕ. Therefore, it would only be non-question begging to say that Σ^* necessitates E if we could add something else, I^*, to Σ^* and still get E. But this is the very move that is supposed to be ruled out by this strategy as a way of avoiding the argument that this I^* could prevent E.

WHAT IF DETERMINISM IS TRUE?

It may be objected to the account that we are assuming too much in an essentially a priori consideration of causation. In particular, are we assuming in our theory that causal determinism is false and thereby deciding a priori on a thesis that may be an a posteriori matter? What, for instance, if physics were to tell us eventually that the whole history of the universe was determined? If the truth or falsity of determinism is an a posteriori matter, then no philosophical account of causation should rule it out.[9] How should we respond?

In the first place, it should be noted that causal necessitarianism—the thesis that causes necessitate their effects—is not the same thing as determinism. One could accept that all causes necessitated their effects without being a determinist simply if one accepted that some events are uncaused. Determinism would require, therefore, that not only do all causes necessitate their effects but also that all events are caused. This shows that causal necessitarianism does not entail determinism.

But does determinism entail causal necessitarianism? We have argued that causes should be understood as disposing towards their effects and that because dispositions can be prevented from manifesting, they should therefore be understood as not necessitating their effects. If causal determinism is true, however, everything that happens is causally fixed by what has happened earlier. But this would still be consistent with the possibility that any individual causal process can be prevented, and in that sense the argument against the necessity of effects stands. There is still a very real sense in which any causal process can be naturally prevented. The determinist, however, would then have to say that where an individual, token causal process is prevented, it was determined that it was so prevented. What did the preventing, according to the powers theorist, will always be a countervailing power. What has been said of necessity applies also to this countervailing power. Although its actual effect is to prevent a certain process, our countervailing power could itself have been prevented from operating and in that sense did not necessitate its effect. The causal determinist again will say that whether or not it does so—whether or not something else prevents it—is an entirely determined matter.

If this kind of determinism is true, then everything that happens naturally is fixed, including which causal processes are prevented and which are not. This brings necessity in the sense that nothing could have been different. It is a very strong claim, however. There would be no probabilistic causation at all. Were we to be told on a posteriori grounds that the world is indeed this way, we would beat a tactical retreat to a position in which the possibility that things could have been different would be either purely logical, metaphysical or epistemic. It could no longer count as a natural possibility. Yet there would also be enough of our core argument that remained. Any individual causal process could still have been prevented had things been different and by our lights is thus not necessary. In that sense, causation is not necessary. What brings the necessity is the fixity of everything else: all the background conditions and processes are set so that it is determined what causes what. With Anscombe, it cannot be derived simply from the concept of causation that the world is like that.

> "If A comes from B, this does not imply that every A-like thing comes from some B-like thing or set-up or that every B-like thing or set-up has an A-like thing coming from it; or that given B, A had to come from it, or that given A, there had to be B for it to come from. Any of these may be true, but if any is, that will be an additional fact, not comprised in A's coming from B" (Anscombe 1971: 136).

The deterministic assumption has to be added and cannot be derived merely from the notion of causal production alone. The notion of causal production developed in the section 'Causal production' is consistent both with determinism and indeterminism and it seems quite correct that any theory of causation should be likewise open to both possibilities.

PROBABILISTIC CAUSATION

The thesis that causes do not necessitate their effects has thus far been independent of an assumption of indeterminism and also of probabilistic causation. The thesis does not rest on such things. Nevertheless, probabilistic causation has to be acknowledged as a possible kind of causation that may indeed occur and even be widespread according to some theories. It is relatively easy to understand probabilistic cases once one accepts the essentially dispositional nature of causation.

By probabilistic causation we do not mean completely random chance events, which may best be described as uncaused. Rather, we mean causation that is chancy yet probabilistically constrained. Let us assume, as a model of such causation, a coin that when tossed has a 50:50 chance of landing heads or tails. Not all probabilistic causes of course have only two outcomes: a dice roll has six. And not all probabilities are equal: a loaded coin may have a disposition to land heads more frequently than tails. The simplest case, however—two outcomes with equal probability—contains all the features we need.

Our preference would be a propensity interpretation of this kind of probabilistic chance (see Mellor 1971). The propensity interpretation makes it sensible to ascribe a chance to an individual coin toss instead of talking about frequencies but also, according to the dispositional ontology, any truths about what is most likely for a whole group of coin tosses would ultimately rest on the dispositions of the individual coins. A probabilistic disposition could be plotted as a single double-headed vector, disposing partly towards F and partly towards G (see Figure 9.5, next page). A 50:50 propensity will point to both in equal measure but other propensities could point more towards one outcome than another.

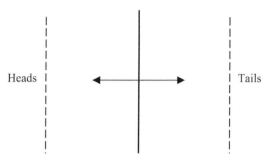

Figure 9.5   A probabilistic case with two possible, equally likely, outcomes.

It is important that this be a single, probabilistic disposition rather than two distinct dispositions. This would explain, for instance, why the combined probabilities must always add up to one. It would be a disposition for a certain distribution between possible outcomes, where all such outcomes comprise a single whole. The single, double-headed vector also distinguishes this kind of power from a regular, non-probabilistic one. Once a probabilistic power is involved, the rules of the game for vector addition are changed. A resultant can still be calculated, but now more than ever it needs to be understood that the resultant only disposes towards that outcome. If at least one probabilistic power is involved, then there remains a chance of other possible outcomes.

Understanding irreducibly probabilistically constrained causation is not easy unless one accepts that it involves a dispositional connection that is neither entirely necessary nor entirely contingent. Our coin tends towards a 50:50 distribution, but in a sequence of trials there could be any distribution of heads and tails. We know that an actual 50:50 distribution is unlikely, especially when the number of trails is low. But we also know that if the number of trials is high then a distribution wildly at odds with an equal distribution is highly unlikely. There is a principle of probabilistic distribution that, applied to this case, says that the proportion of heads and tails will tend to 50:50 as the number of tosses tends to infinity; or, the higher the number of tosses then the closer to 50:50 the distribution is likely to be. This principle is appealing and yet we might wonder why it is true. Is it just some brute fact about the world or does it have a truth-maker? The powers theory offers a truth-maker for the principle. The coin has a tendency to land heads and tails with equal chance, a tendency which manifests itself over a sequence of trails. But this is 'only' a disposition towards such a distribution. It does not necessitate it, as we know when we acknowledge that any actual distribution is possible for any sequence of tosses. Yet the distribution is not entirely contingent either, as we know when we acknowledge that distributions at variance widely from 50:50 are unlikely, proportionate to the number of trails.

The case of probabilistically constrained causation thus corroborates our account. It is noteworthy in so far as the account seems to accord entirely with what we already accept pre-theoretically to be the data of chancy causes.

CAUSATION BY ABSENCE?

A theory in which causation is essentially dispositional suggests the onto-logical reality of powers and that causation occurs when powers manifest themselves. In that case, causation could look like the passing around of powers (see Mumford 2009). There is an objection to this, and to many similar theories of causation, that sometimes causes are absences, such as when lack of water causes a plant to die or the lack of a nail causes a horseshoe to come loose (see Schaffer 2004). Were there to be causation by genuine absences, that is, by nothing at all, then it would indeed seem to create a problem for the present account. Absences are nothing and how can *nothing* have causal powers?[10] Powers, like properties, must be instan-tiated by something.

It is not, however, necessary to invoke absences as real causes. Why they are sometimes invoked as such can be explained and justified by the powers theory. The solution we offer to this difficulty resembles that of Dowe (2001) though with powers at its centre. The claim would be that all cases of genuine causation involve the manifestations of dispositions. Where an absence is invoked, what we have in mind is a counterfactual that the effect would not have occurred had the removed or absent power been present. In Figure 9.6 below, for instance, power *b* is removed, such as when I stop watering my plant. When *b* was present, the plant was in balance, disposing overall neither to death by drowning (F) nor death by dehydration (G). Once we remove the water, it now disposes towards death by dehydration, but note that what kills the plant is the remaining pow-ers, *c* and *d*. The surrounding atmosphere had the power, for instance, to suck moisture out of the roots, soil and leaves. This power is operative on the plant and leads to its death. The absent water does nothing. The the-sis that all causation involves the exercise of powers could therefore still remain. Considering the vector model, however, we can see that had the water been present, the plant would not have dehydrated, which is why its absence is explanatorily useful.

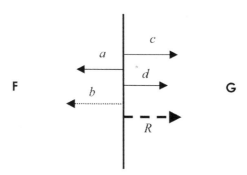

Figure 9.6   Causation 'by absence.'

WHERE HUME REALLY WENT WRONG

Hume's account of causation has proved immensely seductive to such an extent that even those who would refute him have nevertheless accepted many of his starting assumptions. Hume produced an objection for his opponents, to those who believed that there were real causal powers and that causation was something more than constant conjunction. They, Hume insisted, were people who believed in a "necessary connexion" (1739: 77). This move was made with little ceremony as follows:

> "[W]e must be able to place this power in some particular being, and conceive that being as endow'd with a real force or energy, by which such a particular effect necessarily results from its operation. We must distinctly and particularly conceive the connexion betwixt the cause and effect, and be able to pronounce, from a simple view of the one, that it must be follow'd or preceded by the other" (1739: 161).

But he was then able to argue that

> "Such a connexion wou'd amount to a demonstration, and wou'd imply the absolute impossibility for the one object not to follow, or to be conceiv'd not to follow upon the other" (1739: 161–2).

There was no such thing, he concluded.

We have used the same argument as Hume but against the claim that causal production entails causal necessitarianism. However, it would be a mistake to acquiesce in Hume's characterization of powers. Those who believe in real causal powers should not at all accept that they involve necessary connections between events. Hume has effectively wrong-footed his opponents, saddling them with a position they should never and need never adopt. Realists about dispositions have long rejected the so called conditional analysis of dispositions (see especially Martin 1994). But they have not yet been as ready to reject a necessitarian version of the same view: that a disposition ascription means that if a certain stimulus occurs then a certain effect will be necessitated. Just as much, this is an attempt to reduce the dispositional to something else, supposedly more familiar. Anti-Humeans should instead believe in causal connections that are short of necessity, yet more than contingent. This connection is anti-Humean enough, but we should not be misled by his talk of necessity to go further than we ought. The main point is that dispositionality has an important, real, and irreducible modal force of its own. Any attempt to replace it with something non-dispositional will miss the most important thing about dispositionality and, as we argue here, causation.

Indeed, we think that Hume was also incorrect to think that constant conjunction was a part of the notion of causation.[11] That we experience the kind of constant conjunction that Hume had in mind is a dubious claim. Even in his perfect instance of causation, the billiard table (1740: 137), it is implausible that an absolute constant conjunction is really to be found. The object ball that is struck, he claims, always moves away across the table towards the pocket. It never flies into the air, he protests. But we know that there are cases where it does precisely that: where there is an unexpected 'kick' of the kind feared by professional snooker players.

The possibility of exceptions is something that Hume admits when he considers cases where there are only "inferior degrees of evidence" (1739: 403) of causation. But of cases where there is a less than constant conjunction he surmises that

> "supposing that the usual contrariety proceeds from the operation of contrary and conceal'd causes, we conclude, that the chance or indifference lies only in our judgement on account of our imperfect knowledge, not in the things themselves, which are in every case equally necessary, tho' to appearance not equally constant or certain" (1739: 403–4).

Such cases, we argue, are the norm, not the exception. What they show is that constant conjunction, contrary to what Hume elsewhere routinely claims, is not a part of our immediate experience. Instead, constant conjunction is something that is inferred from our experience of less than constant conjunction. And as the previously quoted passage reveals, that inference is of a highly theoretical nature. It would seem that it is motivated by nothing more than an assumption that wherever there is an exception to a constant conjunction it is because there is some other constant conjunction at work, of which we are ignorant. Having made that assumption, Hume then immediately goes back to his usual claim that the idea of cause and effect arise from "the experience and the observation or their constant union" (1739: 405). We urge that a true consideration of the situation shows that *constant union* is not something that confronts our experience of causation. The union, we argue, is always less than constant and is instead of what Hume calls *inferior* degrees. Where it is not inferior, we argue the union is most likely not causal but rather something else such as classification, essence or identity. The assumption that there is always a concealed constant union at work in causation therefore looks under-motivated.

CONCLUSION

We hope to have shown in this chapter that causal production is not the same as causal necessitation. This claim should be no threat to our pre-existing causal thinking. All that has been advanced should be consistent with common sense. The idea that causes dispose towards their effects is natural and makes sense of certain phenomena that by other theories will be philosophically problematic. The dispositional theory of causation shows that the possibility of preventions and exceptions is not something that has to be explained away but something that should be accepted as central to the nature of causation, showing its essentially dispositional character.

A cause can then be understood as a disposition towards an effect, where causal powers are doing their work and manifesting themselves. This is what we think should be basic to a dispositional theory of causation and we take to be a promising this-worldly alternative to Lewis counterfactual dependence account of causation. Assessing whether this or the counterfactual dependence account is the best theory of causation could be done only after careful consideration of the relative merits of each and while we are optimistic about how the dispositional theory would come out of such a consideration, we will leave that work for elsewhere.

ACKNOWLEDGEMENTS

Earlier versions of this chapter were presented at the Metaphysics of Science workshop in Münster, Germany, the Powers, Causation & Laws conference at Durham University, the Nottingham dispositions group, the University of Köln, the University of Athens, Bogazici University, the Powers, Dispositions and Singular Causation conference in Buffalo and the University of Warsaw. We thank all who gave comments. This research was conducted with the financial support of the AHRC-funded Metaphysics of Science project and the Norwegian Research Council (NFR). We also thank Manuel de Pineda, Markus Schrenk, Matthew Tugby, and Charlotte Matheson for helpful support and criticism.

NOTES

1. Examples are too numerous to list in full but for one contemporary instance see Sosa: "What there is in common to all forms of causation is, it appears, necessitation" (Sosa: 1980: 241). Historical examples are to be found in Aristotle, *Metaphysics* IX 5, Spinoza 1677 I, ax. iii: 46, Kant 1781 book II, chap. II, sec iii, second analogy, Mill 1843: III, V, sec 6, Russell 1913: 2, Ducasse 1924: 55, Davidson 1967: 698, Popper 1972: 91 and Mackie 1980: 62.
2. Aquinas uses the terms *inclinatio* and *appetitus*. See Geach 1961: 101.
3. Empiricists tend to prefer events as the relata of causal relations while Mellor (1995) argues that the relata are facts. Either view is consistent with a threshold account.
4. The understanding of causation along the lines of vector addition appears in Cartwright (1983: 59; 1989: 163), though she rejects it on various grounds. She does not think that forces in the world, for instance, literally add. She thinks that only resultant forces are real because they can be measured. In contrast, she thinks that component forces have no separate existence

because if they did there would be a systematic over-determination. Cart-wright's view, applied directly to powers, is rejected in Mumford and Anjum (forthcoming).

5. A precedent for the argument is to be found in Schrenk (2008). It is also deployed by Hume (1739: 161) against the powers view, though we argue in §7 that it works against powers only when they are misconceived. The argu-ment also bears similarities to Bird's (1998) antidote case, where we could call *I* an antidote to the disposition(s) that would produce *E*.

6. Our thanks to Maria Jose Encinas for developing this line of objection.

7. Both these examples occur when Hume tries to show that we (people) are as much subject to causation as inanimate matter. If constant conjunction could be shown for the most difficult case of persons, even with their apparent free will to resist it, then it would seem also established for inanimate matter.

8. Such a suggestion has been made to us by Matthew Tugby, following an idea of Alexander Bird's.

9. Thanks to Stephen Barker for raising this point.

10. One might of course try to defend the line that an absence can have causal powers. David Lewis's (2004) deadly void, for instance, might have a causal power to kill, but we do not think it is necessary to make this move to account for such cases.

11. We believe that Hume's condition of temporal priority was also a mistake. We do not think that causes precede their effects but that they are simultane-ous with them. We have not the space to discuss this claim in detail here.

10 Causation and the Manifestation of Powers

Alexander Bird

It is widely agreed that many causal relations can be regarded as dependent upon causal relations that are in some way more basic. For example, knocking down the first domino in a row of one hundred dominoes will be the cause of the hundredth domino falling. But this causal relation exists in virtue of the knocking down of the first domino causing the falling of the second domino, and so forth. In such a case, A causes B in virtue of there being intermediate events $I_1 \ldots I_n$ such that A causes I_1, I_1 causes I_2, $\ldots$, I_{n-1} causes I_n, and I_n causes B. Cases of this sort include my putting my foot on the brake causing the car to slow, the smoke from a fire causing the fire brigade to be alerted, and so forth. In other cases the more basic causal relations may not be inter-mediate (or at least it is debatable that they are). My seeing that it is raining may cause me to want to stay inside, and this causal relation depends upon more basic causal relations among various components of my brain. But it does not seem possible to analyze this in terms of my perception causing cer-tain brain events, which cause other brain events, which eventually cause my desire. Rather it seems as if the principal causal relation, between perception and desire, is constituted, rather than mediated, by the more basic causal rela-tions in the brain. The same is true of the operation of the dynamo causing the current to flow. Again there are not intermediate events, but rather the causal relation between them is constituted by the motion of the charged particles in the wires moving though a magnetic field, which causes an electric field, which causes the charges to move in the wire.

There are thus at least two kinds of complex causal relation: the chain kind and the constitution kind. If we wish to understand causation, we need to understand the basic causal relations, at least as found in the chain kind. That is, to understand what it is for A to cause B when the latter is a causal relation of the chain kind, requires understanding what it is for the intermediate, basic causal relations to hold. In the case of a complex causal relation of the constitution kind, it is may be that understanding what it is for A and B to be causally related does *not* require understanding what it is for the constituting causal relations to hold. For a complex causal relation of the constitution kind may be itself regarded as basic relative to its own level of explanation.

This kind of distinction is implicit in David Lewis's account of causation (Lewis 1973a), according to which there is a basic causal relation, counterfactual dependence, and that the general causal relation is the ancestral of this basic one: A causes B when A and B are related by a chain of basic causal (counterfactual dependence) relations. However, Lewis's motivation for this approach does not arise from the sorts of consideration given before but from the fact that counterfactual dependence fails to be a general account of causation thanks to the problem of pre-emption. Another motivation is the conviction that causation is transitive. Lewis ensures this by making causation the ancestral of counterfactual dependence.

* * *

What is the motor or cement of the universe? In David Armstrong's metaphysics it is the laws of nature (Armstrong 1983). For Lewis (1973b), there is a sense in which nothing is—all there is at the bottom is the Humean mosaic. Out of the latter he constructs the laws of nature, thence counterfactuals, thence causation. A third approach regards potencies (powers, essentially dispositional properties) as providing the ontological foundation. These different views *could* all agree on the analysis of causation—for example by agreeing with Lewis's analysis in terms of counterfactuals; arguably they might also agree on the analysis of counterfactuals in terms of possible worlds and laws ('and laws' because laws play a central role in determining the proximity of possible worlds). The different metaphysical views would then disagree on the analysis of lawhood: second order relations of necessitation; systematizations of the Humean mosaic; regularities generated by the potencies. However, one might wonder whether a more direct approach would be possible, identifying causation more directly with activity of the underlying ontology.

Consider then the ontology of potencies. Such entities are properties that are dispositional (and essentially so). Thus they are disposed to yield a manifestation in response to some stimulus. The fragile vase is disposed to break when struck, the elastic piece of rubber stretches readily when pulled. Wheras fragility and elasticity may or may not be parts of our basic ontology, these properties illustrate the relation of disposition to manifestation and to stimulus. Furthermore, these examples seem to indicate a causal relation: the striking of the vase caused it to break, the pulling on the rubber band caused it to stretch. So one simple proposal for an account of causation is as follows:

(SD) A causes B when A is the stimulus of some disposition and B is the corresponding manifestation.

Let us call this the simple dispositional analysis of causation.

The simple dispositional analysis of causation has interesting features. Given the presence of the dispositions and the absence of any interferers (finks and antidotes), the stimulus *suffices* for the effect. This sufficiency of, is a subjunctive kind (were the cause to occur, the effect would occur), and so has modal force, but less than full metaphysical necessitation. Nonetheless, this subjunctive sufficiency of causes for their effects does mean that (in this subjunctive way) causes necessitate their effects. The latter is a plausible idea—causes make their effects happen—but it is an idea that has been largely ignored in recent literature, which has concentrated on the Humean idea developed by Lewis that rather than being sufficient for their effects, causes are (counterfactually) necessary for their effects.

The counterfactual approach to causation has counterintuitive consequences, e.g. that the Big Bang is the cause of everything, that my birth is the cause of my death, that my being fed as a child is a cause of this chapter being written, and so forth. The simple dispositional account avoids such consequences, since the first event in each pair is not a stimulus to a disposition whose manifestation is the second event: I did not have the disposition to write the chapter in response to the stimulus of being fed earlier in life. Thus while the counterfactual approach makes no distinction between cause and condition, regarding our natural inclination to make such a distinction as explicable in terms of a pragmatic difference, the dispositional account respects a genuine difference: when the smoke sets off the fire alarm, the smoke is the cause whereas the presence of the alarm is just the condition, which corresponds to the fact that the smoke is the stimulus to the disposition of the fire alarm to sound when smoke is detected.

*   *   *

The simple dispositional account thus has certain advantages, which I elaborate on elsewhere. I shall now indicate a problem with the account. Dispositions can be mimicked: I strike an iron pot; attached to the iron pot is a bomb, which explodes just as I strike, destroying the pot. It looks as if the pot is fragile, although it is not. For this example is is not even required that the striking cause the detonation of the bomb; they may be entirely coincidental. Now consider that the same scenario might occur, even with a fragile glass vase. I strike the vase. It is fragile. It shatters. But the cause of the shattering is not my striking, it is the bomb. So it looks as if we can have a scenario where some x is disposed to manifest Mx in response to stimulus Sx, stimulus Sx occurs, manifestation Mx occurs, but Sx is not the cause of Mx.

One response to the situation described in the previous paragraph is to focus on the details of the processes involved in the manifestation of a disposition. In the case where a striking does cause a fragile vase to shatter, there is a chain of cause and effect between striking and shattering, involving a certain pattern of stress originating at the point of striking which leads to small fractures, then to larger ones, which eventually join up, resulting in the shattering. In such a case the disposition has an underlying physical basis; that physical basis is ready to undergo the process described, when is activated by the stimulus. In the case where the bomb causes the shattering, this process might start but is superseded by a distinct pattern of causation starting from the bomb. Therefore one might distinguish the first case from the second by requiring that each stage in the process that is the activation and playing out of the underlying basis of the disposition is completed.

While that answer may be satisfactory as far as it goes, it is insufficient, since the same problem might arise with basic dispositions which have no complex causal basis. Such basic dispositions or powers are simple properties, not constituted by any complex of properties. As a result the response of the previous paragraph has no purchase. But, arguably, the same problem may arise. If two distinct basic dispositions may have the same manifestation (as seems plausible) then we might have a situation where both dispositions receive their stimuli, but the manifestation is the effect of only one of these. Yet we cannot distinguish between the two dispositions on the basis of one having a complex basis that is fulfilled and the other having a complex basis that is only partially fulfilled., since neither has a complex basis. The case is similar to that of trumping preemption, due to Jonathan Schaffer (2000: 165):

> SPELL: It is a law that the first spell cast on any given day is enacted at midnight. At 1200 Merlin casts a spell to turn the prince into a frog and at 1800 Morgana casts a spell also to turn the prince into a frog. At 2400 the prince becomes a frog.

As the law dictates, the midnight transformation of the prince is an effect of Merlin's spell, not Morgana's. Schaffer specifies that the spell works directly, without intermediary events. Hence one cannot distinguish between Merlin's spell and Morgana's on the basis specified in the preceding paragraph. Schaffer shows that such examples reveal inadequacies in the counterfactual approach to causation, since it is false that had Merlin not cast his spell, the prince would not have become a frog (since Mogana's spell would have done the job). The problem for the dispositional account is different. Both spells have the power to transform the prince; both are enacted by the wizards; the manifestation appropriate to both occurs. Yet the manifestation (the transformation) is the effect of only one.

One might hold that SPELL is also a counterexample to the dispositional account, since in Morgana's case we have a manifested disposition without causation. To respond to this problem precisely it will help to get clearer about what the disposition and stimulus are. One possibility is that the disposition is a power belonging to the sorcerer, so each of Merlin and Morgana has the power to turn the prince into the frog, the stimulus of which is the uttering of the spell. In this case we can say that Morgana's power was *not* manifested; the appropriate event occurs, but not as a manifestation of *her* magical power. The correct conclusion to draw is that a disposition can receive its stimulus and an appropriate event of the manifestation-type will occur, without that event being a manifestation of that disposition-token. (In effect we have a combination of an antidote (mask) to the disposition plus a mimic, as in the case of the fragile vase with bomb attached, considered earlier in this section.) Thus Morgana's power is no counterexample to (SD) so long as we interpret (SD) to mean that the effect event, B, is in fact a manifestation of *that* disposition, not merely an event of the manifestation-type.

Alternatively, the disposition in question is a disposition of the prince to turn into a frog, in response to the spell being uttered. In this case the changing of the prince into a frog is indeed a manifestation of that disposition. But it is not a manifestation in response to Morgana's utterance, but rather in response to Merlin's utterance. So (SD) and (SD') need further to be understood such that B is a manifestation-token of that disposition *in response to A*.

What SPELL and examples like it *do* show is the following: there is a difference between in fact being the manifestation-token of that disposition-token and merely being an event of the manifestation-type in terms of counterfactual or subjunctive conditionals. Likewise there is a difference between a disposition being manifested in response to this stimulus-token rather than that stimulus-token, so that only one really simulates the disposition. The discussion of SPELL shows that SPELL shows that we cannot account for such differences in terms of counterfactual or subjunctive conditionals. The conclusion we must draw, in my view, is that the relation 'Mx is the manifestation of disposition Dx in response to stimulus Sx' is ontologically basic and is not reducible.

*   *   *

Now let us return to the idea that there are basic causal relations and complex ones. Consider:

> DOMINOES: A row of one hundred dominoes has been set up so that the knocking down of the first domino causes the second domino to fall, causing the third to fall, . . . , causing the hundredth to fall.

The knocking down of the first domino caused the falling of the hundredth. Is there a disposition somewhere such that the knocking of the first is the stimulus and the falling of the hundredth is the manifestation? Arguably the row of dominoes taken as a whole has such a disposition. But one might also think that there are cases of complex causation where it is less plausible to attribute a single disposition:

SPILLED TEA: My elbow knocks over my cup of tea; the tea runs between the cracks in the floorboards; it shorts the lighting circuit; that trips the fuse; the lights go out in the kitchen.

So, it might be claimed, my moving my elbow caused the lights to go out in the kitchen; but one might be disinclined to say that there was a disposition for the lights to go out in response to my moving my elbow. Such a case is a counterexample to the simple dispositional analysis of causation.

It seems at least defensible to reject the causal claim here, and to retain the simple dispositional analysis. Is it really that clear that the movement of the elbow caused the lights to go out? Such a claim seems less intuitively assertible, that that the movement of the elbow caused the tea to spill, that the spilling of the tea caused tea to run between the floorboards, that the tea between the floorboards caused a short-circuit, and so forth. In 1879 Lt. John Rothery survived the battle of Isandlwana, at one point avoiding death by ducking to avoid a Zulu assegai. In 2008 his great-great-grandson writes an article about causation. A chain of causes therefore links the two events; nonetheless it seems distinctly odd to say that ducking an assegai in 1879 is the cause of the writing of the paper in 2008. The transitivity of causation is far from obvious, despite Ned Hall's assertions to the contrary (Hall 2004: 181). There are other well-known counterexamples in the literature (see McDermott 1995 for several cases). The general structure of many such counterexamples is that A causes B, where the function of B is precisely to negate the consequences of A-like events by causing C. Since C is incompatible with the continuation of A, A is generally not a plausible cause of C. For example (note that nothing in the example depends on the final outcome being an absence:

WASTEBASKET FIRE: A fire in a wastebasket causes the sprinkler system to operate, thus preventing (causing the absence of) a conflagration.

But the fire in the wastebasket is hardly a cause of the lack of conflagration. It strikes me therefore that there is ample room for simply denying the transitivity of causation. In which case we may hold that the movement of my elbow does not cause the lights to go out, and this parallels the lack of a dispositional connection between them. More generally one might suppose that our reluctance to ascribe causation in cases of chains of causes arises when one is reluctant to regard that chain as belonging to a single structure that could be regarded as the bearer of a disposition. In the case of the dominoes, they are set up precisely so that there will be a chain from the first domino to the last, and so is seen as a single system. Long separated historical events are not parts of one single system or structure. Events such as the wastebasket fire and the non-conflagration are most obviously not parts of the same system, since the first lowers the chance of the second.

Note that in this case these events can be seen as components of overlapping systems: the sprinkler system has the wastebasket fire as its trigger; it also has the non-conflagration as its effect.

David Lewis (1973a) builds transitivity into his account of causation: the causal relation is the ancestral of the counterfactual dependency relation. One of the principal attractions of transitivity for Lewis is the fact that it allows him to escape certain pre-emption counterexamples to regarding causation as identical with counterfactual dependence. As a reason for favoring transitivity, this seems *ad hoc*, although Lewis does later give a defense (Lewis 2000). Nonetheless, if one does hold that it is clear that in SPILLED TEA the movement of the elbow caused the lights to go out, then one ought to make the parallel move to Lewis's, to regard causation as the stimulus—manifestation relation referred to in (SD), thus making our account of causation:

> (SD') A causes B when there is a sequence of dispositions $D_1, \ldots, D_n$ such that for each D_i and D_{i+1}, the manifestation of the former is the stimulus to the latter, and A is the stimulus of D_1 and B is the manifestation of D_n.

Thus in SPILLED TEA we can say the the first event caused the last, since the position of the cup was such that it was disposed to fall if I moved by elbow, the gaps between the floorboards was such that they were disposed to let tea run between them if spilled, and so forth.

* * *

In the last section we saw two approaches to SPILLED TEA. Either one could deny that there is causation between the first and last event, holding that there is causation only between the neighboring events in the sequence and that this is not transitive. Or one could hold that there is a causal relation between the first and last events, in addition those causal relations between the neighboring events, and that causation is transitive. Either way, our focus must now be on the component or basic causal relations, those which the dispositional approach, whether as (SD) or as (SD'), holds are to be understood as the stimulus and manifestation of a disposition. For these (SD) gives the right answer. But does it provide any insight into causation? Furthermore, we saw as a result of considering SPELL that the stimulus-disposition-manifestation relation must itself be considered basic and metaphysically unanalyzable, and so additional insight cannot be provided by further analysis of the right hand side of (SD).

One might argue that (SD) provides no insight into the nature of (at least basic) causal relations. We wanted to understand the causal relation but have just replaced it with the stimulus-disposition-manifestation relation. The latter is very much the same sort of thing as the causal relation, so we don't seem to have moved much further forward. And if anything the stimulus-disposition-manifestation relation is less well understood than the causal relation.

If what one wants from an analysis of causation is a reduction of the concept of causation in simpler, more familiar terms, then (SD) does not provide such a thing. Indeed, aspiring to such a thing seems rather a forlorn hope. What could be more basic or familiar than causation? Indeed, there is evidence that the concept of causation is innate, or that we are primed to acquire it very early on in life, within months at most. So even if there is a respectable philosophical task of conceptual analysis, causation does not look like the sort of concept that is going to get analyzed in other terms. (This is a point made very effectively by Michael Rota (2009).) The only context in which the analysis of causation looks like a sensible project is one where one is laden with the baggage of empiricist assumptions about the nature of concepts: that all our concepts are ultimately derived from experience, and causation is not the sort of thing one can experience. Against that background it makes sense to find concepts which do derive directly from experience, and to try to analyze the concept of causation in terms of those. But if one does not share such empiricist presumptions, one has no reason to reject the thought that among our concepts, the concept of causation is about as basic as one can get.

The task of metaphysical analysis is a different matter. One might gain metaphysical insight into some X by relating X to more general or basic ontological category or entity Y, even if the *concept* of Y is less basic than the *concept* of X. That might occur because X is composed of Ys or because Y is a more general category or kind than X. Either way, our understanding of the metaphysics of Xs may be increased by placing it in a broader metaphysical framework. Thus, for example, Armstrong (1983) hold that laws of nature are structures of first-order universals being related by a second-order relational universal (N) of necessitation. As a conceptual analysis this would be a disaster, since the concept of N is less familiar than concept of law. Furthermore, this doesn't seem much of an analysis since N and lawhood seem very similar sorts of thing. But such criticisms (parallel to those in the second paragraph in this section) miss the point of the exercise. If Armstrong is right we discover that laws are complex entities, and what they are complexes of, we discover what kinds of entity are required to be basic, including the crucial component 'N'. Furthermore, this provides, Armstrong argues, insight into other philosophical questions (such as the nature of properties and of causation, the problem of induction, and the Ravens Paradox).

Returning now to causation, we can see that similar responses are appropriate. While the analysis in terms of dispositions provides no conceptual reduction, it does provide insight into the metaphysics of causation. We know (if the account is correct) what causation *is*—it is the stimulation and manifestation of a disposition. I have suggested that we must take some dispositions as basic natural properties. And this in turn links to a more general metaphysics of powers or potencies, and thence to the metaphysics of laws. This much is non-trivial (it is inconsistent with most other accounts of causation). Furthermore, we gain insight into some of the philosophical problems of causation, for example, the distinction between cause and condition. Articulating all these details is work for another occasion.

ACKNOWLEDGEMENTS

I am very grateful to Michael Rota and audiences in Oxford and Buffalo for their comments.

11 Antidotes for Dispositional Essentialism

Markus Schrenk

THE COUNTERFACTUAL ANALYSIS OF DISPOSITIONAL PREDICATES

Humean minded philosophers have argued: if dispositions, like, for example, fragility and solubility, were real properties they would bring an anti-Humean element to the world. The disposition would somehow point towards its manifestation and thereby generate a connection in nature, a necessity between wholly distinct entities, the existence of which Hume, allegedly, proved to be nonexistent. Consequently one should, as a Humean, deny the existence of dispositional properties.

One way to get rid of dispositions is, presumably, to eliminate them at a very early stage, namely already at the level of discourse: one should, as a Humean, aim to show that dispositional talk can be translated into terms of a language free from dispositional predicates (as famously the logical empiricists tried to do). Preferably, a simple reductive analysis along the following lines would suffice:

> x has the disposition D ↔ if x were exposed to the test T, x would show the reaction R, i.e.: Dx *iff* Tx □→ Rx.
> For example: x is fragile ↔ if x were dropped, x would break.

If a semantic reductive analysis of dispositional predicates along these lines is successful then the existence of dispositional properties is, so the Humean, put into doubt. Yet, anti-Humean dispositionalists—that is, those philosophers who believe that dispositions are irreducible, real properties—have launched forceful counterexamples to such counterfactual analyses which are supposed to show that no such analysis can succeed. Some of these counterexamples have reached folkloric status within analytic metaphysics.

FINKS AND ANTIDOTES

The simple counterfactual analysis saw, for example, its downfall with C. B. Martin's seminal paper 'Dispositions and Conditionals' (Martin 1994).

Martin has convincingly shown that a pure counterfactual conditional is neither sufficient nor necessary for an object to be disposed to react. His example is a live wire (live being the disposition in question) to which a machine—Martin calls it an "electro-fink"—is connected. This machine is built in such a way that it stops the power supply immediately if the wire is touched by a conductor. The conditional analysis of "x is live", taken to be "if x were touched by a conductor, then electric current would flow from x to the conductor" is inadequate, since the wire is live *ex hypothesi*, but the conditional is not true due to the fink. So, the conditional is not necessary. We can rephrase the story *mutatis mutandis* such that a reverse-electro-fink is operating on a non-live wire and thereby show that the conditional is not sufficient either.

A forceful counterexample of a different nature, to a counterfactual analysis of a more sophisticated kind, has been given by Alexander Bird in his 'Dispositions and Antidotes' (Bird 1998). Bird's counterexample was targeted at David Lewis analysis in 'Finkish Dispositions' (Lewis 1997) which was supposed to handle at least Martin's finks. Both Bird's and Lewis's efforts have been duly discussed in the literature and I wish to spare the reader the details here.[1] Suffice it to say that what Bird calls an 'antidote' is an interference with the temporal succession of causal events starting with the disposition's stimulus *s* and (possibly) ending with manifestation *r*. The difference between finks and antidotes is that finks destroy the disposed object's internal structure so that the disposition is lost when triggered. Bird's antidotes, however, leave the disposed object in tact. (This is not important for the considerations in this chapter, though.)

One of Bird's examples is a uranium pile (cf. Bird 1998: 229). It has the disposition to chain-react catastrophically (*r*, the response) when above critical mass (*s*, the stimulus). Yet, there is a safety mechanism—the antidote—which lets boron moderating rods penetrate the pile in case radioactivity increases. The boron rods absorb the radiation and so, although the stimulus *s* is given (uranium is above critical mass) and although the intrinsic structure of the uranium pile is not altered (it remains disposed to chain react) the uranium will not display the disposition's manifestation *r*.

Bird concludes:

> "The existence of the causal basis plus stimulus will never be enough to guarantee the required response nor, if the response comes into being, that it came about in the right way. *A causal chain can always be interfered with*" (Bird 1998: 233; my emphasis).

Needles to say, there have been further attempts to rescue the counterfactual analysis. One version of such attempts aims to exclude the peculiar intervention of finks and antidotes by upgrading the counterfactual's antecedent with some proviso clause and thereby restore the analysis' reductive force: "Conditionals which give the sense of power ascriptions are always understood to carry *a saving clause.*" (Martin 1994: 5; my emphasis). Specifically targeted at his own example Martin offers: "If the wire is touched by a conductor *and other things are equal*, then electrical current flows from the wire to the conductor" (Martin 1994: 5). In formulae: Dx *iff* Cx & Tx $\Box\rightarrow$ Rx (where C holds *other things*, i.e., external influences fixed, or states some adequate conditions, or . . .).

However, it proved to be doubtful whether this move is successful for, as Martin could show, it seems impossible to spell out explicitly and adequately what is meant by such a *"saving"* or *"ceteris paribus"* or *"other things are equal"* clause: a complete explicit (extensional) exclusion list, C, of all finks, all antidotes and all other unwanted interferers would possibly be infinite and thus not available to us. Bird agrees with Martin on this point: "It is certain that the circumstances c, whether rare or common, are not finitely specifiable" (Bird 1998: 233). This, however, would seem to be a necessary requirement for a reductive analysis.

Unfortunately, also a general (intensional) characterization of finks and other interferers seems impossible: Martin points out that the only one feature the to-be-excluded interferers share is that each of them brings it about that it is not the case that the disposition manifests itself (cf. Martin 1994: 6). However, if we take this feature to characterize the interferers and enhance the counterfactual analysis of the dispositional predicate accordingly we end up in a circular, tautological characterization (here again targetting Martin's original example): The wire is live *iff*

> "if the wire is touched by a conductor, and nothing happens to make it false *that the wire is live* [. . .] then electrical current flows from the wire to the conductor" (Martin 1994: 6; my emphasis).

As a consequence Martin, and with him many other proponents of dispositional realism, see the counterfactual analysis ultimately fail. Their conclusion is radical and pessimistic: "Counterfactuals have a place, of course, only as clumsy and inexact linguistic gestures to dispositions and they should be kept in that place" (Martin 1994: 7–8). Consequently many dispositionalists have taken the (alleged) failure of the analysis as good evidence and great motivation for the belief that dispositions are irreducible, real properties.[2]

Of course many further suggestions to save the reductive analysis and more counterexamples have been given. In fact, the analyses vs. counterexamples rivalry can soon compete with the 'Gettier industry' in epistemology.[3] While some Humeans remain optimistic that some reduction will eventually succeed it seems to be consensus among dispositionalists that "the problem of providing a way of specifying C [. . .] has so far found no satisfactory solution" (Bird 2007: 38).

I do not want to judge who is right here, the dispositionalists or the Humeans. Rather I would like to show next that *if* the dispositionalists' arguments against the reductive counterfactual analysis along the lines of Tx $\Box\rightarrow$ Rx are successful and the analysis has to be dropped *then* so must convictions (some) dispositionalists themselves hold. In more detail, a dispositionalist cannot both believe in the failure of the counterfactual analysis and also be a dispositional essentialist of a certain strong kind that links the dispositional power too closely to a metaphysically necessary conditional (see, for example, Bird and Ellis). The two next sections introduce the doctrine of *dispositional essentialism*. The mentioned friction between dispositionality and necessity will emerge *en passant*.

A FURTHER, INDEPENDENT SOURCE OF ANTI-HUMEAN CONNECTIONS IN NATURE

Independent of the debates surrounding dispositions, a further anti-Humean element in metaphysics has gained strength in the past decades: many philosophers subscribe to the ideas put forward by Kripke and Putnam who have made acceptable the belief in a conceptually contingent, *a posteriori*, *de re* connection in nature, namely *metaphysical necessary*. On the basis of Kripke's and Putnam's arguments many people saw the chance of a revival of anti-Humean metaphysics of a broad kind. Stathis Psillos, for example, comments:

> "It was *Kripke's liberating views* in the early 1970s that changed the scene radically. By defending the case of necessary statements, which are known a posteriori, Kripke [1972] made it possible to think of the existence of *necessity in nature* which is weaker than logical necessity, and yet strong enough to warrant the label necessity" (Psillos 2002: 161; my emphasis).[4]

Kripke and Putnam's claims include *theoretical identifications*, that is, the identity of properties, "water is necessarily H_2O"; *one's origin*, "I necessarily originated from a particular sperm and ovum"; *individual objects possessing properties*, "This desk is necessarily made of wood"; and *natural kinds possessing certain features*: "Tigers are essentially mammals".

The details of Kripke's (et al.) arguments surrounding externalist semantics, direct reference, rigid designation, etc. are well known and there is no need to discuss them here at large. For the sake of the argument of this chapter I accept them uncritically.[5]

DISPOSITIONAL ESSENTIALISM

Unsurprisingly, among those who defend essentialism there are also many dispositionalists and the combination of the two, called *"dispositional essentialism*", leads to the claim that natural kinds have some of their *dispositional* features *essentially*. For example: "Necessarily, salt is soluble", where NaCl is the natural kind and solubility the respective disposition.[6]

A particularly strong form of dispositional essentialism goes beyond this mere combination of the two doctrines. This strong version not only says that dispositions are possessed by kinds with necessity but they merge necessity and dispositionality, i.e., they bring together the anti-Humean connection that dispositions bring to the world and *de re* necessity: not only do kinds possess their *dispositional* features *necessarily* but, also, a triggered disposition is said to *metaphysically necessitate* its manifestation. Both the atemporal correlations of kinds and their dispositional features and the diachronic causal events from the trigger to a manifestation of a disposition are considered to be necessary.

We find explicit expression of this belief in the writings of, for example, Brian Ellis and Alexander Bird:

> "Therefore, [. . .] for all x, *necessarily*, if x has p [MS: the power], and x is in circumstances of the kind C, then x will display an effect of the kind E" (Ellis 2002: 158; my emphasis).
> "*Necessarily* if the potency is instantiated and receives its stimulus, then the manifestation will occur" (Bird 2007b: 64).

Note that, ironically, these statements are not dissimilar to the Humeans' reductive analyses in that they closely relate the disposition to a conditional: the Humean offers the reductive Dx *iff* (Tx $\Box\!\!\rightarrow$ Rx) which is said to have failed; the dispositional essentialists give us: $\Box$(Dx & Tx $\supset$ Rx).

There are important differences between the two, though. The first, is that Bird's and Ellis's statements use an anti-Humean metaphysically necessary conditional instead of the weaker counterfactual conditional and, in this respect, make a stronger claim; the second, is that their formulation does not completely exhaust the disposition's character. In this respect their version is weaker. This is visible in that Bird and Ellis do not offer an explicit semantic explication along the lines of, for example, the bi-conditional Dx *iff* $\Box$(Tx $\supset$ Rx) for the dispositional predicate D.[7] Rather, they make the having of the disposition a (crucial)[8] part of the antecedent of the conditional: $\Box$(Dx & Tx $\supset$ Rx). Thereby, they give (at most) a *partial* definition of what it means to have that disposition. I come back to this point in the section following 'Reductive sentences'.

FINKS AND ANTIDOTES FOR (STRONG) DISPOSITIONAL ESSENTIALISM

I will now show that Bird's and Ellis's strong form of dispositional essentialism—which does not only state that properties have their dispositional powers essentially but that also, qua the dispositional power, a disposition's manifestation is *necessitated* by its stimulus—are problematic. I will then, in the next section, introduce a strategy to counter the worries here raised. This strategy might be successful but it will also reveal that the relation between dispositionality and necessity is not straightforward.

The cause for trouble is rather ironic: dispositionalists who believe that antidotes, finks, and the like are convincing arguments against the counterfactual conditional analysis of dispositional predicates (counterfactually linking trigger and manifestation) cannot also believe the stronger claim that there is a necessary link between a triggered disposition and its manifestation. Clearly, the two statements that "Necessarily if the potency is instantiated and receives its stimulus, then the manifestation will occur" (Bird 2007b: 64) and "A causal chain can always be interfered with" (Bird 1998: 233) do not go together well.

In other words, if the dispositionalists' arguments against the counterfactual analysis are taken seriously (and most dispositionalists do take them seriously) then there is no reductive counterfactual (not even a sophisticated one that is backed up by proviso clauses) along the lines of "if x were touched by a conductor, then electric current would flow from x to the conductor". However, if this is taken for granted then it is even less plausible to believe that a logically stronger conditional "necessarily, if x is live and touched by a conductor then electric current flows from x to the conductor" can hold: if the dispositionalists' arguments are successful against counterfactuals along the lines of Dx *iff* $Tx \; \square\!\!\rightarrow Rx$ then they must, *a fortiori*, also prove wrong the stronger necessity claim $\square(\, Dx \; \& \; Tx \supset Rx \,)$.

A DIFFERENCE BETWEEN REDUCTIONIST ANALYSES AND (MERE) INFORMATIVE EXPLICATIONS

I wish to suggest a way in which the dispositional essentialists might be able to defend their suggestion. Previously I said that (i) their claim is, in one respect, stronger than the Humeans' analysis—it proposes a metaphysically necessary conditional where the Humean used only a counterfactual conditional—but also that, (ii) in another respect, their statement is weaker: the dispositionalists neither mean their claim to be a *reductive* analysis nor could they, because, it does not come in the form of an explicit definition.

The crucial idea to defend the dispositionalists against the trouble the stronger aspect of their statement, (i), causes is to utilize the modesty, (ii), their proposal displays in this other respect. Here is how this defense might work.[9]

The fink and antidote examples to the counterfactual analysis let us too easily forget an important, if trivial, fact: ontologically, there clearly are conditions in which, for example, fragile glasses always break, live wires do conduct electricity, salt definitely dissolves, etc. The trouble is not that these conditions do not exist, the trouble is that we fail to be able to spell out exactly what they are in such a way that we arrive at a non-gappy, non-empty, non-circular counterfactual analysis which can be said to reductively analyze the dispositional predicate.

But again, the fact that we, epistemically and/or semantically can't get a good grip on these conditions for the strict requirements of a *reductive* semantic analysis does neither mean that these conditions do, ontologically, not exist[10], nor that a less demanding, maybe benignly circular, yet still informative *characterization* (as opposed to a *strictly reductive analysis*) of dispositions can be given. And, so, the dispositional essentialist might claim that the requirements for the soundness of their metaphysically informative statement about dispositions are weaker than the prerequisites for reductive semantic analyses. In other words, they could claim that some informative, non-reductive statement along the lines of $\Box(\text{Dx \& Tx \& Cx} \supset \text{Rx})$ is possible, where C are just vaguely described conditions that guarantee the absence of any interference.[11]

As Martin showed, this would be hopeless for the reductively interpreted Dx *iff* Tx & Cx $\Box\!\!\rightarrow$ Rx because the bi-conditional analysis would turn out to be unacceptably circular—we most probably have to mention the disposition itself in the characterization of what the absence of any interference is—but for the dispositionalist's statement the disposition may well be mentioned again in the characterization of C. There's no circularity to fear for there is no ambition to spell out explicitly what the disposition is in its entirety.[12]

REDUCTION SENTENCES

Surprisingly, the dispositionalists' $\Box(\text{Dx \& Tx \& Cx} \supset \text{Rx})$ together with much that has been said in the previous section is reminiscent of one of the early empiricist attempts to get hold of dispositional predicates, namely of Carnap's reduction sentences. Having convinced himself that an explicit definition of dispositional predicates along the lines of a material conditional—Dx *iff* (Tx $\supset$ Rx)—would not work, Carnap offered, in his *Testability and Meaning* (Carnap 1936/1937) the statement Tx $\supset$ (Dx $\supset$ Rx) as a step towards an analysis of dispositional predicates (mostly accompanied by the additional Tx $\supset$ (¬Dx $\supset$ ¬Rx)). These so called "reduction sentences" are only *partial* or *implicit* definitions of dispositional predicates for they do not enable us to replace "D" wherever it occurs, as, for example, the explicit definition Dx *iff* (Tx $\supset$ Rx) with its equivalence between *definiendum* and *definiens* would:

> "[T]he terms introduced in this way have the disadvantage that in general it is not possible to eliminate them, i.e. to translate a sentence

containing such a term into a sentence containing previous terms only"
(Carnap, 1936: 443).

In order to overcome or, at least, minimize the resulting indeterminacy
(and deficit in reductive power) Carnap suggested to gradually add further reduction sentences to the original single one and thus offer a whole
list of partial definitions capturing more and more of the disposition's
(dispositional predicate's) character. We might, for example, want to add
$T^*x \supset (Dx \supset R^*x)$ and further statements with yet different trigger-reac-
tion pairs. This could be inspired both by further conceptual analysis—we
might find that the dispositional predicate should also (partially) *mean* that
test T^* is followed by reaction R^*—or, indeed, by empirical research: we
might find out that also $T^*x \supset (Dx \supset R^*x)$ is correct for all objects for
which $Tx \supset (Dx \supset Rx)$ holds. Carnap was aware of the fact that conceptual
analysis and the acquisition of empirical knowledge go hand in hand at this
point and that, thus, the partial definitions, taken together, have empirical
content (cf. Carnap 1936: 444).

The dispositional essentialists' $\Box(Dx \,\&\, Tx \,\&\, Cx \supset Rx)$—or, equiva-
lently, and in line with Carnap, $\Box(T_Cx \supset (Dx \supset Rx))$[13]—is also only a
partial and implicit explication of the disposition in the sense that it (only)
gives some information about some (crucial) aspect of the disposition,
namely that necessarily, when triggered with T in the right circumstances,
C, the disposed object, D, will react with reaction R. Yet, it does by no
means exhaust what the disposition D is and can otherwise give rise to. It
remains silent about, for example, all those interesting cases where the conditions, C, are not ideal and the disposition does not quite deliver R but a
partial manifestation only. Also, just like Carnap's reduction sentences, the
dispositional essentialist's claim does not entitle us to replace the predicate
"D" wherever it occurs.

This should be perceived as no disadvantage for the dispositional essentialists for it is anyway not in their aim to reductively analyze dispositions
(dispositional predicates). On the contrary, dispositions are meant to be
real properties in their own right for which no such analysis (and later
replacement) is wanted.[14]

In fact, Carnap's idea to accumulate additional reduction sentences for
the same dispositional predicate should suit the dispositional essentialist
well. Not only might the very same disposition D give raise to further, different trigger and reaction events—electric conductivity might turn out to
be linked also to heat conduction—more importantly, as mentioned briefly
before, we have to remember that $\Box(T_Cx \supset (Dx \supset Rx))$ captures only a
disturbance-free trigger and a pure reaction. However, disposed objects are
rarely in such ideal circumstances and, so, rarely show a disposition's pure
manifestation. Yet, a dispositional essentialist would surely want to say
that what happens in those impure cases happens, too, necessitated by the
disposition. In other words, $\Box(T_C{}^* \supset (Dx \supset R^*x))$ shall hold just as much

as the pure case, where, here, $T_C{}^*$ is a trigger in not quite disturbance-free circumstances and R^* is not quite the disposition's pure manifestation.

A sheer infinity of such statements could, in principle, be added but clearly no subset exhausts the disposition D's whole character. Yet, this is perfectly in line with the dispositionalist's credo that dispositions are real properties in their own right that cannot be analyzed away.

EVALUATION: THE RELATA AND THEIR DIACHRONICITY, THE MONOTONICITY OF NECESSITY

I wish to shed some more light on what the conditions C commit us to. Some tension between metaphysical necessity and dispositionality will emerge that might be a little worrisome for the dispositionalist's version of Carnapian reduction sentences despite the positive assessment given so far.[15]

The Relata *and their Diachronicity.* It has to be noted that the dispositional essentialists' claims bring, due to circumstances C, a whole new type of metaphysically necessary statements to the Kripke and Putnam classes of statements. Circumstances C, so we have granted the dispositionalist, can be described as those conditions a disposed object has to be in such that no interferer (antidote, fink, mask, etc.) is or will be present at least till it is certain that the reaction comes about (i.e. C has to take care even of very late preventions). What this tells us about C, ontologically speaking, is that C has to fix whatever is in the light-cone just before R so to make absolutely sure that no interference can sneak in. Note, that C has to encompass also what might *actually* seem to be causally irrelevant for the disposition's manifestation: already space-time regions that could only *possibly* house a potential interferer have to be, so to speak, silenced pre-emptively because we wish to make a statement that is not only factually true but *necessarily* true i.e.in all possible worlds. And, so, we have to exclude also interferers that are merely *possible*.[16]

This is a major commitment for C and also for what the necessity operator holds together: in $\Box(Dx \,\&\, Tx \,\&\, Cx \supset Rx)$, metaphysical necessity not only binds the disposition and a simple trigger to a reaction but, rather, whole world states to a succeeding world state.

Moreover, we must not forget that statements of dispositional trigger-manifestation correlations should bear time variables, which have so far been omitted for simplicity. Instead of $\Box(Dx \,\&\, Tx \,\&\, Cx \supset Rx)$ we should rather write something like $\Box(D(x, t) \,\&\, T(x, t) \,\&\, C(x, t) \supset R(x, \Delta t))$[17]. However, none of the Kripke/Putnam cases is about diachronic successions in time. Remember that Kripke and Putnam's original examples are all similar to the timeless "water is necessarily H_2O", "I necessarily originated from a particular sperm and ovum", "This desk is necessarily made of wood", or "Tigers are essentially mammals".

Taking now both considerations together—that the *relata* are not individuals or kinds or properties but also include world state types and events *and* that we are confronted with successions in time rather than with atemporal statements—we might start to doubt whether Kripke and Putnam's metaphysical necessity is at all applicable here: the transfer of metaphysical necessity to the dispositional cases—from static, eternal facts to the necessary connections among events in the natural world—seems only permissible either if it can be shown that Kripke-Putnam style arguments which might be successful in synchronic or atemporal relations of individuals, kinds, and properties can also be applied effectively to diachronic succession cases linking world states and events, or failing a direct application of the Kripke-Putnam machinery of direct reference, rigid designation, etc., if we can give an otherwise plausible argument for why we should assume that metaphysical necessity is also the binding force in these diachronic über-events.

Monotonicity of Necessity. There is a further worry that needs to be addressed. It questions not the nature of the *relata* and their diachronicity but the robustness of the metaphysical necessity under consideration. Take, for comparison, one of the orthodox statements of metaphysical necessity as found in Kripke and Putnam and their followers: "necessarily, electrons are negatively charged". If true then, since it is in the essence of electrons to be so charged, any particular electron will be charged *no matter what*: whether it is surrounded by a magnetic field, or in the presence of a neutron, or being subjected to gravitation, etc. In other words, one could, in principle, add anything one pleases to the antecedent of a conditional like "necessarily, if x is an electron then x is negatively charged". It still holds with necessity that if x is an electron *and in a magnetic field, and in the presence of a neutron and . . .* then x is negatively charged. Necessity is, to take a notion normally applied to logical entailment, *monotonic*: antecedent strengthening does not affect the original necessary conditional regarding electrons and negative charge. One might even be tempted to suggest that antecedent strengthening is a test for the alleged necessity: if it is true that electrons are negatively charged, come what may, then you are justified to state a necessary relation between electrons and negative charge.

Things turn out to be crucially different in the case of dispositions, their triggers and their manifestations. Here, not everything goes.[18] On the contrary, it proved to be important to add to the first envisaged antecedent, Dx & Tx, an exclusion clause C such that unwanted additional factors are debarred. In fact, the conditions C in $\Box(Dx \mathbin{\&} Tx \mathbin{\&} Cx \supset Rx)$ are there to disallow antecedent strengthening because the presence of a fink, an antidote, or other interferences would make the conditional false. The relation between Dx & Tx and Rx is only robust, that is, *of necessity*, if no antecedent strengthening is allowed, i.e., if the previously described envisaged necessity-robustness test is, with the help of C, forbidden by *fiat*.

I will leave it an open question whether, therefore, necessity has been obtained surreptitiously only, but I believe the last word has not yet been spoken on the metaphysical necessity of dispositionality.

CONCLUSION

Within the last ten–fifteen years dispositionalism, the view that dispositions are real irreducible properties, has gained a lot of support. This is partially due to a debate between Humean minded philosophers, who aim to give reductive analyses of dispositional predicates, and anti-Humean oriented dispositionalists, who have launched forceful counterarguments against this eliminative analysis.

There has been a second anti-Humean movement in current analytic metaphysics: Kripke's arguments in *Naming and Necessity* have encouraged people to believe in metaphysical *de re* necessity and, related, in a modern version of essentialism.

When these two strands of anti-Humean reasoning are combined they culminate in what has frequently been called "*dispositional essentialism*". This is the stance that (all or most) properties or kinds have their *dispositional roles necessarily*.

A stronger version of dispositional essentialism aims to bring necessity and dispositionality even closer together in that it sees the disposition involved in a necessary conditional featuring the trigger and the manifestation of the disposition: "*necessarily*, if something has power P and is triggered, it displays the power's manifestation".

In this chapter I have shown that the tenability of this statement is debatable for precisely the reasons the Humean reductive analysis was problematic. However, I have also shown that strong dispositional essentialism might escape these problems because the strict rules for reductive semantic analyses might not apply to mere metaphysical explications or characterizations of dispositionality.

Yet, other grave difficulties still remain: the alleged metaphysical necessity of $(Dx \,\&\, Tx \,\&\, Cx \supset Rx)$ bears some strong dissimilarities to those cases of necessity Kripke and Putnam originally introduced: the *relata* are different and it is a diachronic business rather than being synchronic or atemporal. Moreover, it is not entirely clear whether the robustness of the alleged necessity has been properly earned or whether it has been obtained surreptitiously.

ACKNOWLEDGMENTS

Thanks are due to Stephen Mumford, Matthew Tugby, Charlotte Matheson and Rani Lill Anjum for invaluable discussions.

NOTES

1. The history of the ups and downs of the reductive analysis is well documented. See for example, (Malzkorn 2001) and (Schrenk 2010). Detailed analyses of Lewis's, Bird's and many other attempts can be found in the literature listed in footnote 2.

2. Which consequences we should really draw from the (alleged) failure of a semantic analysis is, of course, more controversial than we suppose here. Inspired by logical empiricists' (anti-)metaphysics, their epistemology, and verificationist semantics people have assumed that if Humeans should be able to provide a watertight analysis that answers to all possible counterexamples then dispositions are not real and vice versa. Yet, outside the constraints of empiricism/verificationism, conclusions from semantics to metaphysics are not so straightforward. John Heil, for example, points out: "Even if you could concoct a conditional analysis of dispositionality impervious to counter-examples, it is not clear what you would have accomplished. You would still be faced with the question, What are the truth makers for dispositional claims? Suppose you decide that 'object o is fragile' implies and is implied by 'o would shatter if struck in circumstances C '. You are not excused from the task of saying what the truth maker might be for this conditional. Presumably, if the conditional is an analysis, its truth maker will be whatever the truth maker is for the original dispositional assertion. This is progress?" (Heil, 2005: 345). Be that as it may, all that is needed for the argument of the rest of the chapter is, in any case, only the assumption that the counterfactual analysis is under threat by finks, antidotes, and other possible interferences whether or not this amounts to an argument against such analyses and for dispositional realism or not.

3. To name but a few: (Molnar 1999), (Malzkorn 2000) with a reply by (Mumford 2001), (Gunderson 2000) with a reply by Bird (Bird 2000), (Choi 2003, 2006).

4. I am not saying here that Psillos is an anti-Humean. I quote him because he gives expression to the view that Kripke was significantly involved in the anti-Humean revolution the defenders of essentialism and *de re* necessity have attempted.

5. Yet, I wish to add that I am generally not convinced by the original Kripkean arguments and that I rather endorse Humean or conventionalist intuitions in regard to (metaphysical) necessity.

6. I will set aside generally important but here irrelevant distinctions between essences and necessary properties (cf. Fine 1994, 2002).

7. Note that this is at variance with my (Schrenk 2009) where I have taken the dispositional essentialist to mean the stronger "Dx *iff* $\Box(Tx \supset Rx)$" and where I discuss the inadequacy of that formulation.

8. I say "an (essential) part of the antecedent" because the essentialist dispositionalist would probably want to deny that $\Box(Tx \supset Rx)$ holds just by itself for, on their dispositionalist account, it is precisely x's having of the disposition that powers the reaction from stimulus to manifestation. Thus, the conditional is itself conditional on Dx.

9. Another possible move to reconcile dispositionalism with the dispositionalist's necessary conditional is to point out that for an important set of dispositional properties—namely, for the fundamental, basic, perfectly natural ones—there are no finks (and many other interferers). Bird endorses this line of argument in his *Nature's Metaphysics* (Bird 2007b: chap. 3.3). (However, he also concedes that antidotes might be possible even on the fundamental level and therefore still be problematic.)

10. To deny their existence seems almost to deny the uniformity of nature: repeat again everything involving a disposed object and the same will again happen to that object.

11. To be fair to Ellis I have to confess that I omitted a line from his quote where he already attempts to exclude interferences in this fashion: "Therefore, [. . .] for all x, necessarily, if x has P, and x is in circumstances of the kind C, then x will display an effect of the kind E, *unless there are defeating conditions that would mask this display*" (Ellis 2001: 286; my emphasis). As I will show now, this is still problematic.

12. There is a danger here, of course, that (Dx&Tx&Cx⊃Rx) turns out to be analytically rather then (merely) metaphysically necessary due to an unfortunate definition of C. One would hope that analyticity can be avoided.

13. I have merged Tx and Cx into T_Cx and given a formulation that is logically equivalent to the dispositional essentialist. A remaining dissimilarity to Carnap is, of course, the necessity operator.

14. Unless, of course, the dispositional essentialist really would like to see dispositions and dispositionality completely reduced to metaphysical necessity. Yet, see (Schrenk 2009) for the hopelessness of this aim.

15. For further charges see my (Schrenk 2009).

16. This is, of course, no new argument: already Russell argued in his famous "On the Notion of Cause" (Russell 1912/2003) that "in order to be sure of the expected effect, we must know that there is nothing in the environment to interfere with it. But this means that the supposed cause [corresponding to a minimal antecedent in a disposition; my addendum] is not, by itself, adequate to ensure the effect." (Russell 1912/2003: 169)

17. Cf. the formulations with time variables Lewis and Bird introduced in (Lewis 1994) and (Bird 1998).

18. Kit Fine observes similarly: "It would be harder, for example, to break the connection between the truth of P&Q and the truth of P than the connection between cause and effect." (Fine, 2002: 278–79).

Contributors

Rani Lill Anjum is a Norwegian Research Council Post-Doctoral Research Fellow in Philosophy at the Universities of Tromsø and Nottingham. Her primary research interests are causation and dispositions, as well as philosophy of logic and language.

Alexander Bird is Professor of Philosophy at the University of Bristol. He is the author of *Nature's Metaphysics: Laws and Properties* (2007) and many papers on dispositions and powers, including 'Dispositions and Antidotes' (1998) and 'The Regress of Pure Powers?' (2007).

Brian Ellis is Emeritus Professor at La Trobe University and Professorial Fellow in Philosophy at the University of Melbourne. He is the author of three books on the essentialism and scientific realism: *Scientific Essentialism* (2001), *The Philosophy of Nature* (2002), and *The Metaphysics of Scientific Realism* (2009), as well as three other books, and many papers in philosophical journals and professional collections.

Toby Handfield is a Senior Lecturer in the School of Philosophy and Bioethics at Monash University. His primary areas of research are metaphysics and ethics. He is currently writing a monograph on the nature of chance.

John Heil is Professor of Philosophy at Washington University in St Louis and an honorary Research Fellow at Monash University. He works chiefly in metaphysics and the philosophy of mind.

Kristina Engelhard is currently a Research Assistant at the Department of Philosophy at the University of Cologne. Her area of specialization is contemporary metaphysics, in particular dispositions. Her research interests also include Leibniz, Kant and German Idealism. She is the author of a book on Kant's theory of matter and the second antinomy: *Das Einfache und die Materie* (2005), and co-editor of *Kant—Key Concepts* (2010).

E. J. Lowe is Professor of Philosophy at Durham University, and specializes in metaphysics, philosophy of mind and language, philosophy of logic and language, and early modern philosophy. His authored books include: *Kinds of Being* (1989), *Subjects of Experience* (1996), *The Possibility of Metaphysics* (1998), *A Survey of Metaphysics* (2002), *Locke* (2005), *The Four-Category Ontology* (2006), *Personal Agency* (2008), and *More Kinds of Being* (2009).

Anna Marmodoro is a British Academy Post-Doctoral Fellow in Philosophy at the University of Oxford and a Junior Research Fellow at Corpus Christi College. Her primary research interests span ancient and contemporary metaphysics and the philosophy of mind. She has published in these areas and also in medieval philosophy and philosophy of religion.

Jennifer McKitrick is an Associate Professor of Philosophy at the University of Nebraska–Lincoln. Her primary research interests intersect metaphysics and philosophy of science. She has published in these areas and also in feminism and political philosophy.

Stephen Mumford is Professor of Metaphysics at the University of Nottingham. He is the author of *Dispositions* (1998) and *Laws in Nature* (2003). His current work is on causation and powers.

Markus Schrenk is a German Research Foundation (DFG) Post-Doctoral Fellow on a project focusing on causation, laws, and dispositions. In addition to contemporary analytic metaphysics of science, he is also interested in philosophy of mind, philosophy of language, and epistemology. He is the author of *The Metaphysics of* Ceteris Paribus *Laws* (2007) and (in German) an *Introduction to the Philosophy of Language* (2008).

Neil E. Williams is an Assistant Professor of Philosophy at the University at Buffalo (State University of New York). His primary area of research falls at the intersection of metaphysics and the philosophy of science, but his interests extend to general questions of metaphysics and ontology as they arise in a wide range of domains. Recent publications cover these areas, as well as the philosophy of medicine.

Bibliography

Anscombe, G. E. M. (1971), 'Causality and Determination' (Cambridge University Press), reprinted in *Metaphysics and the Philosophy of Mind. Collected Philosophical Papers* Vol. II (Blackwell), 1981: 133–147

Aristotle. (1985), *The Complete Works*, Vol. II, J. Barnes, ed., (Princeton University Press)

Armstrong, D. M. (1961), *Perception and the Physical World* (Routledge)

———. (1968), 'The Headless Woman Illusion and the Defense of Materialism' *Analysis* 29: pp. 48–49

———. (1973), *Belief, Truth, and Knowledge* (Cambridge University Press)

———. (1983), *What is a Law of Nature?* (Cambridge University Press)

———. (1997), *A World of States of Affairs* (Cambridge University Press)

———. (1999), 'The Causal Theory of Properties: Properties According to Ellis, Shoemaker, and Others'. *Philosophical Topics* 26: pp. 25–37

———. (2004), *Truth and Truthmakers*, (Cambridge University Press)

Barker, S. (2009a), 'Dispositional Monism, Relational Constitution and Quiddities' *Analysis* 69: pp. 1–8

———. (2009b), 'The Emperor's New Metaphysics of Powers'. Available online at: http://www.nottingham.ac.uk/philosophy/staff/Stephen-Barker.php

Berkeley, G. (1710/1998), *A Treatise Concerning the Principles of Human Knowledge*, J. Dancy, ed. (Oxford University Press)

Berlin, I. (1966), *The Hedgehog and the Fox: An Essay on Tolstoy's View of History* (Simon and Schuster)

Bhaskar, R. (1975), *A Realist Theory of Science* (Leeds Books Limited)

Bird, A. (1998), 'Dispositions and Antidotes', *Philosophical Quarterly*, 48: pp. 227–234

———. (2000), 'Further Antidotes: A Replay to Gundersen', *Philosophical Quarterly* 50: pp. 229–233

———. (2005), 'Laws and Essences', *Ratio* 18: pp. 437–461

———. (2007a), 'The Regress of Pure Powers?' *Philosophical Quarterly* 57: pp. 513–534

———. (2007b), *Nature's Metaphysics: Laws and Properties* (Oxford University Press)

———. (2009), 'Structural Properties Revisited' in T. Handfield, ed., *Dispositions and Causes* (Oxford University Press), pp. 215–241

Black, R. (2000), 'Against Quidditism', *Australasian Journal of Philosophy* 78: pp. 87–104

Blackburn, S. (1984), *Spreading the Word: Groundings in the Philosophy of Language* (Clarendon Press)

———. (1990), 'Filling in Space' *Analysis* 50, pp. 62–65

Block, N. (1990), 'Can the Mind Change the World?' in George Boolos, ed., *Meaning and Method: Essays in Honor of Hilary Putnam* (Cambridge University Press), pp. 137–170

Bostock, D. (1994), *Aristotle: Metaphysics. Book VII and VIII* translated with commentary (Clarendon Press)

Bostock, S. (2003), 'Are All Possible Laws Actual Laws?' *Australasian Journal of Philosophy*, 81: pp. 517–533

Bradley F. H., (1893), *Appearance and Reality* (Swan Sonnenschein & Co.)

Broad, C. D. (1933), *Examination of McTaggart's Philosophy* Vol. 1 (Cambridge University Press)

Burks, A. W. (1951), 'The Logic of Causal Propositions', *Mind*, 60: pp. 363–382

Butterfield, J. (2006), 'Against Pointillisme about Mechanics' *British Journal for the Philosophy of Science* 57: pp. 709–753

Cameron, R (2008), 'Turtles All The Way Down: Regress, Priority and Fundamentality in Metaphysics' *Philosophical Quarterly* 58: pp. 1–14

Campbell, K. (1976), *Metaphysics: An Introduction* (Encino: Dickenson Publishing Co.)

Carnap, R. (1936), 'Testability and Meaning I', *Philosophy of Science* 3: pp. 419–471

———. (1937), 'Testability and Meaning II', *Philosophy of Science* 4: pp. 1–40

Cartwright, N. (1983), *How the Laws of Physics Lie* (Clarendon Press)

———. (1989), *Nature's Capacities and Their Measurement* (Oxford University Press)

———. (1999), *The Dappled World* (Cambridge University Press)

———. (2007), 'What Makes a Capacity a Disposition?' in M. Kistler and B. Gnassounou, eds, *Dispositions and Causal Powers*, Ashgate

———. (2009), 'Causal Laws, Predictions, and the Need for Genuine Powers' in T. Handfield, ed., *Dispositions and Causes* (Oxford University Press)

Chalmers, D. (1996), *The Conscious Mind: In Search of a Fundamental Theory* (Oxford University Press)

Choi, S. (2003), 'Improving Bird's Antidotes', *Australasian Journal of Philosophy* 81: pp. 573–580.

———. (2006), 'The Simple vs. Reformed Conditional Analysis of Dispositions', *Synthese* 148: pp. 369–379

Collins, J., Hall, N. and Paul, L. (2004), 'Counterfactuals and Causation: History, Problems, and Prospects, in J. Collins, N. Hall, and L. Paul, eds, *Causation and Counterfactuals* (MIT Press), pp. 1–57

Corry, R. (2009), 'How is Scientific Analysis Possible?', in T. Handfield, ed., *Dispositions and Causes* (Oxford University Press)

Crane, T. (1996), 'Introduction' in T. Crane, ed., *Dispositions: A Debate* (Routledge)

Dancy, J. (2000), 'The Particularists Progress' in B. Hooker and M. Little, eds, *Moral Particularism* (Oxford University Press), pp. 130–156

Dauer, F. W. (1972), 'How Not to Reidentify the Parthenon' *Analysis* 33: pp. 63–64

Davidson, D. (1967), 'Causal Relations', *Journal of Philosophy* 64: pp. 691–703

———. (1980a), 'The Individuation of Events', in D. Davidson, ed., *Essays on Actions and Events* (Oxford University Press)

———. (1980b), *Essays on Actions and Events* (Oxford University Press)

Dipert, R. R. (1997), 'The Mathematical Structure of the World: The World as Graph' *Journal of Philosophy* 94: pp. 329–358

Dowe, P. (1992), 'Wesley Salmon's Process Theory of Causality and the Conserved Quantity Theory', *Philosophy of Science* 59: pp. 195–216

———. (2000), *Physical Causation* (Cambridge University Press)

———. (2001), 'A Counterfactual Theory of Prevention and "Causation" by Omission', *Australasian Journal of Philosophy* 79: pp. 216–226

Dretske, F. I. (1988), *Explaining Behavior: Reasons in a World of Causes* (MIT Press)

Ducasse, C. J. (1969), *Causation and the Types of Necessity*, first published 1924 (Dover)

Eagle, A. (2009), 'Causal Structuralism, Dispositional Actualism, and Counterfactual Conditionals' in T. Handfield, ed., *Dispositions and Causes* (Oxford University Press) pp. 65–99

Ellis, B. (2001), *Scientific Essentialism* (Cambridge University Press)

———. (2002), *The Philosophy of Nature* (Acumen)

Ellis, B. and Lierse C. (1994), 'Dispositional Essentialism', *Australasian Journal of Philosophy* 72: pp. 27–45

Esfeld, M. (1998), 'Holism and Analytic Philosophy', *Mind* 107: pp. 365–380

Fara, M. (2001), *Dispositions and Their Ascriptions*. Doctoral thesis. Princeton University.

Feynman, R. P. (1985), *QED: The Strange Theory of Light and Matter* (Princeton University Press)

Fine, K. (1994), 'Essence and Modality', *Philosophical Perspectives* 8: pp. 1–16

———. (2002), The Varieties of Necessity' in T. S. Gendler & J. Hawthorne, eds, *Conceivability and Possibility* (Oxford University Press), pp. 253–282

Foster, J. (1982), *The Case for Idealism*. London: Routledge and Kegan Paul

Freeman, A., ed. (2006), *Consciousness and Its Place in Nature: Does Physicalism Entail Panpsychism?* (Imprint Academic)

French, S. and Krause, D. (2006), *Identity in Physics: A Historical, Philosophical, and Formal Analysis* (Clarendon Press)

Furth, M. (1985), *Aristotle: Metaphysics Books Zeta, Eta, Theta, Iota (VII–X)*, translated (Hackett)

Geach. P. T. (1961), 'Aquinas', in G. E. M. Anscombe and P. T. Geach, eds, *Three Philosophers* (Blackwell), pp. 65–125

Gunderson, L. B. (2000), 'Bird on Dispositions and Antidotes', *Philosophical Quarterly* 50: pp. 227–229

Hall, N. (2004), 'Causation and the Price of Transitivity' in J. Collins, N. Hall, and L. A. Paul, eds, *Causation and Counterfactuals*, (MIT Press), pp. 181–204

Handfield, T. (2008a), 'Humean Dispositionalism', *Australasian Journal of Philosophy* 86: pp. 113–126

———. (2008b), 'Unfinkable Dispositions', *Synthese* 160: pp. 297–308

———. ed. (2009), *Dispositions and Causes* (Oxford University Press)

Harré, R. (1970), 'Powers', *British Journal for the Philosophy of Science* 21: pp. 81–101

Harré, R. and E. H. Madden. (1975), *Causal Powers: A Theory of Natural Necessity* (Blackwell)

Hawthorne, J. (2001), 'Causal Structuralism', *Philosophical Perspectives* 15: pp. 361–378 (reprinted in J. Hawthorne, ed., *Metaphysical Essays* (2006; Oxford University Press)

———. (2006), Metaphysical Essays (Oxford University Press)

Hawthorne, J. and Cortens, A. (1995), 'Towards Ontological Nihilism', *Philosophical Studies* 79: pp. 143–165

Healey, R. (1991), 'Holism and Nonseparability', *Journal of Philosophy* 88: pp. 393–421

Heil, J. (2003), *From an Ontological Point of View* (Oxford University Press)

———. (2005), 'Dispositions', *Synthese* 144: pp. 343–356.

———. (2008a), 'Critical Notice of Peter Unger's *All the Power in the World*', *Noûs* 42: pp. 336–348

————. (2008b), 'Anomalous Monism' in H. Dyke, ed. *From Truth to Reality: New Essays in Metaphysics* (Routledge), pp. 85–98

Heil, J. and Robb, D. (2003), 'Mental Properties' *American Philosophical Quarterly* 40: pp. 175–196

Hitchcock, C. (2001), 'The Intransitivity of Causation Revealed in Equations and Graphs', *The Journal of Philosophy* 98: pp. 273–299

Holton, R. (1999), 'Dispositions All the Way Round', *Analysis* 59: pp. 9–14

Horgan, T. and Potrc, M. (2008), *Austere Realism* (MIT Press)

Horsten, L. (forthcoming), 'Criteria of Identity: Predicative and Impredicative', *Philosophy and Phenomenological Research*

Hume, D. (1739), *A Treatise of Human Nature*, L. A. Selby-Bigge, ed., 1888. 2nd edition, with text revisions by P. H. Nidditch (Clarendon, 1978)

————. (1740), 'Abstract of a Treatise of Human Nature', in *An Enquiry Concerning Human Understanding*, P. Millican, ed., (Oxford University Press, 2007), pp. 133–145

————. (1748), *An Enquiry Concerning Human Understanding*, P. Millican, ed., (Oxford University Press, 2007)

Hüttemann, A. (1998), 'Laws and Dispositions', *Philosophy of Science* 65: pp. 121–135

————. (2004), *What's Wrong With Microphysicalism?* (Routledge)

————. (forthcoming), 'Dispositions in Physics' in G. Damschen, R. Schnepf, and K. R. Stuber, eds., *Debating Dispositions: Issues in Metaphysics, Epistemology and Philosophy of Mind*, (Walter de Gruyter)

Johnson, W.E. (1924), *Logic, Part III. The Logical Foundations of Science.* (Cambridge University Press)

Johnston, M. (1992), 'How to Speak of the Colours', *Philosophical Studies* 68: pp. 221–263

Kant, I. (1781), *Critique of Pure Reason*, N. Kemp Smith trans., (MacMillan, 1929)

Kim, J. (1976), 'Events as Property Exemplifications' in M. Brand and D. Walton, eds, *Action Theory* (Reidel Publishing Co.)

————. (1988), 'Explanatory Realism, Causal Realism, and Explanatory Exclusion', *Midwest Studies in Philosophy* XII pp. 225–239

Ladyman, J. (2007), 'On the Identity and Diversity of Objects in a Structure', *Proceedings of the Aristotelian Society*, Supplementary Volume 81: 23–43

LePore, E. and McLaughlin, B. (eds) (1985), *Actions and Events: Perspectives on the Philosophy of Donald Davidson* (Blackwell)

Lewis, D. K. (1973a), 'Causation', *Journal of Philosophy* 70: 556–567. Reprinted in D. K. Lewis *Philosophical Papers. Volume 2* (Oxford University Press, 1986: 159–172)

————. (1973b), *Counterfactuals* (Blackwell)

————. (1986a), *On the Plurality of Worlds* (Blackwell)

————. (1986b), *Philosophical Papers. Volume 2* (Oxford University Press)

————. (1997), 'Finkish Dispositions', *Philosophical Quarterly* 47: 143–158. Reprinted in D. K. Lewis, *Papers in Metaphysics and Epistemology* (Cambridge University Press 1999): pp. 133–151)

————. (1999), *Papers in Metaphysics and Epistemology* (Cambridge University Press)

————. (2000), 'Causation as Influence', *Journal of Philosophy* 97: 182–197

————. (2004), 'Void and Object', in J. Collins, N. Hall and L.A. Paul, eds, *Causation and Counterfactuals*, (MIT Press, 2004), pp. 277–290

Lewis, D., and Langton, R. (1998), "Defining 'Intrinsic'". *Philosophy and Phenomenological Research*, 58: pp. 333–345. Reprinted in D. K. Lewis, *Papers in*

Metaphysics and Epistemology (Cambridge University Press, 1999: pp. 116–132)

Linnebo, Ø. (2008), 'Structuralism and the Notion of Dependence', *Philosophical Quarterly* 58: pp. 59–79

Locke, J. (1975), *An Essay Concerning Human Understanding*, P. H. Nidditch, ed., (Clarendon Press)

Lotze, H. (1884), *Metaphysics, in Three Books: Ontology, Cosmology, and Psychology* (1879), B. Bosanquet ed. and trans., (Clarendon Press, 1884; 2nd edition, 1887)

Lowe, E. J. (1989a), 'What is a Criterion of Identity?', *Philosophical Quarterly* 39: pp. 1–21

———. (1989b), 'Impredicative Identity Criteria and Davidson's Criterion of Event Identity', *Analysis* 49: pp. 178–181

———. (1998), *The Possibility of Metaphysics: Substance, Identity, and Time* (Clarendon Press)

———. (2002), *A Survey of Metaphysics* (Oxford University Press)

———. (2003), 'Individuation', in M. J. Loux and D. W. Zimmerman. eds, *The Oxford Handbook of Metaphysics* (Oxford University Press)

———. (2005), 'Identity, Vagueness, and Modality', in J. L. Bermúdez, ed., *Thought, Reference, and Experience: Themes from the Philosophy of Gareth Evans* (Clarendon Press)

———. (2006a), *The Four-Category Ontology: A Metaphysical Foundation for Natural Science* (Clarendon Press)

———. (2006b), 'Powerful Particulars: Review Essay on John Heil's *From an Ontological Point of View*', *Philosophy and Phenomenological Research* 72: pp. 466–479

———. (2007), 'Sortals and the Individuation of Objects', *Mind and Language* 22: pp. 514–533

Mackie, J.L. (1965), 'Causes and Conditions' *American Philosophical Quarterly*, 2: pp. 245–265 (reprinted in E. Sosa and M. Tooley, eds, *Causation*, Oxford University Press, 1993: pp. 33–55)

———. (1980) *The Cement of the Universe* (Oxford University Press)

Malzkorn, W. (2000), 'Realism, Functionalism and the Conditional Analysis of Dispositions', *Philosophical Quarterly* 50: pp. 452469

———. (2001), 'Defining Disposition Concepts: A Brief History of the Problem', *Studies in History and Philosophy of Science* 32: pp. 335–353

Martin, C. B. (1980), 'Substance Substantiated', *Australasian Journal of Philosophy* 58: pp. 3–10

———. (1993), 'Power for Realists' in J. Bacon, K. Campbell, and L. Reinhardt, eds, *Ontology, Causality and Mind. Essays in Honour of D. M. Armstrong* (Cambridge University Press), pp. 175–186

———. (1994), 'Dispositions and Conditionals', *Philosophical Quarterly* 44: pp. 1–8

———. (1997), 'On the Need for Properties: The Road to Pythagoreanism and Back'. *Synthese* 112: pp. 193–231

———. (2008), *The Mind in Nature* (Oxford University Press)

Martin, C. B. and Heil J. (1999), 'The Ontological Turn', *Midwest Studies in Philosophy* 23: pp. 34–60

Martin C.B. and Pfeifer K. (1986), 'Intentionality and the Non-Psychological', *Philosophy and Phenomenological Research*, XLVI pp. 531–554

Maudlin, T. (2007), *The Metaphysics Within Physics* (Oxford University Press)

McDermott, M. (1995), 'Redundant Causation', *The British Journal for the Philosophy of Science* 46: pp. 523–544

McKitrick, J. (2003), 'A Case for Extrinsic Dispositions', *Australasian Journal of Philosophy*, 81: pp. 155–174

———. (2005), 'Are Dispositions Causally Relevant?', *Synthese* 144: pp. 357–371

Mellor, D. H. (1971), *The Matter of Chance* (Cambridge University Press)

———. (1974), 'In Defence of Dispositions', *Philosophical Review* 83: pp. 167–182

———. (1982), 'Counting Corners Correctly', *Analysis* 42: pp. 96–97

———. (1995) *The Facts of Causation* (Routledge)

———. (2000), 'The Semantics and Ontology of Dispositions', *Mind* 109: pp. 757–780

Menzies, P. (1999), 'Intrinsic Versus Extrinsic Conceptions of Causation' in H. Sankey, ed., *Causation and Laws of Nature*, (Reidel), pp. 313–29

Mill, J.S. (1967), *A System of Logic* (Longmans)

Molnar, G. (1999), 'Are Dispositions Reducible?', *Philosophical Quarterly* 49: pp. 1–17

———. (2003), *Powers: A Study in Metaphysics* (Oxford University Press)

Mumford, S. (1998), *Dispositions* (Clarendon Press)

———. (1999), 'Intentionality and the Physical: A New Theory of Disposition Ascription', *Philosophical Quarterly* 49: pp. 215–225

———. (2001), 'Realism and the Conditional Analysis of Dispositions: Reply to Malzkorn', *Philosophical Quarterly* 51: pp. 375–378

———. (2004), *Laws in Nature* (Routledge)

———. (2009), 'Passing Powers Around', *Monist* 92: pp. 94–111

Mumford, S. and Anjum, R. (forthcoming) *Getting Causes from Powers* (Oxford University Press)

Oppy, G. (2000), 'Humean Supervenience?', *Philosophical Studies* 101: pp. 77–105

Pearl, J. (2000), *Causality: Models, Reasoning, and Inference* (Cambridge University Press)

Place, U.T. (1996), 'Intentionality as the Mark of the Dispositional', *Dialectica* 50: pp. 91–120

———. (1999), 'Intentionality and the Physical: A Reply to Mumford', *Philosophical Quarterly* 49: pp. 225–231

Popper, K. (1972), *Objective Knowledge* (Clarendon Press)

———. (1990), *A World of Propensities* (Thoemmes, Bristol)

Priestley, J. (1777/1972), 'Disquisitions of Matter and Spirit' in *The Theological and Miscellaneous Works of Joseph Priestley*, Vol. 3. (Kraus Reprint Co.)

Prior, E. (1985), *Dispositions* (Aberdeen University Press)

Prior, E. W., Pargetter R., and Jackson F. (1982), 'Three Theses about Dispositions', *American Philosophical Quarterly* 19: pp. 251–257

Psillos, S. (2002), *Causation and Explanation* (Acumen)

———. (2006), 'What Do Powers Do When They Are Not Manifested?', *Philosophy and Phenomenological Research*, Vol. LXXII, No. 1, pp. 137–156

Quine, W. V. (1969a), 'Existence and Quantification' in W. V. Quine *Ontological Relativity and Other Essays* (Columbia University Press)

———. (1969b), 'Speaking of Objects' in W. V. Quine *Ontological Relativity and Other Essays* (Columbia University Press)

Rota, M. (2009), 'An Anti-reductionist Account of Singular Causation', *Monist* 92: pp. 136–155

Russell, B. (1913) 'On the Notion of Cause', *Proceedings of the Aristotelian Society*, NS, Vol. 13 (1912–1913), pp. 1–26 (reprinted in S. Mumford, ed., *Russell on Metaphysics*. Selection from the Writings of Bertrand Russell (Routledge 2003)

———. (1927), *The Analysis of Matter* (London: George Allen and Unwin)

Salmon, W. C. (1984), *Scientific Explanation and the Causal Structure of the World* (Princeton University Press)

———. (1998), 'Causation without Counterfactuals', in W. C. Salmon, *Causality and Explanation* (Oxford University Press) pp. 248–260

Santayana, G. (1930), *The Realm of Matter* (Charles Scribner's Sons)

Scaltsas, T. (1994), *Substances and Universals in Aristotle's Metaphysics* (Cornell University Press)

Schaffer, J. (2000), 'Trumping Preemption', *Journal of Philosophy* 97: pp. 165–181

———. (2003), 'Is There a Fundamental Level?', *Noûs* 37: pp. 498–517

———. (2004), 'Causes Need Not be Physically Connected to Their Effects: The Case for Negative Causation', in C. Hitchcock (ed.) *Contemporary Debates in Philosophy of Science* (Blackwell), pp. 197–216

———. (2005), 'Quiddistic Knowledge', *Philosophical Studies* 123.1–2: pp. 1–32 (reprinted in F. Jackson and G. Priest, eds, *Lewisian Themes: The Philosophy of David K. Lewis* (2004), Clarendon Press, pp. 210–30)

———. (2010), 'Monism: The Priority of the Whole', *Philosophical Review* 119.1

Schewe, P., J. Riordon, and B. Stein. (2003), 'A Water Molecule's Chemical Formula is Really Not H2O'. *Physics News Update* 648. Available online at: http://www.aip.org/enews/physnews/2003/split/648-1.html.

Schrenk, M. (2009), 'Hic Rhodos, Hic Salta. From Reductionist Semantics to a Realist Ontology of Forceful Dispositions' in G. Damschen, R. Schnepf, K. Stueber, eds, *Debating Dispositions: Issues in Metaphysics, Epistemology and Philosophy of Mind* (Berlin: De Gruyter)

———. (2010), 'The Powerlessness of Necessity' forthcoming in *Noûs*

Shoemaker, S. (1980a), 'Causality and Properties' in P. van Inwagen, ed., *Time and Cause* (Dordrecht: Kluwer) reprinted in E. Sosa, ed., *Properties* Oxford University Press 1997, pp. 228–254

———. 'Properties, Causation and Projectability' in L. J. Cohen and M. Hesse, eds, *Applications of Inductive Logic* (Oxford University Press) pp. 291–312

———. (1984), *Identity, Cause, and Mind: Philosophical Essays* (Cambridge University Press)

———. (1998), 'Causal and Metaphysical Necessity', *Pacific Philosophical Quarterly* 79: pp. 59–77

———. (2003), *Identity, Cause, and Mind* (Oxford University Press)

Skow, B. (2007), 'Are Shapes Intrinsic?' *Philosophical Studies* 133: pp. 111–130

Smart, B. (1972), 'How to Reidentify the Ship of Theseus', *Analysis* 32: pp. 145–148

Smart, J. J. C. (1963), *Philosophy and Scientific Realism* (Routledge and Kegan Paul)

Sosa, E. (1980), 'Varieties of Causation', in E. Sosa and M. Tooley, eds, *Causation* (Oxford University Press) pp. 234–242

Spinoza, B. (1677), *The Ethics*, R. H. M. Elwes, ed., (Dover) 1955

Swinburne, R. (1980), 'Properties, Causation, and Projectability: Reply to Shoemaker' in L.J. Cohen and M. Hesse, eds, *Applications of Inductive Logic* (Oxford University Press) pp. 313–320

Teller, P. (1995), *An Interpretive Introduction to Quantum Field Theory* (Princeton University Press)

Unger, P. (2006), *All the Power in the World* (Oxford University Press)

Whittle, Ann (2009), 'Causal Nominalism' in T. Handfield, ed., *Dispositions and Causes* (Oxford University Press), pp. 242–285

Williams, N. (2005), 'Static and Dynamic Dispositions', *Synthese* 146: pp. 303–324

Williams, N. and Borghini, A. (2008), 'A Dispositional Theory of Possibility', *Dialectica* 62: pp. 21–41

Wilson, J. (forthcoming) 'What is Hume's Dictum, and Why Believe It?', *Philosophy and Phenomenological Research*

Zimmerman, D. (1997), 'Immanent Causation', *Philosophical Perspectives* 11: pp. 433–471

Index

Printed in the USA/Agawam, MA
February 6, 2014

585009.038